Pulpo, Pig & Peppers

- travels around Galicia

Lisa Rose Wright

Pulpo, Pig & Peppers
Copyright © Lisa Rose Wright 2022
ISBN 979883360741

The right of Lisa Rose Wright to be identified as the author of this work has been asserted by her in accordance with the Copyright Designs and Patents Act 1988

All rights reserved. No part of this publication may be reproduced, transmitted, or stored in a retrieval system in any form or by any means, without permission in writing of the author.

*Any queries please contact me at
lisarosewright@msn.com*

*Cover photograph La Torre de Hércules, A Coruña
Cover design and all photographs © Lisa Rose Wright*

For S –
Thank you for introducing me to Galicia, and for walking by my side, always.

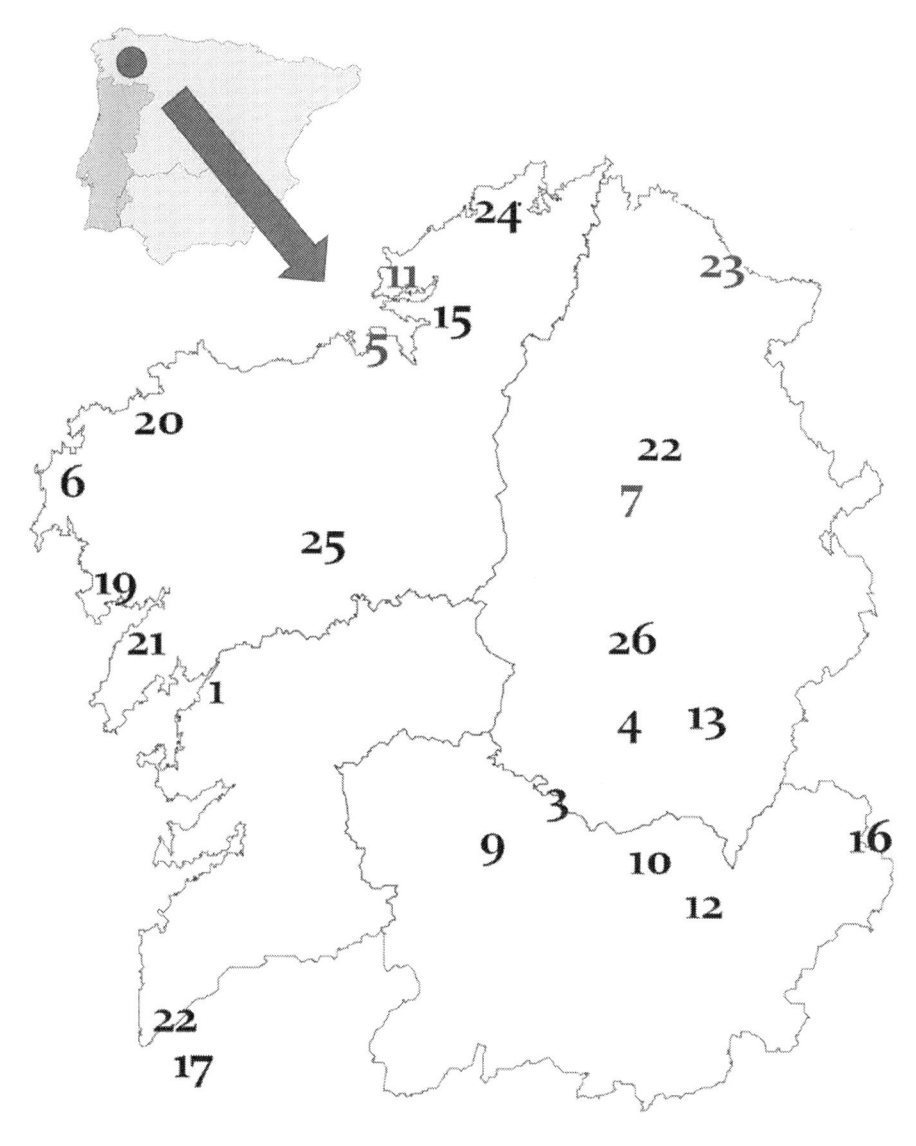

Location of chapters around Galicia, and beyond

CONTENTS

Introduction: 1
1 Catoira - the Vikings are coming 4
2 Gastronomic fiestas - *pulpo*, pig & peppers 13
3 Os Peares - el *Día de la Madre*, and the three rivers 24
4 La Ribeira Sacra - Galicia's sacred rivers 32
5 A Coruña and the Tower of Hercules 42
6 Muxía - the wild Atlantic coast 50
7 The Roman city of Lugo - the very first time 62
8 Return to A Coruña - walking the City of Glass 70
9 Ramón's city of Ourense 82
10 Castro Caldelas - castles and CLOPso 92
11 Ferrol - el Castillo de San Felipe 99
12 Cabeza de Manzaneda - top of the world 110
13 O Courel part I - two feet in the past 120
14 O Courel part II - *castros*, castles, and a forest 130
15 Fragas do Eume - flipflopping through the forest 139
16 Las Médulas - gold diggers 152
17 Caminha - and why we can't return to Portugal 161
18 A trip to Salamanca - bonus chapter 173
19 Carnota - the longest beach in Galicia 186
20 Camelle to Laxe - the Walk of Death 195
21 A Castro da Baroña - a Celtic hillfort 210
22 Celtic *castros* - Iron Age settlements 219
23 Foz, and the Lucense coast 230
24 The Ortigueira Peninsula 241
25 Los Caminos de Santiago 252
26 *A Casa do Campo* - a walk through the seasons 261
Please consider leaving a review: 270
DISCLAIMER 271
COMING NEXT 272
ACKNOWLEDGEMENTS 273
ABOUT THE AUTHOR 274

Introduction:

Galicia, in the remote northwest of Spain: a land of mists and mysteries, green fields and greener forests; of vines and vistas, rivers and *rías*; of erratic weather and warm hospitality.

Galicia is a surprisingly well-kept secret to those of us who live here. Except for the Camino de Santiago pilgrim route and the Madrileños who descend on the coast near to Santiago in summer, Galicia is not well-known as a tourist destination. This means that the inland areas in particular are unspoilt and definitely off the beaten track. Even the beautiful coastline is all but empty outside the July-August high season. You can potter around much of Galicia without any crowds to spoil the enjoyment of everything she has to offer.

Part of the problem, and the charm, of Galicia is that it is not 'on the way' to anywhere. The next destination westwards is the expanse of the wild Atlantic Ocean. To the south, separated by the mighty river Miño is Portugal, whilst to the east, beyond the mountains, lies the mass of the Iberian Peninsula.

This is the place I and my husband Stewart (known throughout my books as 'S') have called home since we bought our wreck of a stone farmhouse in the summer of 2007.

Our adventures renovating *A Casa do Campo* (the country house), defying bureaucracy to marry in Galicia two years later, and renovating a second house for my then 84-year-old mother, who moved to Galicia in 2015, are described in my *Writing Home* series of travelogue memoirs: *Plum, Courgette & Green Bean Tart*, *Tomato, Fig & Pumpkin Jelly* and *Chestnut, Cherry & Kiwi Fruit Sponge*.

Whilst working on that series, I was acutely aware that many of the places we have discovered over the years

Introduction:

wouldn't fit into those stories. Thus was born this book. It is still a travelogue memoir – of places, events, and attractions we have visited and enjoyed. Each place I wrote about elicited a memory, an anecdote, or a yarn which turned this book into a labour of love – for all the wonderful places in our adopted homeland.

    This book is divided into sections which can be read in any order, or dipped in and out of as you choose. From Viking festivals to undiscovered beaches, Celtic roundhouses to Galician peppers, and from mountain villages to ancient forests – each chapter is devoted to one trip, one experience, one more enjoyable adventure here at the end of the world.

There is also an accompanying E-photo album to this book.

Travels around Galicia, the album
https://smarturl.it/travelsaroundGalicia

Finally, I must apologise for the places I've missed. We've still not explored Vigo or the Cies islands for instance, and we hope to one day rectify those omissions. In the meantime, I hope you enjoy our wanderings and might be inspired to visit our beautiful green Galicia.

Lisa

SECTION ONE - FABULOUS FIESTAS

1 Catoira – the Vikings are coming

It was a blistering hot summer's day when we set off in search of Vikings.

We expect August to be warm, even up here in the rainy northwest of Spain, but 2016 blew the record books by experiencing highs of 42°C at the normally cooler coast. Cars and people overheated and I'd booked a hotel with no air-conditioning...

Summer is made for festivals. This was Mum's second summer living in Galicia and her first in her new home. We'd had a big party in a local restaurant for her 85th Birthday in July. All our, and Mum's, friends came to eat, drink and wish her well. Earlier that same year, shortly after Mum had moved into *A Casita* (the cottage), and two years almost to the day since we bought it in a ruinous state, we'd all visited our local Roman Festival, Arde Lucus.

For four days in June, the city of Lugo is time shifted 2,000 years backwards to its Roman beginnings for one of its biggest festivals of the year.

Lugo's documented history goes back to 14 BCE with the founding of Lucus Augusti (the grove of Augustus) by the emperor's representative Paulus Fabius. The 2nd century walls were built to protect the city from marauding attackers and became a UNESCO World Heritage Site in 2000. Soon afterwards, the festival of Arde Lucus (burn Lugo) was born. Arde Lucus is always held on the third weekend in June (unless some official randomly decides the first weekend in July would be better – as happened one year after a number of people had booked to visit us especially for the festival).

My favourite thing about Arde Lucus is the way everyone gets into the spirit of the occasion. There are barbarians stalking the streets with painted faces, and Roman senators in robes and purple sashes drinking coffee. Lepers beg for alms, acrobats perform incredible feats of balance, and stalls line the streets selling everything from posies to swords, pig meat to helmets.

And then there are the Roman Legions.

Each Legion has its own uniform, which provide a wonderful touch of colour to the streets as they march past. The Praetorian guard, dressed all in black, are guardians of the Roman gates, the only entrances to the old town. They are frighteningly realistic with their gleaming helmets and polished armour plate.

Our Workawayer that year, a lovely polite southern American lad, had gallantly agreed to go with us wearing a toga (read dress) that Mum had whipped up for him. And very good he looked too! All in all, it was a fun day out.

Less expected in Celtic Galicia is a Viking Festival. But on the first Sunday in August, the quiet town of Catoira on the west coast (population 3,500) turns into a Viking stronghold – the number of horned helmets only matched by the furs of the barbarian hordes come to pillage Christendom.

In the late Middle Ages, various Viking incursions occurred along the Ría de Arousa on Galicia's west coast, searching for the riches known to be stored at the town of Iria Flavia (now Padrón) by the bishopric. Catoira, at the mouth of the Río Ulla became important for the strategic defence of the coastline and preventing those forays reaching the religious capital up river.

Fortified strongholds were constructed at the mouths of the western *rías*, including the reconstruction of Roman fortifications at Catoira. The Torres de Oeste, or Western Towers, are still visible and an important part of the annual celebrations. Despite the fortifications, incursions continued and are one of the reasons the Galician capital was moved to Santiago de Compostela, an unusual capital city in that it is not built on a river.

1 Catoira – the Vikings are coming

The stronghold at Catoira was undoubtedly important and the festivities, which began as a small gathering in 1960 of a local literary and history forum, are now a major festival.

By 1989, the Viking festival had grown so large that the local authority decided to get on board and take over its running. They twinned the town with Frederikssund in Denmark, which has a strong Viking tradition, and instigated the building of Viking longships.

Mum has had a fascination with Vikings ever since she first saw the 1958 Kirk Douglas film of the same name. She has even gone so far as to state that she wants a Viking burial on a longboat complete with flaming arrows. I just hope she times her demise for the Catoira Viking weekend when we would at least have chance to purloin a boat!

As soon as I discovered the *Romería Vikinga* that summer, I'd looked on Booking.com for accommodation. Every flat, *pensión*, hotel and homestay within spitting distance of Catoira had apparently been booked up for months. Eventually, I found a motel in Caldas de Rei which seemed okay, even if the rooms appeared a bit – red. There was garage parking and breakfast was included, so I duly booked.

By the time we reached Caldas, the temperature was reading 44°C on the car's dash and I was grateful once more that we had recently bought a car with the luxury of air conditioning. Our 20-year-old Ford Escort would have been as hot inside as out and the engine would probably have been overheating by now. The only downside of air-con is the sudden shock when one opens the door. Our tea break had been short. The café interior was cool inside the thick stone walls, but the car was sitting in the full sun and even with air conditioning it took a while to cool down again.

After two passes on the main road, we eventually found the rather overly discreet sign for the motel and drove up a narrow track alongside a high stone wall. Despite craning my neck, I was unable to catch any glimpse of the building. At the end of the wall was a firmly closed gate and an intercom. They seemed to take security very seriously for the usually safe and laid-back Galicia. The disembodied voice directed us to block 3C and told us to wait there.

Curiouser and curiouser!

We drove through the gate and alongside the first of a number of two-storey, square accommodation blocks. Each block had two units separated by a garage with a closed roller door. By the time we had trawled around the site looking for the appropriate block, a smiling lady was standing outside with our keys.

She showed Mum into her cosy, cool unit, to the left of the garage, before opening the door to our room on the other side.

I entered a pre-heated oven.

"Oh crikey! Where's the air-con?" I gasped, as S pushed past and started to turn knobs on the unit positioned on the wall.

"*Está roto*," muttered our host.

Broken? On a day with the highest temperatures ever known in Galicia?

"Then move us to a different unit."

"It is not possible, they are all full," said the lady, no longer smiling.

"This is ridiculous, I can't sleep in here," I grumped, menopausally. "I'm going to look for somewhere else."

Of course, I'd already tried that a few days before so I knew it was highly unlikely I'd find anywhere.

I didn't.

The lady returned to ask if we were staying and offered to find a fan for the room.

"Okay, I suppose so. Two would be better," I added, hopefully.

1 Catoira – the Vikings are coming

The lady disappeared after asking us to put our passports through a hole in the wall in the corridor outside. I caught a quick glimpse of a concrete wall beyond, before the hatch was dropped back in place.

I turned to examine our sauna of a room. It was of a reasonable size, dominated by a large double bed covered in faux silk sheets of a dark plum colour. The walls and ceiling were also dark plum. The carpet had some interesting looking stains on it. The whole ensemble looked how I imagined a porn movie studio might be decorated.

"Wait a minute. Have you seen the bathroom?" called S, popping his head out.

This room was tiled in black, with smoked glass mirrors around the walls. The comfort kit included toothbrush, comb, and some paper wrapped articles which Mum later told me she'd thought were shower caps. They were certainly not made for that sort of head at all.

My whirring thoughts were interrupted by the nice lady bringing a tall stand fan. Bliss.

"Where is the restaurant for breakfast?" I remembered to ask.

"Breakfast is served in your room. The menu is next to the telephone, just dial and give your order and the time you want it," she replied.

"Oh. Okay." Stranger still!

The fan thankfully reduced the overnight room temperature to just above 30°C, and the noise drowned out some of the more unusual nocturnal comings and goings that night.

At our requested breakfast time there was a discreet knock on the door. When I opened it, there stood a driverless hostess trolley piled with fruit salad, croissants and tea. For Spain it was a good breakfast, but I marvelled at all the cloak and dagger stuff.

"I wonder if guests need a good breakfast to keep their energy levels up?" I mumbled to S as we packed.

"That was an odd place," reflected Mum, as we drove away. "I think there were cats screeching outside, and cars were going past at all hours."

I thought this was an appropriate point at which to narrate a story I'd remembered the previous night...

Our friend Leo had told me of arriving in Spain from Canada with his young family and booking into a motel. In North America, and in the UK, a motel is a family-friendly motoring hotel – usually with on-site parking and convenient for main trunk roads. In Spain, a motel will often charge by the hour and is discreet because the (often married) guests demand it. It is, in short, a bordello, a knocking shop, a rumpy-pumpy hotel.

"I wonder how much we could've made last night, Mum?" I said, grinning.

After our exciting night, Catoira could have been quite a let-down. But it wasn't. In fact, it was a magical place.

Catoira is built at the mouth of the Río Ulla, one of the longest rivers in Galicia, which passes close to our house on its way to the sea. The road bridges as we approached Catoira, spanned a delta of mud and silt.

In spring and autumn, this is an important wetland site for migrating birds. At this time of year, the poor things would likely be speared by a mad barbarian. Everywhere we looked, horned helmets and furs vied with swords and double-headed axes.

As we pulled into a serendipitously vacated space, we were passed by a tall chap in full Viking regalia, sword and shield at the ready, fur cape draped over his back and a two horned helmet perched on his head. A swarm of Celts, their faces painted in black stripes and swirls, yelled from across the way. They were also dressed in fur and I was wondering at what point they would all collapse with heat exhaustion.

The parking space we'd found was on the wrong side of the railway line for the entertainment, and the short cut everyone was using was straight across the tracks.

1 Catoira – the Vikings are coming

We managed to get our recently 85-year-old across safely, without any of us being run down by a train, and emerged into a Viking village.

There were various workshops set up under canvas with Norsemen making tea and generally being domestic in the background. Through a wooded path we emerged onto a newly built boardwalk across marshland, and into a clearing full of people. I could imagine that at other times of the year this spot would be perfect for bird-watching. Today, there was a large and busy market taking place beyond the estuary and the scents of *pulpo*, *churros* and barbecued meats mingled to great effect.

"Fancy a bit of *pulpo*, Mum?" I said, pointing at the vats of boiling octopus.

Mum shuddered.

"What about a nice deep-fried *churro*?" teased S, as my parent held her nose.

Poor Mum isn't keen on doughnuts either, even the delicious long thin Spanish *churros*. Luckily the main show was approaching.

The Viking invasion was set to occur at 1pm. By noon, the bridge over the river was full from end to end with the waiting masses. We wandered along the river bank, hoping for a shady spot in which to wait. We failed dismally. The sun beat down mercilessly and our water bottles were soon depleted. We stood with thousands of other spectators waiting to be entertained. Next to me, a middle-aged man looked incongruous in shorts and T-shirt, sporting a huge and ill-fitting Viking helmet and carrying a large wicker shopping basket. Beyond him were a couple, their offspring's pushchair decorated as a Viking warship complete with roundels on the sides.

A cry went up and two longboats appeared, rowing against the current toward the crumbling tower.

"Look, Mum," I shouted. "The Vikings are coming!"

There were over fifty people aboard the boats, all dressed in full Viking costume and shouting barbarous insults at the waiting Christians. The atmosphere was only slightly spoilt by the flotilla of small pleasure craft full of camera-clicking tourists which dogged the longboats, their outboard motors chugging.

The Longboats used in Catoira are reconstructions of genuine Viking ships or *drakkars*. The first *drakkar*, *Torres de Oeste*, was built in 1993 by local artisans who travelled to Denmark to learn traditional building methods. The second boat, *Drakkar Frederikssund*, is a reconstruction of a known longboat found in Norway, the *Gokstad*. They certainly looked authentic enough as they rowed up the *ría* that day.

Suddenly, a red and white striped sail was unfurled and the first boat began to turn towards the mud flats of the shore line. Many of the waiting spectators headed onto the mud to watch the ensuing battle more closely. Sandals squelched invitingly as they hurried towards the action. We were sadly just too far away to see clearly, but the cries and clanging of steel suggested it was a hard-fought battle.

By now the midday heat had topped 40°C and we were ready for lunch. We left the hordes, and the Viking warriors, to their battles and made our way to the thankfully cool interior of a pizzeria for a well-earned lunch – and a ponder on the numerous festivals which make up our tiny part of the world.

That afternoon we drove down the western coastline of Galicia, stopping at the seaside town of Vilagarcía de Arousa for a paddle.

Mum sat in the shade of a large tree whilst S and I donned swimsuits and lay sunning ourselves on the beach. Every ten minutes or so we'd jump into the icy Atlantic Ocean at our feet to cool our burning skin.

Mum indicated she was getting ice creams.

"Yes, please!" I yelled over.

1 Catoira – the Vikings are coming

She kindly brought them to us. Dripping from their cones and in danger of becoming milk shakes, they were nevertheless welcome.

Back home, *A Casa do Campo* seemed icy inside its seventy-centimetre-thick stone walls. I gave a sigh of relief as I had a tepid shower in our white bathroom – devoid of smoky mirrors, strange shower caps, or Vikings.

We all agreed it had been a most interesting, informative, and unusual trip.

2 Gastronomic fiestas – *pulpo*, pig & peppers

I sometimes think that with a little planning, one could visit a fiesta or festival in Galicia every day of the year. Certainly, my battered 'guidebook to the *fiestas*, *ferias* and *romerías* of Galicia' is more of a novella than a leaflet, and that only includes a fraction of the total number.

In addition to the costume spectaculars such as those mentioned in the first chapter, each parish celebrates their saint's day. This celebration can be as simple as mass in a tiny village church, followed by a parade of the saint's statue around the square – as in our own parish's Día de Asunción on the 15th of August. There may be a community barbecue afterwards, or the festival could be a four- or five-day celebration with full *orquestas*. In Galicia, an 'orchestra' is the name given to the travelling shows which tour the provinces over the summer months. Arriving in pantechnicons which barely fit the narrow streets, their arrival is often as exhilarating as their music.

Many Galician festivals have their origins in pagan rituals surrounding the four elements and the changing seasons. Often, these were adapted by the early-Christian church to underpin their power. Festivals also keep the Galician identity strong, reinforce bonds between neighbours, and are a great excuse to let your hair down.

Galician festivals traditionally included a market of artisan products. Many of these markets had their beginnings in necessity – they acted as a sort of mobile shop for rural villagers who were able to buy produce from the furthest corners of the region. This was especially true of those festivals held in autumn and spring, when stores could be laid in for the harsh winter months or depleted ones restocked.

2 Gastronomic fiestas – pulpo, pig & peppers

It is these markets which gave rise to the gastronomic festivals of Galicia – festivals which celebrate the special products of each area, whether from the sea, the land, or the rivers.

Galegos are rightly proud of their produce, much of which has the coveted D.O (*denominación de origen*) – the equivalent of the British Protected Geographical Status. For me, a self-confessed foodie, Galicia's gastronomic festivals are some of the best there are. From *pulpo*, pig, and peppers to wine, bread, and cheese, there is something for everyone.

§

Pulpo a feria has to be the national dish of Galicia. The quickest way to a *Galego's* heart is to answer '*Si, claro,*' (yes, of course) to the oft-asked question; "Do you like octopus?"

Pulpo (or *polbo* in Galego) is sold in specialised restaurants called *pulperías*, and at every fair or market in the region. It is served the Galician way – sprinkled with sea salt, paprika and rich olive oil, the juices mopped up with fresh crusty bread.

I once tried to work out how many octopuses are consumed annually in Galicia. There are usually two markets a month in each small town or village; the one in our local town of Taboada is the 4th and 20th of the month, our next nearest town is the 5th and 21st, the next one the 3rd and 19th, and so on. At each market there will be at least three *pulpo* stalls which do a brisk trade between around 11am and 2pm.

These pop-up stalls consist of a brightly-coloured awning over a huge copper cauldron of boiling water. The water is heated by a gas burner which is itself connected to a gas bottle placed a few feet away – its rubber hose trailing across the pavement where customers are going to walk. Nearby will be a teetering stack of wooden platters and a pair of stout scissors. In the early days of our life here, this teetering stack often had a cigarette butt balanced on the edge of a platter, waiting for its owner to have a hand free once more. The cleaned but whole octopus is plunged into the boiling water and, once ready, cut up onto a wooden platter. The platters each have the initials of the restaurant burnt into them and are usually cleaned by being dipped into the octopus water.

Eaten in the open air, under a tent-like canopy, *pulpo a feria* is one of the best market treats there are. It is a treat too, as the prices have shot up in recent years with a small platter now costing upwards of twelve euros.

Anyway, back to my calculations. One platter of *pulpo* is one 'arm' so that's eight portions from each octopus. I reckon each stall sells around thirty platters including the hefty take-away trade, so that's ninety platters a day at each market and there will be a market somewhere in Galicia every day, 365 days a year. I reckon that's almost 34,000 platters or 4,000 octopuses a year.

The first time we ate *pulpo* was at a market in a small town called Baralla when we were house hunting back in 2006. At that time, a platter was a modest six euros and included bread and wine. We sat at a long wooden bench sipping wine out of a *cunca*, or small earthenware bowl, until the *pulpo* was ready. Keeping the olive oil from spilling all over the table was quite a feat, needing prodigious use of napkins and pieces of spongy Galician bread to prop the platter up as the benches were anything but level. Someone passed round a large wheel of cheese. We all used our ever-present penknives to cut off a chunk of hard, strongly-flavoured cheese then passed it on. It was a great meal and one which had us falling in love with Galicia all over again.

Often the *pulpo* stalls park up outside a local bar on market day. Each stall has its own particular site. Customers order *pulpo* from the stall then go inside the adjacent bar to eat, ordering wine, bread and any side dishes from the bar. This can be a very convivial way to

2 Gastronomic fiestas – pulpo, pig & peppers

enjoy *pulpo* but also an expensive one by the time all the inevitable extras have been consumed and paid for. It's much cheaper to order a menu of the day plus a *pulpo* platter to share... though that requires a huge appetite, even by Galician standards.

Carballiño, a small town in Ourense province, is known as the *pulpo* capital of Galicia. Carballiño borders one of the ancient Camino de Santiago pilgrim routes, The Silver Way, which passes the nearby monastery of Oseira. It is a friendly town with a reputation for serving the best octopus in Galicia. As Galicia is a small area with a huge appetite for this seafood delicacy, that is some recommendation. Carballiño's *Fiesta del Pulpo* is held on the second Sunday in August and well worth a visit.

For the best seafood in Galicia, the festival of seafood (*Exaltación del Marisco*) in O Grove is hard to beat. Held over the first two weeks in October, there are stalls serving the very freshest mussels, oysters, clams, and goose barnacles – Galicia's renowned *percebes* – most just landed that morning from the port not ten metres away.

O Grove is a lovely town, described bizarrely in one of the famous travel guide series, as 'like Blackpool'. It has a seaside vibe, lovely beaches, thermal spas and the best seafood in the world – and there's not a kiss-me-quick hat in sight.

If sardines are more your thing, then Galicia in June is the place to be. On the eve of St. John the Baptist's Day, many towns and villages hold a festival called a *sardiñada*. As the name suggests, this fiesta involves cooking and eating large quantities of sardines. If ever a miracle of loaves and fishes was needed it is in Galicia on the 23rd of June, when vast quantities of sardines, bread, wine, and *bizcocho*, a deliciously lemony sponge cake, are consumed. In the city of A Coruña on this date, the *Hogueras de San Juan* involves not only sardines but huge bonfires along the beaches, invoking a truly magical evening.

Galicia also offers trout festivals, oyster festivals and *bonito* (tuna) festivals throughout the year – so whatever your fishy desires they can be catered for here.

§

Pigs are a mainstay of Galician country life. Almost every home in the *campo,* or countryside, will keep a pig over the summer, ready for slaughter around St Martinmas on the 11th of November. In recent years, the annual *matanza,* or killing day, is often later. Fine autumn weather means an early slaughter would lead to flies and spoilt meat.

When we first came to Galicia, during our winter house hunting in 2006, we were startled to see pig carcasses hanging in garages open to the street in the centre of the market town where we stayed.

I couldn't imagine such a thing in Britain in the 2000s.

Years ago, when my godmother was a child, her family kept pigs at the end of the garden behind their terraced house, as did many of their neighbours. They kept chickens too, and grew their own vegetables. Other than the possible exception of the vegetables, all that has disappeared in Britain, under an outflow of bureaucracy and supposed health issues.

Here in Galicia, there were murmurs years ago of the central government stopping people growing and killing pigs at home. It was never enforced, and was frankly unenforceable in a region with thousands of tiny settlements too small to be villages but big enough for a few pigs. The threat to the Galician *campesinos'* way of life has yet to materialise.

2 Gastronomic fiestas – pulpo, pig & peppers

Like the *campesinos,* we too eat local where we can. Besides growing many of our own vegetables, fruit, and nuts, each year our friend and neighbour grows us a pig. We arrive to 'assist' in the slaughter before taking the carcass away to turn into a year's worth of sausages, pies and roasts.

I know these animals are well-fed on organic-grown vegetables and humanely-kept. They have no long journey to a slaughterhouse, and are dispatched quickly and quietly. As a meat eater, I believe this is the way to enjoy a sustainable feast.

Because every part of a pig can be eaten, it is a good cheap option for a peasant family. There are many Galician recipes involving pork products, and many of Galicia's foodie festivals are based around pig meat.

There is a splendid book entitled '*Everything but the Squeal'* by John Barlow, a Yorkshireman living in Galicia. In it, the author spends a year trying to eat every part of the pig. That he succeeds is a testament to both his iron constitution and the Galician love of all things porcine.

And Mr Barlow missed out the most famous of all Galician piggy festivals.

Our local town of Taboada holds its *Festa do Caldo de Ósos,* or bone stew festival, on the first Sunday of *Entroido* or *Carnaval*, the beginning of lent. It is a wonderful day of pork and bean stew, pork ribs, and local piggy products.

Near to Taboada, the week before the bone stew festival, there is the *Feria del Cocido* in Lalín. *Cocido* is a traditional Galician stew of pork, potatoes, greens, and chickpeas (garbanzos) cooked together. The meat and vegetables are served separately to the stock, the long cooking converting simple ingredients into something magical.

Churrasco, or grilled meats, are another Galician staple which were taken across the Atlantic to the Americas by

Galician émigrés. This platter of carnivores' delight is a feature on almost every *menú del día* in the area.

In Moraña, in Pontevedra province, *churrasco* is taken to new heights in the *Fiesta Carneiro ó Espeto*. Here, on the final Sunday in July, whole lamb carcasses are 'skewered' in butterfly fashion and slow roasted around huge bonfires. The barbecued carcasses are sold for up to 300 euros apiece – the price including bread, wine, and Galician *empanadas*. The meal is shared between groups of friends or family in a convivial atmosphere. This festival began in the 1960s; the recipe was brought back from Argentina by returning emigrants, so Galician *churrasco* has crossed the ocean and returned again.

Empanadas, a flat Galician pie filled with seafood, fish, or meat with a bread-like crust, feature in a number of festivals of their own. Beware though, if you visit the *empanada* festival in Chantada you need to take your own pies as there are bizarrely none to buy. A problem we discovered one disastrous day out with Mum early in our life here in Galicia.

§

Don't panic if you're not a fan of seafood or meat; even Galicia caters for non-carnivores, and some of the best D.O (*denominación de origen*) foodstuffs fall into this category.

By far the best known are *Pimientos de Padrón*. A small green pepper which is deep fried and sprinkled with sea salt, they are often called the 'Russian roulette of peppers'. Padrón peppers are generally innocuous little things, but every tenth one or so has a chilli bite which can make your eyes water. It's usually my chilli-and-heat-hating hubby, S, who gets this one.

Franciscan monks are said to have brought seeds from Mexico in the 16th century from which they developed the strain of peppers known today.

2 Gastronomic fiestas – pulpo, pig & peppers

The proportion of 'hot' peppers can vary with area, and with the weather in any given year. I've found that some years my Padrón peppers are all chilli hot, in others as mild as a bell pepper.

One year our friends invited us to lunch. Dawn had grown Padrón peppers for the first time and prepared them the traditional Galician way. S took his first bite, turned puce and started to cough. I laughed at him and took a bite of my own pepper – it was as hot as a jalapeño. I love spice so happily munched, offering S any I thought weren't too spicy. There weren't many that day.

Over 15,000 kilogrammes of Padrón peppers are grown yearly in the region and over 2,000 kilogrammes are given away during the *Fiesta del Pimiento de Herbón*, held each year in the town of the same name, near to Padrón, on the first Sunday in August.

The next town to Carballiño, of *pulpo* fame, is San Cristovo de Cea. An even smaller town, it has some fifteen bakeries and the reputation of baking the best bread in Galicia. Cea's breadmaking history stretches back to the 13th century – the preparation and cooking has changed little in that time. Like most artisan Galician bread, the ingredients are simple: flour, salt, water and *masa madre* (a starter culture or *pate fermentee* used by bakers). The bread is baked in a traditional wood-fired oven and has a tough crust and deliciously spongy interior.

Céa has a bread festival, *Exaltación de Pan*, in July of each year. Participants can not only try the famous bread but take a guided walk along *la ruta dos fornos* (the oven route), which takes in ancient threshing areas, restored stone-built bread ovens, and the history of the area.

Cheese is another Galician delight. Locally we have the D.O Arzúa-Ulloa cheese – a soft creamy, slightly acidic cheese, made in a traditional one kilogramme wheel. We are lucky enough to have a cheese lady deliver our cheese to the door every two weeks for a ridiculously low price, direct from the dairy.

There is an annual cheese festival run by the three councils which make up the Ulloa district. Sadly, these councils can rarely agree on a date for the festival which consequently changes each year and requires sharp eyes to spot the advertisement!

Arzúa, one of the last towns on the Camino de Santiago and the convergence of many pilgrim routes, holds its own *Fiesta del Queso* on the first Sunday in March, selling the same Arzúa-Ulloa D.O cheeses. It's well worth a visit to stuff yourself with dairy delights.

Queso San Simón da Costa is another Galician cheese holding a D.O. This slightly smoked cheese is made in the Terra Cha – a high, flat area in Lugo province, sixty kilometres north of us. San Simón is known as *tetilla,* or tit cheese, due to its shape – which looks remarkably like Madonna's cone bra from her Blond Ambition tour.

If you want to check this phenomenon out, the *Fiesta del Queso de San Simón da Costa* is usually held in April, in the town of Vilalba.

§

If all this talk of food makes you thirsty, Galicia boasts plenty of festivals catering to quenching that thirst.

One of the first festivals we visited when we moved to Galicia was a local cider festival in our nearby town of Chantada. When we finally found the event, there was a row of stalls dispensing cider for free. Customers bought a glass for something like two euros then visited each stall, drinking as much cider as could be imbibed. I was amazed that there were no displays of drunken behaviour that evening.

2 Gastronomic fiestas – pulpo, pig & peppers

More common here are the various wine festivals, where each festival celebrates the wine of its area. The *Feria del Vino de Amandi*, is held in Sober, in Lugo province, on Palm Sunday. The long-windedly titled, *Feria-Exposición de Exaltación del Vino de O Ribeiro*, is held in Ribadavia, in Ourense province, at the beginning of May. And the *Fiesta del Vino Albariño*, Galicia's premier white wine, is held in August in Cambados, in Pontevedra province.

Our own town of Taboada held a wine fair one year. There were a dozen fifteen-litre boxes of wine on a trestle table and hand-painted *cuncas* for a euro fifty. We filled our ceramic bowls from the tap below the first box, returning as often as we wished to top up or try another wine. It was low-key, simple, and a delight.

§

There is a sentence in my well-thumbed guidebook which sums up Galician festivals beautifully:
"*Lo sacro y lo profano, entre altar y una buena mesa.*" The sacred and the profane, between altar and a good table.

What more could we ask for?

As a last postscript, there are also what I call 'pop-up' festivals. These are festivals or fiestas with no set date and often no rhyme nor reason – they just pop up one year with little fanfare or advertising, only to disappear once more. Our own tiny council area has, at various times, enjoyed tapas trails, tortilla festivals, Celtic festivals, chestnut festivals, and beer festivals. These events can be some of the most authentic and fun ones because they are simply an excuse for locals to have a good time.

Serendipity and open ears can be your best friends in Galicia.

SECTION TWO – SACRED RIVERS

3 Os Peares – el *Día de la Madre*, and the three rivers

"Where shall we take Mum for Mother's Day?" I asked.
"Is it Mother's Day?"
"Yup. *El Día de la Madre* is next week, in Spain."

It was a sunny Sunday at the beginning of May. I had been pondering where to go when a chance encounter online brought the town of Os Peares to mind. We invited a couple of our friends along and set off.

Os Peares is a small town around an hour south-east, and a whole world away, from our own small market town of Taboada. Whereas our village sits at 500 metres above sea level, Os Peares is nestled in a deep valley, at the confluence of three rivers. The influence of those rivers, the Miño, the Sil, and the smaller Búbal, on the climate of the town is obvious.

That morning had been bright and sunny at home, after an annoying late frost overnight. My runner beans, the six tomatoes I'd sacrificed to test the weather, the newly emerging leaves on my early potatoes, and the tips of the walnut leaves, were blackened like dead men's fingers. In Os Peares the bright lemons, huge oranges, and half-grown figs mocked me, while the grape vines were fully two feet long. Mine were at most an inch, and being optimistic at that.

The road to Os Peares is one of my favourite drives, full of surprises and stunning scenery. Once we'd left the main Lugo to Ourense highway behind, the narrow road passed through woodland of chestnut, oak, and walnut. The stately oaks were already cloaked in Lincoln green, the walnuts showed bronzed new growth, beautifully backlit by the sunshine, whilst the gnarled, late-blooming chestnuts stubbornly remained as bare as winter. The road wound below the canopy, shaded and damp in the morning air, and we crisscrossed narrow rivers on even narrower bridges, back and forth, ever downhill. We passed through tiny hamlets of a couple or three houses and larger villages boasting a shop, a bar, or a *tabac* – often the same place.

Just beyond the wonderfully named village of Chaos, a roe deer stood in a field watching us, before, with a twitch of white rump, it disappeared, melting into the tree line. On the right, the trees gave way to a steep slope and the vista abruptly opened out over a deep valley. In early May the heavily wooded valley was clothed in greens of every hue from dark forest to pale moss. The sun shone on the vegetation and sparkled from the red roofs of houses, dotted here and there on the steep slopes.

This sight caused my girlfriend and I to both exclaim, simultaneously, "How do they get *there*?"

The further one drives, the more startling this valley is. We were following the course of the river Búbal. A small river which arises a little to the west of the main N540, Lugo to Ourense road, the Búbal ends its life at Os Peares. Although a relatively short river, the Búbal has carved a deep valley. The scenery is dramatic and has been likened to Switzerland or Austria with its precipitous, abundantly green slopes and tiny villages.

An almost invisible right turn began a vertiginously steep downhill section. We were now heading into the Os Peares valley zigzagging through, not broadleaved woodland, but eucalypt forests with tight, hairpin bends and a steep drop away to the valley floor. The trees blocked the view until we reached the first houses above the town.

A small pull-in allowed a photo opportunity next to a pretty house with summer flowers, a lemon tree, and grape vines already clambering up their supports. Still some 300 metres above the valley floor, the view took in the Búbal below us and the distinctive blue wrought iron railway bridge which crossed the river Miño beyond. The huge concrete structure of the main N120

3 Os Peares – el Día de la Madre, and the three rivers

road bridge spanned the valley in the distance, almost on a level with our viewpoint, dominating the little town below.

We drove the final, short but steep, zig-zag to the river, avoiding two pedestrians loitering on a narrow 180-degree bend, and parked in the shade beside a small fountain.

Beyond the stone bridge over the river Búbal which we had just crossed was a *casa rural,* beautifully restored in grey granite stone with deep-red shutters. A short concrete ramp led to a grassy area next to the river.

The Búbal is fast-flowing, perfectly clear and quite shallow here. In July a set of sluice gates is lowered into a framework downriver of this section to provide a safe, and icily cold, river pool. Just right for a deliciously refreshing dip.

In late spring, the river had no barriers and romped joyfully over the rocks. Beyond the small weir, vegetation grew thickly in the sunny shallows before trees moved in to shade the river for the last part of its journey.

Our little party followed a walkway alongside the Búbal, below the canopy of the riverside trees. To our right the river dived over a waterfall, the spray splashing us with droplets and the noise drowning out conversation. To our left chickens pecked happily below a set of grape vines, no doubt eating bugs for the grateful owner. Above, a Muscovy duck sat on the topmost vines, eyeing the hens below.

A *finca*, further on the left, fascinated me. The small vegetable patch was completely fenced in from the path with a long set of steps up to a gate at road level, way above us.

"You'd have to be fit to cultivate this plot," I mumbled, largely to myself.

I've often thought the population of Os Peares must be one of the fittest in Galicia, as every house, shop and *finca* is on a slope. There are slopes up to the bar, and the sports centre is at the very top of an almost vertical track. We had to walk up to that sports centre to catch a bus following a ten-kilometre sponsored walk one year; that gradient is etched into my memory!

Our short walk on that particular sunny May day brought us to our lunch stop where I'd booked a table. The Acea do Búbal is a restaurant and hotel set on the banks of the river in an old chocolate factory. There is a sort of museum in a back room, though sadly all remnants of chocolate have long since gone (though the chocolate pudding was pretty good – but I'm getting ahead of myself). The restaurant on the upper floor has a narrow balcony with views over the three rivers. There is a sunny terrace at the front of the property and to the rear a shady terrace was laid, just for us. Our table was on its own open deck, built out over the river directly below us. The setting was perfect and the food rivalled it.

The waitress presented us with a menu before going off in search of essentials – *vino*, water and bread. She returned without the bread but we failed to notice until our starters were consumed, leaving tasty juices which cried out for our elusive *pan*. I hung on to my empty plate until our waitress returned with delicious crusty, slow-risen Galician bread to mop up the garlicky juices from my grilled baby squid (*chipirones*). Mum had chosen *huevos rotos* for her starter. A scrambled egg mixture poured over a huge plate of chips and mixed with small chunks of *chorizo*, it was a sort of deconstructed sausage, egg and chips.

For mains, the three of us chose chicken, pot roasted with peppers, herbs and more garlic. The whole leg was nearer to a quarter chicken and full of rich flavours. Our friends opted for *albóndigas*, Spanish meatballs.

A second bottle of wine sustained us through dessert. My chocolate mousse pie was rich, chocolatey and heavenly. Mum enjoyed her coffee *flan* (a Spanish crème

3 Os Peares – el Día de la Madre, and the three rivers

caramel) and our friend his *natillas*, or Galician custard. We had our coffee on the sunny terrace at the front as it was getting a bit cool in the shade out there over the water, and Mum's fingers were turning blue.

After a lunch that size, we needed a walk so headed over the iron railway bridge. Halfway across we heard an ear-splitting horn and a non-stop express train hurtled past, less than an arm's span from us, rattling the metal walkway with its vibrations. We were crossing the Miño now. To our left, the Búbal poured into this much bigger river while to our right, beyond the train tracks, the Sil also flowed along to meet its end in the tumble of the Miño. At this point, in this tiny town, these three rivers join to become one for their final journey to the Atlantic Ocean, forming the border between Spain and Portugal further downstream.

The town of Os Peares has the unique distinction in Galicia of having four mayors. This settlement of less than 200 inhabitants is split, not only between two provinces, Lugo and Ourense, but four municipalities; those of Carballedo and Pantón to the north, and A Peroxa and Nogueira de Ramuín to the south. Unsurprisingly, this makes for much controversy and little action.

On the other side of the bridge, we entered the municipality of Pantón, north of the river Sil and east of the Miño. The skyline here is dominated by the huge concrete pillars of the main N120 road bridge, 356 metres above our heads. The bridge creates a permanent shadow over this part of the town; yet, ugly as the concrete is, there is a magnificence to this bridge, a statement from man of his engineering prowess.

From here we could walk across the small road bridge over the river Sil into Ourense province. We stood on the bridge for a while, one foot in each province, admiring the vineyards on the steep hillsides above the railway tracks and the cantilevered roadway which seemed to lean precariously toward the valley floor. Not one of our little group volunteered to go up there for a photo opportunity.

Our walk into Ourense province took us maybe ten minutes from our lunch stop, but until 2016 that same trip would have taken longer by car. The railway bridge we used to cross the Miño has a pedestrian walkway but no vehicle access. To drive from one province to the other used to be an eight-kilometre trek.

The now leader of the *Xunta da Galicia*, the Galician council, is a local of Os Peares, and one of Señor Feijoo's promises to his home town was a new road bridge linking the two provinces.

We recrossed the blue railway bridge over the Miño, and walked under a tunnel beneath the railway line. Doubling back towards the station with its one stopping train a day, we climbed a short, steep path and arrived on a level with the railway tracks once more but on the opposite side. Here a wide road dead-ended at a cluster of derelict-looking houses.

I use the word 'derelict-looking' deliberately as we have been caught out many times here in Galicia. A house with broken window panes, rotten doors and overgrown *finca* may suddenly sprout a line of washing, blowing in the breeze. One can never assume! Still, these did look pretty derelict. The first house had no door and an empty space where the old wood-burning range, or *cocina*, would once have been. There were rusted bedsteads on the rotten floorboards, and beyond the open door at the rear a beautiful view over the river Miño – now joined by the Sil and the Búbal on their journey to become the river Minho at Portugal.

We followed the road back towards the station at its far end. On our right was the railway line, on our left a line of beautiful, abandoned two-storey houses with square walls, high, ornate, wooden doors, and wrought-iron balconies above. Amongst this dereliction was the odd, neatly renovated and obviously lived-in house, and a large church. Many of the buildings had painted signs,

3 Os Peares – el Día de la Madre, and the three rivers

long since faded. There was a jeweller's shop, and others too damaged to identify. A car service centre stood with its metal concertina doors wide open onto a vast space overlooking the river at the rear.

I stood, fascinated. It seemed such a special spot – the fronts of the buildings overlooking the railway and the backs dropping away steeply to the Miño behind. Many of the properties had four or even five storeys at the rear. Some had a *finca* below, on a level with the river. In those gardens there were orange trees, the fruit bigger than my fist. The views behind were stunning but more than fifty percent of the properties seemed abandoned. Why didn't the council (we were in Carballedo now) do something to renovate the area? It was a mystery to me.

A double and a triple-fronted property together were for sale. My mind whirled with possibilities. I let my imagination run wild, envisaging Victorian-era ladies taking a *paseo* along this parade, dripping with jewels and furs – maybe choosing a new brooch from the jewellers as they promenaded past.

I would love to go back in time and see this area as it was in its heyday, bustling with life – the steam from the trains mingling with the mist from the waters below.

I was happy to see a bar-restaurant, the Barra Miño, had reopened since we were last there; they used to do lovely tapas but we were way too full to contemplate any food so continued to wander as far as the new bridge.

This is Feijoo's promised link between the two halves of the town. Completed in 2016 and costing in the region of 2.8 million euros over five years, the bridge is low, and surprisingly narrow at just five and a half metres, and gaudily striped in grey and red brick pavers. The bridge begins at the end of the parade we had been walking along and I hoped its construction might help generate business for more shops along this neglected stretch.

To get to the railway station we would need to follow the cars below the railway tracks through a hair-raisingly narrow and twisty underpass. I thought it must be chaos in rush hour, but this is Galicia so rush hour is not likely to consist of more than a half dozen cars and they probably know each other's schedules like their own. As the only train was not due for hours yet, we wandered back along my dream parade and through the streets of the town, past the pharmacy and the old-fashioned grocery shop to our car, waiting patiently in the shade.

As I looked over at the Búbal once more, I pondered the mix that is Os Peares; a testament to both nature and to man, with its three rivers, its four bridges and its hydroelectric dam. And this unusual town is so much more interesting for that.

4 La Ribeira Sacra – Galicia's sacred rivers

The Galician writer and geographer, Ramón Otero Pedrayo, called his homeland '*os país dos mil ríos*', the land of a thousand rivers. *Rías*, rivers, brooks, and streams crisscross the landscape like skeins of silk forming a sparkling cats' cradle through the Galician countryside. Abundance of water, whether from the sky or underground, is the reason Galicia is so green and verdant – and of all her riparian landscapes, the Ribeira Sacra is one of the most blessed.

An area bounding the mighty Miño and Sil rivers and encompassing parts of Lugo and Ourense provinces, La Ribeira Sacra (literally The Sacred Riverside) is home to Galicia's 'heroic viticulture' and the fresh young Ribeira Sacra wines. The continental climate of long hot summers and the moisture-laden air which forms above the rivers contribute to the fresh taste of these D.O (*denominación de origen*) wines. Some 1,250 hectares (3,000 acres) of steep hillsides are planted with grape vines; in autumn, those hillsides come alive with people carrying crates of blood red or virginal white grapes up and down the vertiginous slopes to waiting lorries.

In all, twenty councils make up the Ribeira Sacra region – from Portomarín in the north to Castro Caldelas in the south and Quiroga in the east. In addition to the two main rivers there is the Cabe which flows through Monforte de Lemos; the Lor in the east, which extends into O Courel; and the tiny Búbal, the third of the rivers which pass through the intriguing town of Os Peares.

Since 2005 the region has had its own tourism council to promote this beautiful and unspoilt inland area and was proposed for candidacy as a UNESCO biosphere site in 2021. The creation of this new biosphere reserve would bring to seven the total number in Galicia, with 35% of Galician territory within a biosphere reserve and 42% having some kind of protection.

When we first saw our home to be, *A Casa do Campo*, we had no idea we were lucky enough to be in this stunning area of heroic viticulture and brooding rivers. We also had no idea that we had already fallen in love with another house in the Ribeira Sacra region, some three years earlier.

It was 2004. We had set off to walk the *Camino de Santiago* that spring, along the coastal route. We overpacked and undertrained for the walk. Having reached Galicia via the fishing town of Ribadeo, we realised we wouldn't make it to Santiago in the time we had left. Instead, we turned inland – to view houses with an estate agent whose details I just happened to have with me.

Many people walk the Santiago pilgrim routes and have some kind of epiphany. Our epiphany took a slightly different direction; we fell in love with Galicia and, though we didn't know it, the Ribeira Sacra region.

The estate agent, Antonio, showed us many houses that first week, all were ridiculously cheap and all were totally unsuitable for our needs – bar one.

Nogueira de Ramuín is one of the councils making up the Ribeira Sacra region. It is one of the highest councils in the area, sitting at some 640 metres above sea level. When we first visited the house in Nogueira, we were amazed how the vegetation changed as we drove up the twisting hillside. In the Sil valley below, there were chestnut trees and oaks. As we climbed, non-native eucalyptus plantations emerged. Then came the pine plantations. At the very top were rocky outcroppings, thrusting through gorse and heather.

The house we fell in love with overlooked the river below (from one very small corner of the balcony, balancing on tiptoes and craning my head eastwards). At the front it had two storeys with a long wrought-iron balcony on the first floor. At the rear there was only one storey; the lower floor was only half the width of the upper, being built into the granite hillside behind.

4 La Ribeira Sacra – Galicia's sacred rivers

Upstairs, a corridor ran the length of the house. To the front were two good sized rooms, one a living room and one a bedroom with a tiny but functional en-suite. To the rear was a small kitchen and two further small, dark rooms.

Outside there was some land next to the house and, my hubby's favourite part, a remote woodland. This woodland was not one which was going to generate us an income, being mainly scrubby oak and birch with the occasional too tall eucalypt poking through. It did have some magnificent boulders in it though. Some of these rocks were the size of a small car and perfect for clambering on. Hence S' joy. A number of houses in that village were built into the rocks and at least two had glacial erratic boulders making up one wall of the building.

In the end, the owner of the house could not be traced, so we walked away, and some three years later we moved into our own *A Casa do Campo*, forty kilometres north and west of that first house, in Taboada council, which borders the Miño river to the east.

One of the things I'd liked about Nogueira was the walking route, which started in the village and traced a high course along cliff edges, through tiny villages with ancient stone-built churches, and past a granite quarry.

The Ribeira Sacra is dotted with walking routes, many following one of the river valleys. All have spectacular viewpoints and vary in length from a couple of hours trek to several weeks.

We have followed a few of these routes and would highly recommend them to get a feel for the area. Many of the routes can be found on *Wikiloc* if you are interested.

The Ribeira Sacra also offers driving routes, stopping at some of the wineries in the area. In autumn each year the tourism council runs the *Vinobus*. A coach collects participants from a number of different areas, stopping for wine tastings and talks along the way – always of course with accompanying *tapas*.

One year we joined our friends, Mike and John, and their visitors, two elderly and go-getting ladies, on one such trip. The coach picked us up in Pantón, near to where Mike and John lived. We paid our five euros each, then it drove us back to within ten minutes of home and a winery in Chantada. Despite this it was a good trip.

Each winery gave us a tour and a chat about the winemaking process. Sadly, this talk was entirely in Spanish, of which Mike's visitors understood not a word. Helen was 86 years old, and had no qualms about speaking her mind.

"This is boring, when do we get to taste the wine," she announced part way through, in a rather louder than necessary voice.

I was caught between acute embarrassment and the giggles. The tour guide continued unabated and I stuffed my hand in my mouth.

In typically generous Galician fashion, the tastings included bottles of wine piled onto a table along with chunks of *chorizo* and slices of Manchego cheese, accompanied by hunks of fresh local bread.

Our last visit of the day was to the wine centre in Monforte de Lemos, the second largest city in Lugo Province.

The wine centre is in the historic centre of Monforte. The 1752 stone building also houses a café, an excellent restaurant, a wine shop, and the tourist information office. On the first floor is a museum, interpretation boards, and a short video about the heroic viticulture of this undulating area. The video was in Galego, but luckily we had seats and Helen was silent throughout – I think she may have fallen asleep.

4 La Ribeira Sacra - Galicia's sacred rivers

Monforte is the setting of one of the two *paradores* or state-run luxury hotels in the Ribeira Sacra region, the other being in Nogueira de Ramuín. These historic hotels can be surprisingly well-priced for a luxurious overnight stay. The *parador* in Monforte sits in a commanding position at the top of the 'mont' overlooking the city. It was previously a monastery, with beautiful architecture and comfortable settles.

There are also many stunning *casas rurales* in the area. These rural house hotels are generally stone-built period farmhouses, beautifully restored and often retaining original features such as the open fires, or *lareiras,* and stone threshing areas.

Along the road eastwards from Monforte, lies the town of Quiroga. In the far east of the province of Lugo, on the north bank of the river Sil and poking into Castilla y León like a hernia, Quiroga is an historic and unusual town.

Quiroga is known for its honey and olive oil production, and has a honey and olive oil festival in August each year. The town is just 250 metres above sea level, in its own steep-sided valley, south of the Courel mountains.

When we last visited, the temperature in the valley was some 42°C. The air was completely still that day, humid and choking. Orange and lemon trees grew abundantly alongside some of the most delicious cherries I've ever eaten.

Just beyond Quiroga, and the last place in Galicia heading eastwards, is Montefurado with its Roman walls, its Roman olive oil stores sitting like huge beehives on the landscape, and its Roman gold mine workings.

The name Ribeira Sacra, or Sacred Riverside, comes from the numerous churches and chapels which abound in the area. There are often tours along the sacred rivers, visiting many of the granite *romanico* churches along the way.

For those who enjoy architecture, every one of the councils in the Ribeira Sacra has a unique building – be it a monastery, *pazo* or Celtic *castro*. Taboada has the biggest concentration of *pazos* or old manor houses in Galicia, one of which is close to our home and has a collection of anthropomorphic tombs. All of these are privately owned so can only be viewed from the outside – unless one asks the owner nicely as a young friend of ours once did.

When the first dams were built on the Miño, a number of villages situated along the banks of the river were inundated. Near to us is the village of Mourulle. It occupied a privileged spot close to the river and, I am assured by previous inhabitants, produced the most delicious wine in Galicia. In 2011, when the reservoir had to be emptied to allow work on the dam, this village appeared once more for a brief but memorable few months. We spent hours wandering between still standing, derelict stone homes. The vineyards were still visible; the preserved grape vines looking as if they were simply waiting for the spring sunshine to burst into bud. The whole place had an eerie post-apocalyptic feel to it.

Unlike Mourulle, the town of Portomarín was completely destroyed before being inundated. The locals were so upset about the new dam that officials feared they would return to their homes. At least that was the official line.

The old town of Portomarín lay in a warm valley along the Miño. The houses and 12th century church clustered along a narrow roadway running alongside the river which was crossed by a low bridge. Next to this bridge were the remains of an earlier Roman bridge – its two stepped end pillars standing tall, although much of the centre of the bridge had gone.

4 La Ribeira Sacra – Galicia's sacred rivers

One of those end pillars now stands on a roundabout as pilgrims on the Camino Frances enter Portomarín. Its steep steps lead to the new town, perched on a blustery hilltop above the reservoir. In the new town, on the plaza, sits a magnificent granite-built church with curious numbers written on its stones.

In 1957, the 12th century church of St. Nicolas and St. John was taken down and rebuilt, piece by piece like a painting by numbers. The letters and numbers, still visible some sixty years on, tell a story of both incredible stonemasonry and incredible heartbreak.

The two major rivers in the Ribeira Sacra region (and in Galicia) are a study in contrasts. The Miño is generally wide, its hillsides green and sun-filled. This 340-kilometre-long river arises just north of Lugo, flowing south then west to form the boundary with Portugal as it heads into the Atlantic Ocean at A Guarda. The river Sil arises inland, in the Castilla y León region, flowing 225 kilometres westwards to join the Miño at the town of Os Peares. The Cañon do Sil, or Sil Canyon, is a spectacular, steep-sided, brooding gorge with deep grey waters at its base. The sheer rock walls rise almost 500 metres above the river giving a unique microclimate and the most spectacular scenery in the area.

The 'sacred' rivers lend themselves to messing about in boats. Sadly, neither of the main rivers in the region is navigable for much of their length due to numerous hydroelectric dams, but there are plenty of opportunities for short trips.

Near to us is a nautical club which hires canoes, and occasionally puts on banana boat or water-skiing trips. It was here that S had his stag do the night before our wedding in 2010. Luckily no one ended up in the water that year.

Catamarans operate on both the Sil and the Miño rivers providing two-hour scenic trips which give a totally different perspective of these heroic landscapes.

We have been on the Miño trip twice and enjoyed it enormously. The first time was during Mum's 85th birthday celebrations. We began with drinks in a café on the banks of the river, sitting in the summer sunshine and enjoying the views of the village of Belesar climbing up the hillside opposite. The catamaran left at 11am, taking a large loop to the tip of the world (*O Cabo do Mundo*). The tour guide was a lovely chap, kindly explaining many of the sights in English for us and pointing out derelict villages.

"How many people do you think live in that village?" he asked, pointing at a largish settlement of some fifty buildings on the hill opposite. It was a beautiful looking spot.

"I don't know. Twenty?" I guessed.

"One!"

"Good grief!"

We spent the rest of the trip wondering what the sole inhabitant did alone up there every day, and if he had any friends.

The guide told us that before the Belesar dam was built the river was much shallower and narrower.

"People would use the river to visit each other and to transport goods for sale. Some villages didn't have road access until a few years after the dam was built."

I imagined people cut off from friends and neighbours until the slow wheels of bureaucracy turned and a road was provided.

We returned to the café that day, just in time for lunch. I'd booked a table for us and we ate outside in the shade, overlooking the river and, on my part, imagining how different the way of life was in this area before hydroelectric dams came to Galicia

SECTION THREE -
THE WILD ATLANTIC

5 A Coruña and the Tower of Hercules

"You do have your passport, don't you?"

I don't know what made me ask. We had already been on the road for over an hour and were well on the way to our destination. Some sixth sense maybe.

Mum fiddled in her handbag for a while. "No, sorry. I didn't think I needed it."

I do have these intuitions occasionally. They are never of much use to be honest. Why couldn't my sixth sense have asked the question before we left home?

"You should always carry your passport, Mum. It's your only ID if the police stop us."

At this revelation, Mum looked panic stricken. I had inadvertently triggered her worry mechanism with my ill-advised words.

I smiled. "Don't worry. We can always go back."

Now it was S' turn to look panic stricken at the idea of driving all the way home again.

"I don't think we have a choice," I said. "But I'll ring Frankie."

My niece was still at sea and her phone wasn't picking up, so I messaged my sister-in-law.

"Do you think we'll get away with it?" I asked her.

"I doubt it, the ship is very strict on security," came back the inevitable reply.

I loathe going backwards. Even when we take a walk, I like to do a circular route. On this occasion there was no help for it, we had to return home and collect the errant document if we were to have any hope of visiting my niece's place of work.

We had decided on a trip to A Coruña, the titular capital of Galicia's northwesternmost province, a few months before. My niece had messaged to say the passenger liner on which she worked as a nurse was docking in A Coruña in October. Could we meet up?

We hadn't seen my younger brother's daughter for years and were keen to visit her 'office'. It was also a chance to see a Galician city we'd not yet visited. We decided to keep it a surprise for Mum.

After stopping on the way back home for a quick cuppa at A Parga, it being past our usual morning tea time by now, we collected the missing passport then turned the car around. By the time we reached Rábade, just off the A6 motorway, a second time around – it was lunchtime. We pulled up next to one of the restaurants along the minor road through the town. It was a good choice. A small, dark bar area opened into a bright, clean and large dining room behind. The *menú del día* was a very respectable ten euros a head and our roast rabbit dish was huge.

Suitably fed we continued our journey, arriving in A Coruña at 3.30pm – slightly later than intended.

As the sun was shining, we headed straight for the Torre de Hércules.

This iconic building, which stands on a headland at the very northern tip of the A Coruña headland, is the only working example of a Roman lighthouse in existence and therefore the oldest active lighthouse in the world. The lighthouse was built in the 1st century CE, though nothing of that original building remains in the current façade. In 1788 the deteriorating Roman façade was covered with new stonework. Inside though, the remains of the original stone walls and the Roman chambers with their vaulted ceilings have been preserved.

The entrance to the tower is at the lower level, through an archaeological dig site where the original foundations can be seen. It was rather dark and crowded in there and Mum had soon had enough. She went back outside to sit on a convenient seat while S and I climbed the four storeys and 234 steps (no, I didn't count them, my brochure from the tourist information office below

5 A Coruña and the Tower of Hercules

the tower told me) to the viewing platform at the very top.

The Roman architecture was, as ever, a fascination for me. The square blocks of dressed stone for the walls, the rounder pebbles in the vaulted ceilings, and the huge keystones above the arched doors and windows set my imagination rolling.

From the open rooftop we had a stunning view of A Coruña city, the green peninsular tip on which the tower stands, and the wild Atlantic Ocean. The sky had now turned slate grey and the wind was howling across the headland. Mum sat far below us, huddled on a seat, and my hair was whipping around my face as I tried to photograph the ever-changing shadows on the peninsula.

A Coruña sits on Galicia's Atlantic coast, due north of Santiago. The sprawling city has long since spread beyond the original northeast facing old city. A narrow isthmus, with the port to the east and a long sandy beach to the west, leads to a bulbous headland. The right-hand bulge, incorporating the old town with its narrow alleyways and the Plaza Mayor, sweeps round to the north, partially enclosing the sheltered sea port. The left-hand bulge is a large, rocky green space, out of which the Hercules Tower arises.

The tower was listed as a UNESCO World Heritage Site in 2009. It is 59 metres (193 feet) high, making it 120 metres (393 feet) above sea level, and provides a vital service to shipping along this dangerous coast where sea mists arise out of nowhere and rocks lie in wait for the inexperienced sailor.

In other fascinating facts I discovered that day, the lighthouse emits a group of four white flashes every twenty seconds throughout the night. The light is visible 24 miles away, and the tower is twinned with the Statue of Liberty, 5,283 kilometres or 3,282 miles across the Atlantic Ocean.

The name of the tower arises from a legend which says that Hercules fought with a giant called Gerión who was king of all the lands between the Tagus and Duero rivers. Hercules was, of course, the victor, decapitating the giant and burying his head before ordering a tower to be built atop it. Hercules then founded the city of A Coruña nearby.

There are of course other contrasting legends but that one seemed suitably gory!

By the time I'd photographed each aspect from the top of the tower, including the green park below us and a sculptured circle divided into the seven Celtic nations, and taken the obligatory selfies, my hair was hopelessly tangled.

"I think it's time to rescue Mum," I said.

S pointed. "She's chatting to some young men down there."

"Ah! On second thoughts, she doesn't look like she needs rescuing."

When we arrived, the young men were just packing away their photography gear having spent some time photographing Mum's hands on her stick for a college project. It's an interesting thought that Mum's fingers may one day be on display in A Coruña.

By now the Atlantic was really showing off; the waves bounced on the rocks below the tower, and the wind was ferocious. It was time to find our bed for the night.

I'd booked our hotel online. It was close to the harbour where Frankie's ship was docking the following morning and near to the old town. After two passes of the street where the hotel was supposed to be, I spotted it. The place was built almost directly above a huge four-lane underpass which whisked cars towards the old town. There was no parking nearby so S dropped Mum and me off to ask at the reception.

"We can park in the underground car park opposite for a 'special' rate of 25€," I told hubby, before leaving

5 A Coruña and the Tower of Hercules

him to negotiate the four lanes and the parking whilst Mum and I checked in.

The hotel reception was bright and airy with seating in small groups, free water and juice dispensers, and sweeties in vast bowls. In contrast, our rooms were tiny. There was space (just) for the double beds whilst still allowing access to the bathroom door. They were also airless and roasting hot.

I popped back to reception to ask how to reduce the heating in the room but was told the aircon wasn't working. This seems to be a theme for me and hotel rooms. We pushed open the windows, listening to the sounds of a city at night and a loud disco opposite.

The hotel was not situated quite as conveniently as I'd thought from its photographs on Booking.com (which failed somehow to show the rather obvious underpass) but it was a reasonably level walk for Mum into the old town that evening for an explore, with the promise of *tapas* and wine at the end.

We wandered the alleyways and *tapas* bars, ending our night in the Plaza María Pita sitting on a restaurant terrace, sipping *vino tinto* and enjoying our *tortilla de patatas* as the beautiful and rich promenaded by on their evening *paseo*.

We were awake early the next morning. We'd found the room stuffy and achingly hot with the windows closed, and the city noise unbearable with the windows open. In our little village, we hear nary a sound at night other than owls hooting or the snuffling of night animals.

"Did you sleep well?" I asked Mum, when I popped next door to check on her.

She was sitting in a chair gazing at four huge white funnels poking up above the noisy disco opposite.

"Look, these appeared this morning," she said, pointing in awe.

Although we could only see the top of the superstructure it was obvious that it was massive.

"Shall we go and have a look after breakfast?" I asked.

We opted to walk into the old town for breakfast as S had spotted a *chocolatería* on one of the back streets the evening before. The *chocolate caliente* was everything I'd dreamed of. My spoon stood straight up from the thick mud-coloured liquid and my doughy *churros* sucked loudly as I prised them out of its quicksand-like grasp.

Mum chose toast and coffee.

Afterwards we wandered down to the docks to peer up at the magnificent ship. People were streaming out of the dock area and lining up for their coach tours to Santiago, or to the Torre de Hércules. The ship would dock in each port for maybe a day and most of the passengers would see nothing of the real city, being whisked away to distant tourist sites. It's Wednesday so it must be A Coruña.

My niece had arranged for us all to be added to her visitor list so we could see the ship. None of us had ever been on a luxury passenger liner and I was looking forward to nosing around.

Mum still knew nothing of our plans.

"Let's go and have a closer look," I suggested, heading off against the current of exiting passengers.

"Oh, I don't think we can," replied Mum, her worries surfacing again. I think Mum must have had a strict childhood, sometimes. Or she is simply of a not very daring generation.

"Of course we can. I'll just go and chat to those guards," I said.

The security detail manning the exit from the dock area were delightful. I explained we should be on the manifest for visitors that day and they confirmed we were. I beckoned Mum and S.

"Come on, we can go through," I said.

Mum was still reluctant, expecting, it seemed, to be thrown into jail any minute. And probably expecting us to then do a runner and leave her there – such is her imagination.

5 A Coruña and the Tower of Hercules

Close up, the ship was bigger than I'd imagined. We were dwarfed by the vast whiteness of the structure. Mum loved it, but suddenly refused to go any further.

"I can chat up the guards on the gangplank. I bet they'll let us have a look round," I teased.

But she dug in her heels, so I had to call for reinforcements.

"We're here," I texted to my niece. "But nana won't come any further!!!"

"On my way," came the reply.

Within a few minutes I saw her; red-headed, graceful, and dressed in her 'best' whites, Frankie was virtually on top of us by the time Mum noticed. When she did, the floodgates opened and my photographs of the reunion look like Mum has been recently beaten, with tear-stained face and mussed hair.

The ship was as magnificent as I'd expected and more. It was all wood-panelling, glass, and polished brass, looking like a Victorian gentleman's club. We had tea in one of the lounges. It was served in proper tea pots accompanied by a plate of aniseed biscuits.

The communal area was marble-floored with a wood and brass staircase spiralling upwards to the next level. Below was a display of carved pumpkins for the annual Hallowe'en competition. Some were genuine works of art.

As Frankie showed us around the ship, she told us about her job as one of the nurses on board. It seems a dream job to many but had its difficult moments too.

One of those long, difficult moments was to come the following spring when Covid-19 suddenly descended. The ship was in Australian waters, ready to head to New Zealand when all cruise ships were banned from putting into port. What followed was a six-month long nightmare. The ship had to lie off shore for an eternity before eventually steaming all the way back to Portsmouth, months after everyone's tour had finished.

For now, though, the problems were more routine; heart attacks were common apparently, as were falls and broken bones. There was the odd elderly, confused person who wandered the decks, having to be rescued, and there were sunburns and mosquito bites.

The restaurant was huge. The food apparently varied depending on the clientele and the cruise destinations. Frankie asked us if we would like a pub lunch.

"Well, it would be rude to say no," I said, smiling.

We sat ourselves in the onboard 'English Pub'. I had pie and chips, and half a pint of real ale. Mum chose a huge whorl of Cumberland sausage with mash, whilst S opted for battered fish, chips and mushy peas, and a pint. It was a delicious change.

We left the ship, and my lovely niece, at 3.30pm. A steady drizzle had set in as we headed back to the hotel to check out.

It had been another lovely road trip and I had learnt a valuable lesson - keep passports together and always, but always, check before leaving home!

6 Muxía – the wild Atlantic coast

Galicia's Atlantic coast is a wild and dangerous place, and none of it more so than the area known as the Costa da Morte or Coast of Death. This 200-kilometre stretch, from Muros in the south to Malpica in the north, is littered with the remains of ships sunk off the treacherous rocky shore. It is, however, also a stunning coastline, especially when the sun is shining, and the perfect area for a spring road trip.

"The animals will be okay for a couple of days. What do you think?" I asked over breakfast.

"Sounds good to me," replied hubby, S.

"We should get to Betanzos in time for tea."

Betanzos is a pretty town, near to the beginnings of the west coast *rías*, founded in the 13th century by King Alfonso IX. By the 16th century, Betanzos was the capital of one of seven Galician provinces. The main town is built on a hill overlooking two rivers, the Mendo and Mandeo, which wind in a horseshoe around the base of the hill. The old town, climbing the hillside, is compact with a lively café scene and a large market square on top of the hill.

The square was packed that day. There was some event on, with stalls run by the local councils and tourism boards, bouncy castles, and street vendors selling doughnutty *churros*. We wandered from stall to stall, collecting maps and other goodies.

"Here you go, Mum. Keep the sun out of your eyes." I plonked a bright green baseball cap on Mum's head.

The smiling stall holder offered her a matching green canvas bag with 'Concello de Pontedeume' written on it.

Mum smiled. "Thank you! How much?"

"No. Is free."

Happy with our haul we headed towards the coast.

Unfortunately, the navigator (aka yours truly) missed the slow road turn off and we ended up on the *peaje* towards A Coruña.

We dislike toll roads, not just because of the cost, which is not great, but because we are hopeless at working out the different systems. After twice getting into the wrong lane at the toll booth and having to reverse past waiting cars, we finally escaped at Carballo and headed to the coast at Malpica de Bergantiños.

"Malpica. Is that 'bad peaks'?" asked S.

"Ha. Probably! Or bad bite. Not the most promising name for a seaside town, is it?"

It is nevertheless a popular one. Personally, we found Malpica expensive and touristy.

"All the restaurants seem to be serving seafood. No good for Mum," I'd said as we wandered the streets.

"And have you seen the prices?" added S.

I'd booked our accommodation for the night in the coastal town of Muxía, at the Pensión Alemana, online. Muxía is the self-styled 'heart of the coast of death' and one of the way-points on the triangular extension to the Camino de Santiago, the Muxía-Finisterre Way.

We parked on the main seafront and set off on foot to find our elusive hotel. It was well hidden on a narrow backstreet; the frontage, with its green painted balcony and stone walls, looked inviting and cheerful. The bar area inside was dim and cool, full of old wooden benches positioned around a stone fireplace with a bar to one side.

On hearing Mum was in her eighties, the friendly owners insisted on carrying her case up the stairs for her. They had put Mum on the first floor near to the breakfast room and us on the floor above. Both rooms were clean and bright with colourful rugs on the stone floors, and for us a balcony overlooking the narrow street.

6 Muxía – the wild Atlantic coast

Once settled in, we walked towards the Santuario da Virxe da Barca, which sits on a shoreline at the very tip of the peninsula, looking out to sea. The Sanctuary of the Virgin of the Barge must be the most famous and photographed building in Muxía, lying in one of the most stunning settings of any I've seen. Beyond the creamy stone building with its two towers is a field of rocks. Sheets of wave-smoothed granite make up the shoreline. Odd irregular boulders are bestowed with names and magical properties. The oscillating stone (*pedra de abalar*) wobbles alarmingly, whilst the lovers' stone has obvious properties for those seeking that special bond.

The santuario was built, firstly as a hermitage then a church, on a spot which was sacred to the early Celts as a place of worship and magic. It seems the magic held for the Christian church as the Virgin Mary was said to have arrived on this coast in a stone barge to give inspiration and comfort to St James, who was struggling to convert the pagans of the land. The large erratic boulders along the coastline here are said to be the remains of the Virgin's boat. This legend has many of the same themes as that of the apostle himself, who, it is said, landed in Galicia in a stone barge after his death in the holy lands.

At the santuario we met a couple of pilgrims. After exchanging *holas*, they asked if we knew of a supermarket. Sadly, we didn't. We said goodbye and continued our walk in the opposite direction.

Later, Mum was sitting on a bench in a small square when we saw the same pilgrims. Having now seen a number of supermarkets, I ran to intercept them.

"Hola. *Hay un supermercado allí,*" I puffed, on reaching the young-looking, grey-haired lady.

"*Ah, gracias, mi marido descubre,*" she replied in good but accented Spanish.

"*¿De dónde eres?*" I asked, being nosey me.

"*Australia,*" came the reply.

At that point I switched to English and we both laughed at our attempts to converse in Spanish.

"I love those shoes. What on earth are they?" I asked, pointing to her feet; five toes were visible on each foot, caught in a what looked like a neoprene glove.

"These?" she replied, wriggling her toes. "They're the most comfortable things ever. I always wear them after we've finished walking for the day."

Sue and Howard, it turned out, lived near Brisbane and had walked the Camino a number of times. That year was their 70th birthdays so they were including the Muxía way to Finisterre.

"We've walked to Finisterre a number of times but wanted to extend our *camino* further this time."

"How far is it?" I asked.

"Around 200 kilometres all in all. The leg to Muxía is 80, then 29 along the coast to Finisterre and slightly under 90 back to Santiago."

"Wow! You two make me feel like a layabout!"

I was still talking with Sue when her husband reappeared with provisions from the supermarket and we continued our chat at the bench on which Mum still sat, wondering where I'd gone!

On the way back to our *pensión* we checked out a couple of potential dinner spots, choosing O Prestige which advertised a nine-euro, all day, *menú del día*.

The Prestige is the oil tanker which sank off the Costa da Morte in November 2002 causing one of the worst wildlife disasters in history. The clean-up cost of the 60,000 tonnes of crude oil was estimated to be 2.5 billion euros for the Galician coast alone

The walls of the Bar O Prestige were adorned with pictures of all the shipwrecks off this notorious coast going back to 1596 when twenty ships of the Spanish Armada sank in violent storms with the loss of over 1,700 lives. It was a morbid but ultimately enthralling display, and kept us amused whilst waiting for our meal.

6 Muxía – the wild Atlantic coast

Afterwards, we walked the few hundred yards back to the *pensión*, which had transformed itself from quiet dark pub to heaving, loud and jolly watering hole in the time we'd been away. The bar area was standing room only, but someone soon spotted the 'English' and forced a space for Mum at one of the low tables. It was hot and friendly, and Mum enjoyed her large brandy before bed.

The noise continued below our balcony until extremely late or extremely early, whichever you prefer. In the morning the owner was most apologetic, telling us she had asked the patrons to be quiet when they went outside but to no avail.

I laughed. "Asking a Spaniard to be quiet is impossible. It doesn't matter."

Breakfast was served in the large, and mainly empty, room just across from Mum's bedroom. The cheerful lady there sorted us out with orange juice and tea then made piles of toast which she brought out with jam and butter, urging us to 'eat more' until we were sated and virtually immobile.

After breakfast we drove to the santuarío for a good look around. S and I walked across the sheets of stone which line the shore whilst Mum practised taking photographs with my camera. The stone path up to the Monte Corpiño gave us 360-degree views down to the Atlantic Ocean, the santuarío, Cape Vilán on the headland opposite, and the many beaches along the coast. It was breathtaking.

Our next stop was the small village of Camelle, the last home and resting place of an eccentric German artist called Manfred Gnädinger – better known locally as *El Alemán,* or simply 'Man'.

Gnädinger was born in Bohringer, in Germany, in 1936. He moved to Galicia at the insistence of a friend and initially rented a house, painting the walls black and collecting oddities from his beachcombing sessions. After the owners asked him to leave, the German disappeared. He returned to Camelle some time later wearing nothing but a loincloth.

'Man' is described as tall and thin with long hair and beard, and in pictures wears nothing but his trademark loincloth. He bought a piece of land near to the end of the harbour in Camelle where he built a wooden hut. The hut was still there when we visited, decorated with circles in vivid colours and surrounded by stone cairns built by Man over his years living there without electricity or water.

Man was a rabid collector of flotsam from the beach. In the seventies, he opened his home to visitors. The nominal fee included a pack of pencils and paper for the visitor to record their feelings on seeing Man's work. Some of these visitor drawings are still to be found in the museum dedicated to the artist, with displays of thousands of his carefully annotated notebooks and displays of weird and wonderful sculptures made using debris from the sea shore. This indoor museum opened in 2015, not long before we visited. Man's home itself is sadly no longer open to the public.

Manfred Gnädinger died on the 28th of December 2002, just weeks after the Prestige oil tanker spilled its cargo onto the Galician shores. The oil slick destroyed seabirds and wildlife, and devastated the fishing industry.

When the oil flooded Man's outdoor museum at the end of the harbour he declared that it should be left as it was, saying:

"I say that this must not ever be cleaned. It is an episode of history. It must remain for all to remember who man is because man doesn't love man nor the sea nor the fishes nor the beach."

We walked along the harbour to Man's shack, still visible and surrounded by some of the crazy oil-slicked stone cairns he'd built. It was a poignant sight.

6 Muxía – the wild Atlantic coast

Our accommodation for our second night was in Camariñas, just across the *ría* from Muxía. One disadvantage of booking online is that you don't get a feel for a place before arriving. In Muxía we had been spoilt, in Camariñas we weren't.

There was nothing wrong with our hotel, except the receptionist didn't seem to have time to speak with us, nor to offer us any information about the town, nor even manage to give us directions to our rooms. All minor things and no great issue, but it felt so different to the overt friendliness we'd received at Muxía.

Our rooms were, however, faultless, with pleasant balconies overlooking the sea at an angle and clean white bedlinen. There were even free bottles of water in the room. The restaurant was closed on a Sunday so we headed into the town to find a late lunch somewhere.

"Most of these restaurants seem to be just *tapas* bars," I said, peering at the customers sitting at outside tables laden with mixed plates.

"I like those," Mum replied, pointing at one of the tables none too subtly.

Our *raciones* were tasty, but the service suggested that Camariñas might be slightly jaded with tourists.

Dinner that evening took even more finding. Almost everywhere was closed on a Sunday night and we must have walked in circles for hours before finding a rather swish looking place on one of the umpteen back streets in Camariñas. The Villa Oro was friendly and attentive, the meal huge and delicious. It was a good end to an interesting day.

Breakfast was served in the closed restaurant opposite the reception desk, where we were told to go and help ourselves.

Our first challenge was to find some cutlery, as there was none on the tables. Random opening of a few cupboard doors elicited bowls, glasses, napkins, and eating irons. Breakfast was a slow process. The orange juice consisted of a machine into which one had to feed whole oranges, catching the juice in a jug.

"Five minutes that's taken me," I complained, plonking three glasses of freshly squeezed juice on our table. "I hope no one wants seconds!"

The toaster took forever to brown a piece of bread and the kettle wouldn't boil.

Of the staff there was no sign. Even reception seemed deserted. It was a most bizarre experience.

"Shall we go and look at the *faro*?" I asked over our DIY spread. "I saw a sign yesterday. Google says it's worth a look."

"What's a farrow?" asked Mum.

"The Faro de Cabo Vilán was the first electric lighthouse in Spain when it replaced the steam driven light in 1896. It sits on a rocky outcrop above the wild Atlantic coast with a museum next to it," I read.

"Sounds good."

We drove off into the morning sunshine, and after the third attempt found the correct road to the lighthouse - the narrowest and twistiest of the three options. Obviously.

By the time we arrived at this lonely outpost, the *faro* was entirely surrounded by a dense, cold, penetrating mist and invisible from more than ten yards away. The wind whipped away the door of the car, my cap, and our voices. It was probably delightful in the sunshine.

"It says the light can be seen for over forty miles," I yelled into the wind.

"I can't see more than forty feet!" replied S. "And I think Mum has blown away."

Point taken, we jumped back into the warm car.

Having been bitten by the pioneering spirit, we drove on to look for the Cementerio de Los Ingleses.

"On the 10th of November 1890, the HMS Serpent sank off the Punta de Boi near to Camariñas. The residents of the village of Xaviña quickly arrived to help the survivors, but sadly all but three of the 175 passengers

6 Muxía – the wild Atlantic coast

died that day off the dangerous Costa da Morte. The residents buried the dead. The British Navy later came to erect a stone wall around the 'English Cemetery' and a salute was fired each time a warship passed by the area in grateful thanks to the actions of the local people.

"In gratitude for the help of the locals the mayor of Camariñas was presented with a watch and the priest of Xaviña with a rifle," I read from a leaflet I'd picked up.

"Why a rifle?" asked Mum.

"Who knows!"

The map showed a walking route to the cemetery but the directions for vehicles were vague. After circling the tall wind turbines on the hill, we asked a mother and daughter walking along the narrow road.

"*¿El Cementerio? Si. Es arriba,*" said the elderly lady, dressed from head to toe in black and standing almost as tall as my shoulder. She pointed upwards in an unreassuringly vague manner. "*¿Tenéis familia allí?*"

"No, we don't have family there," I replied. I then struggled to explain why exactly we did want to visit a cemetery to a bunch of people we didn't know. In the end I just shrugged and we continued on our way.

Again, we circled the windmills and even ventured a little way along a rocky dirt track but eventually our pioneering spirit gave out.

"I don't think the car likes this road either," said S, as we bounced along.

We never did find the cemetery of the English, but I'm sure it's worth a trip if you ever find yourself near Camariñas with nothing to do – and in a pioneering frame of mind.

Back at sea level the sun was gloriously hot as we drove towards the small town of Laxe.

Laxe had a delightful sandy, dune-backed beach and a number of shops and restaurants. It felt much more real to me than Camariñas and I liked it immediately.

We wandered up through the old town, along the usual narrow streets and along the wooden boardwalk towards a newly-built complex of villas, me daydreaming about buying a house on the seafront and paddling every day.

"You'd soon get fed up," said S. "The view doesn't change at the coast."

"Of course, it does. The sea changes hourly here. I bet it's wild in winter."

"But it's still just sea."

I sighed. I'd never win that battle, and I do love our ever-changing view of the woodland from our windows at home.

At Laxe, I discovered signs for a long-distance coastal walk.

"That would be a nice walk," I said at the time.

Again, we ended up on the toll road heading back home, and almost ran out of fuel as we hadn't checked the gauge.

Our very vocal cat was awaiting our return and his inevitable goodies. I heard his yowl as I opened the drive gates – a yowl which didn't stop until his bowl was on the ground in front of his nose, full of left-over meat and chips.

SECTION FOUR - CAPITAL CITIES

7 The Roman city of Lugo – the very first time

I fell in love with the Roman city of Lugo the first time I saw it. The year was 2004 and we had just stepped off a coach from Ribadeo, the gateway to Galicia, on the north coast. In front of me, as we exited the bus station, was a magnificent stone wall. It was over twenty metres high, made of granite blocks and slate, and sported clumps of spring flowers. The wall disappeared off in either direction, curving away from us. Directly ahead was a high archway with glimpses beyond of stone buildings and a patch of grass. Along the top of the wall, I could see people walking, jogging, or ambling along chatting to their companions.

"Wow! Can we go up there?" I asked, lifting my too-heavy rucksack onto my shoulders.

"Let's find somewhere to stay first and get rid of these, eh?" replied S.

He had a point. I didn't fancy lugging my rucksack around the city if I didn't have to.

We found the tourist information office, despite the council's attempts to hide it. On that occasion it was in an arcade of shops off the Plaza Mayor. Since then, the office has moved at least three times and each time it has been relocated to somewhere even less prominent than a tiny office snuck in between travel agencies and clothes retailers with no signpost.

When I enquired about a hotel, the lady in the office took one look at our rucksacks and travel-stained clothes and rang a number.

"Sara will meet you by the *Porta Falsa*. She has a very good, and cheap, *pensión* nearby."

We stood in a small plaza next to a large granite-walled school building and a glass elevator down to the underground parking. The latter looked out of place in this city of grey stone. I stared up at the encircling stone walls in awe.

The *Porta Falsa* is one of the five original Roman gates into (and out of) the old city. The tall, pedestrian-only, stone archway led to a short set of steps down to the city ring-road, the Ronda da Muralla, beyond. The walls towered above me, accessed by a stone staircase with a low banister wall. The stones were green with moss and spattled with multi-coloured lichen. I could imagine a sentry standing on the walls, shouting a challenge before slowly creaking open the heavy wooden gate which would have protected the city.

"I can see Roman legions marching up there," I said, pointing.

Before my imagination ran away with me, our host arrived to escort us to her *pensión*, just five minutes' walk away. The Pensión Gran Vía had comfortable rooms and the friendliest of owners. We still stay there when we visit Lugo. On that occasion, we dumped our bags and shot back out to find lunch and to explore this intriguing city.

The tourist information lady had obviously got the measure of us. When I'd asked her to recommend a restaurant for lunch, she immediately directed us to a parade of four such establishments just outside the walls. All had reasonably priced *menús del día*, and the one we chose, Café Recatelo, became our home from home for the next fifteen years, until Andrés and his lovely wife retired.

Lugo was probably founded by early Celtic peoples (Lugos or Logos is a Celtic god). It was named Lucus Augusti, the Grove of Augustus, by the conquering Romans, in 15-13 BCE.

Initially a thriving commercial town in a busy gold mining area, manor houses and hovels tumbled down the hillside in an expansive sprawl as the city rapidly grew. The walls I'd been staring at earlier were not built until the 3rd century CE when the town was fortified against attacks by both local and Germanic tribes.

7 The Roman city of Lugo – the very first time

In the process of creating a defensible, walled city, many of the homes which had grown up on the edges of it were destroyed. Traces of these homes can still be found. When a new auditorium was being built for the University of Santiago near to the cathedral gate, a Roman manor house was discovered. Some of its highly decorated walls were still intact, together with a temple to Mithras, a Roman/Persian deity. The new auditorium was built above the archaeological remains, the lower floor being one of my favourite museums, *El Domus*.

Lugo was declared a UNESCO World Heritage Site in 2000 for the 'finest example of late Roman fortification in western Europe'. The walls totally encircle the old town, being some 2.2 kilometres in circumference and the only complete walls in existence of this era.

As I found that first day, walking the Roman walls in Lugo is a delight, especially for someone of vivid imagination. I spent our walk envisaging myself as a Roman centurion marching with my century, or gazing out of the openings on *A Mosqueira* tower at the barbarian raiders, circling the Ronda da Muralla dozens of feet below.

"This is the best view," I said, as we paused on our circuit of the walls.

Here, there was a break in the array of mixed-era, but mainly ugly, concrete-built apartment blocks. A panorama opened up. From our vantage point I could see the river Miño as a thin ribbon twinkling far below us, and grey-green hills in the distance.

"I can see why it was such a strong defensive position," I said.

The walkway along the top of the Roman walls was gravelled and said to be wide enough for a century of men to walk in formation. The parapet was at knee height with no thought for health and safety. I was at once horrified and fascinated, imagining small children and dogs toppling over the barrier. Looking inwards to the old city below us, I could see tiny alleyways and old stone buildings. Some of the roofs were on a level with us.

"The cats have colonised this one." S pointed at a gaggle of cats of all hues, basking on a black tiled roof.

Many of the buildings here looked abandoned – their roofs collapsed, windows broken, and wooden shutters hanging dejectedly. Some of the buildings sported large lamps, their metalwork painted in a vulgar shade of purple.

"Odd area," I said.

I felt sad at the obvious disrepair of these historic buildings. Some were unbelievably narrow four and five storey high structures squeezed between newer apartment blocks, their roofs patched and covered in tar to waterproof them. A tiny attic window stood open to the elements, its paintwork peeling. Some of the higgledy-piggledy buildings had roofs which crossed at bizarre angles. I could imagine the army of felines wandering the entire city without ever having to descend to ground level.

"Oh, I like these ones."

Next to us, opening onto the walkway itself was a row of terraced houses. From here they were just one storey high but from the alley below, they were at least five storeys.

"Can you imagine opening your door onto a Roman wall every morning?" I asked.

Inside the walls, the old town was compact, with surprises around every corner. In one area I saw those odd purple lamps again. Next to one such lamp was a scantily dressed woman, posing in an erotic fashion. The penny dropped with agonising slowness.

"Red light district," said S.

"No. Purple light district," I replied.

In the centre of the old city was a large square with a central area shaded by enormous topiaried weeping Japanese Pagoda trees (*Sophora japonica 'pendula'*). We

7 The Roman city of Lugo – the very first time

entered the Plaza Mayor up a wide set of steps. At the top was a bandstand and wooden benches.

The *Casa do Concello*, or Town Hall, stood at the far end, its row of flags flapping on long poles. In front of the town hall was a line of cannon balls, each one set a little deeper into the stone-flagged pavement than its neighbour – as if a giant had run along, jumping on the iron spheres. To the left was a row of cafes under a stone-pillared arcade. People sat drinking coffee and people-watching on a terraced area in front of the cafes. On our right, a decorative art nouveau corner building announced itself to be the Círculo das Artes. Diagonally opposite, next to the town hall, stood a pharmacy shop. All wood and decorative glass, it looked as if it had been there for a hundred years. I could well imagine that it had.

A long straight pedestrianised street led to a market hall, closed in the afternoon, and a museum, the Casa dos Mosaicos – also closed. One of the myriad alleyways gave us my favourite discovery of the day. In a dark corner, near to one of the city gates, was a tiny and tangled, ancient shop which sold string, and corks. Nothing else. What a find.

As we sat outside one of the many cafes near to a stone-built fountain in the Plaza de Campo, I mused on this ancient city.

"It's like time's stood still, isn't it?"

Although we were unaware on that spring day, each June, Lugo hosts a Roman festival. The city is the perfect setting with its alleyways and cobbled plazas, its stone buildings and ancient feel. There are Roman forts, Celtic villages, weddings and battles, chariot races, gladiator fights, a parade of the Roman Legions and a firework display. Almost the whole of the city dresses for Arde Lucus, and visitors to the area must wonder that they really have slipped back two millennia in time.

We wandered around the town that evening, sampling bars and listening to the sounds of locals enjoying themselves.

"I like it here," I said.

S nodded. "D'you have that telephone number for the estate agent you found?"

"Of course."

"Good. Let's go see some houses."

§

We saw many houses over the next few days and three years later, in 2007, we finally moved to Galicia.

I still love the city of Lugo. Many of the older houses we saw in 2004 have long since been demolished, but the council has begun to stamp preservation orders on some of the more interesting old buildings and renovation works are ongoing.

It's also good to know that, many years later, Lugo can still show us new sights to surprise us.

Over seventeen years after that first trip, we decided to take a walk along the Paseo Fluvial next to the river Miño and over Lugo's Roman bridge – one historic monument we had never visited. It was a bright and sunny November day. We left the car at Carrefour supermarket before walking downhill towards the park which fronts the river.

The old city was just visible at the top of the hill 100 metres above us; the towers of the Cathedral of Santa María poked up between the concrete blocks of the newer city which sprawled down the hillside, much as that early Roman city would have done.

It was a pleasant walk. The water sparkled, reflecting the low sun. The overhanging trees cast long shadows, even at midday. A short weir tumbled the water with a gentle susurration. People walked their dogs or cycled along the pedestrianised river walk. To our left was a large grassed area. Locals sat in the winter sunshine,

7 The Roman city of Lugo – the very first time

talking or staring at their phones, exercising or reading. Up ahead I saw the distinctive arches of the Roman bridge.

The current bridge is actually of Medieval construction, though it probably replaced an earlier Roman bridge which would have been part of the Via XIX connecting Lucus Augusti to Bracara Augusta (Braga) in Northern Portugal.

At the entrance to the bridge was a full-sized figure of a Roman soldier, cast in polished steel, and looking somewhat skeletal-faced. The trees along the riverbank were clothed in autumn colours. Still in leaf, they shone green, gold, and scarlet, lining the banks like sentinels. The blue of the river reflected that of the cornflower sky, and even the ugly, modern Lugonian apartment blocks on the hill couldn't spoil the view.

Just beyond the Roman bridge we reached the 1st century Roman spa. In a *déjà vu* moment, I realised that it was closed.

The last (and only other) time we'd tried to visit the Roman baths, it had been closed too. That time there had been no lights working, though the door was open. This time the door was firmly closed. A notice stated the spa may reopen in March. I loved the decisiveness of the 'may'.

Despite the closed door, the sulphuric, rotten egg smell still permeated the area. Next to the door and at a lower level, I could see a number of tumbled, moss-green stones lying in a heap. The notice board said the spa was well-preserved – the 'dressing room' where clothes were left and the hot pool, of particular interest. I'd have to take their word for that, as all we could see was the new spa hotel which was built on the site.

In Roman times, spas were often built near to main trunk roads for marching soldiers, or more likely wealthy merchants, to soak away the ache of a long journey.

I sat in the sunshine and thought of our own long journey, to be here, in Galicia, where we all feel more at home than we ever have elsewhere.

"Those Romans knew a thing or two, didn't they?" I mumbled to the ancient stones beneath me.

8 Return to A Coruña – walking the City of Glass

A Coruña is Galicia's second most populous city, after Vigo. It is situated in the west of the province bearing its name, on a northwest facing peninsula that bulges into the Atlantic Ocean, creating its sheltered harbour.

The majority of Coruña's 243,000 population are found in the sprawling new town. We, though, were heading towards the bulge which sprouts beyond the mainland and is joined to it by a narrow isthmus – and an autumn walk.

Looking for all the world like a balloon pushed through a tiny hole and then blown into a flattened bulb, or something a trainee glassblower may produce, Coruña's 'bulge' is not only home to its seaport, but the old town, two beaches, and the iconic Hercules Tower. As one passes through the narrow neck, only half a dozen streets wide, there are some old and elegant buildings fronted by wide *galerías* of metal and glass, giving A Coruña its epithet, 'the City of Glass'.

Popping out on the other side of a road tunnel, the port was immediately visible. Passenger liners sat serenely at anchor, gleaming in the sunshine. Beyond the port, our lovely but annoying navigation system, which I call 'SatGirl', took us on a convoluted route around the back streets of the city.

The road which runs the length of the 'top' of the peninsula has one of those wonderfully long-winded Galician names, which defy reason.

Each time we arrived at a roundabout, which was roughly every fifty metres, SatGirl announced; "At the roundabout take the second exit to continue on Avenida de Paseo Maritima de Alcalde Francisco Vázquez."

This took so long, and her Spanish pronunciation was so dire, that we had inevitably reached the next roundabout by the time she'd got the sentence out and we had to endure a replay. By the time we finally 'reached our destination' at the Torre de Hércules, we were chanting the directions alongside poor SatGirl and giggling like schoolkids.

The latter was not, I felt, a good idea as I desperately needed a wee. Finding a toilet with public access in these post-Covid times was not easy. The portaloos stuck in the car park at the Torre de Hércules were filthy, and I didn't fancy paying entrance to the Torre just to use their loos. I sulked while S relieved his bladder as only men can.

"Go in the bushes," he said, when I complained.

"That's easy for you to say. In case you'd not noticed, we're in a very public place with no bushes suitable for sneaking into and dropping my knickers. Unless you want a crowd of onlookers laughing at your wife, we'll have to find a café."

Of course, the more of a hurry one is in, the more things go awry and today was no exception.

S led us down a track from the tower towards the promenade. Unfortunately, this particular track led only to a hill above a tiny beach. It dead-ended at the cliff edge, looking down on the beach nestling fifty metres below us. I took some photos of the *torre* whilst crossing my legs and hoping I wasn't going to embarrass myself, before back tracking ill-humouredly.

Once we got onto the Paseo Maritima, which parallels the road of the same name, the going was easier and I strode away, trying not to think about my overextended bladder.

"There! That's a café, I think. Is it open?" I asked, peering short-sightedly across two streets and a patch of grass.

"The door's open…" began S, but I was already off, waddling as fast as I could towards the inviting doorway.

"Chamomile, please," I called to my long-suffering hubby over my shoulder as we entered the bar, then,

8 Return to A Coruña - walking the City of Glass

"*Hola*," to the barman as I dashed to the clearly (thank you) signed *aseos*.

Two minutes later I was seated at a small table in the middle of a large, and mainly empty, café.

"Better?" asked S, smiling.

"Hmm. It's alright for you lot," I said, not for the first time – nor for the last.

"D'they do tapas?" I asked. "I'm hungry now my bladder's empty, and I forgot the cake from the car."

"You did stomp off a bit quickly."

"I forgot to change into my sandals and shorts too. It's getting really warm out there."

I wandered up to the counter to look at the offerings. There was the usual Russian salad, and *chorizos*, and a couple of tasty looking, thick round *tortillas*.

"D'you want a bit of *tortilla*?" I asked, returning to the table.

"I'm okay. But you go ahead," S replied.

"I don't like eating alone," I sulked.

"I don't need anything, but you do or you'll be ratty."

"Rattier, you mean?" I asked, wandering back to the bar.

"*Una tapa de tortilla, por favor*," I said, pointing.

"*¿Una?*" the barman asked, holding up one finger.

"*Si.*"

The barman obviously didn't believe me, or thought I was being mean to my poor starving hubby, as he plonked a huge slice of golden-yellow Spanish omelette on a plate, along with two great chunks of Galician bread and a couple of forks.

"You'd better share or I won't eat my dinner," I said, taking my seat.

Replete with creamy potato and egg *tortilla,* we wandered back across the grassy bank, two roads, and a set of tram lines.

"I didn't see them on the way in. Do you think the trams still run?" I asked.

"If so, those cars may be in for a shock." S pointed at the line of cars parked on the tram tracks in front of us. I guess trams are a thing of the past. A pity.

The Paseo Maritima runs for some thirteen kilometres around the south, north, and west side of the peninsula. As the bulge narrows to form the neck, a scalloped bay is cut into the western cliffs creating the golden sand beach of Orzán.

"Are those people? Swimming?" I asked, squinting at the black blobs in the water.

S followed my pointing finger. "Surfers," he replied.

"Not many waves," I said, looking at the milky-calm sea.

As I watched, a huge wave built. It rolled towards the frantically paddling, wet-suit clad figures before crashing over them. A couple of surfers emerged, still paddling, and one of them managed to get to his feet before taking an inelegant dive into the churning water. Three more waves came in rapid succession. Each crashed over the surfers, and each resulted in maybe one of them attempting to ride it.

"They're not very good! Must be a training school," I concluded.

As quickly as they had built, the waves stopped and the sea became calm again. The would-be surfers continued their gentle paddling as we wandered away.

"It's surprisingly peaceful for a big city," I mused. "I think it's 'cos you can look out to sea and avoid people."

"And the pavement's so wide," added S. "You don't need to come into contact with anyone."

By now we were at the narrowest part of the peninsula so it seemed prudent to cross to the east side. I'd seen a Thai restaurant advertised in the centre which was an opportunity too good to miss.

I love Galician food. The meat, and especially the fish, is some of the best quality anywhere – but I do miss the flavours of international cuisine. The closest we get to international in Taboada is our Danish-run pizzeria. In

8 Return to A Coruña – walking the City of Glass

Lugo, there are a couple of Chinese restaurants and a new sushi bar. There's also a good Japanese restaurant in cosmopolitan Ourense, though the one in Lugo was a short-lived experiment.

The idea of Thai flavours of lemon grass and red chillies was exciting. S doesn't like hot food but he enjoys the flavourful Thai dishes, and I guessed that a Thai restaurant in Galicia was unlikely to be as spicy as one in London or Bangkok.

We found the Thai Market easily enough. Inside, it looked as though someone had created a pop-up store inside a derelict building. Bare walls showed crumbling cement render and a huge stainless-steel vent snaked its way along the bare rafters. On one side, planks had been fitted into what looked like doorways joining the space to its neighbour. The wall above had either been partly plastered or some of the existing plaster had fallen off. I wasn't sure which. There were high tables and seats on one side and low tables with stools on the other. Shorty legs me opted for the low stools.

"Oh heck. It's one of those QR reader thingies again," I mumbled. "Whatever happened to paper menus?"

"Covid," replied S.

"I don't see how a printed piece of throwaway paper's a Covid risk," I grumbled.

This wasn't the first time I'd had this particular rant; S wisely kept quiet.

"They were Galician Thai restaurant of the year in 2017," S pointed out, once I'd stopped ranting.

This made me smile. "I can't see it being a huge field, that!"

"*¡Hola!*" said a friendly-faced man, heading toward our table.

"*¡Hola!*" I replied. "*¿Hay una carta?*"

"No, sorry. You can use the QR?" The man replied, switching seamlessly to English.

What was it in those four words which gave me away? I wondered. After fifteen years, our clothes are Spanish, my words may even be Spanish, but we are still, somehow, obviously English.

It may have been the fact that we were sitting in a Thai restaurant which gave us away. As we sat there and enjoyed our Pad Thai bowls (chilli flakes separate - double for Lisa!) I noticed that every single patron spoke English to the waiters, or attempted Spanish in a decidedly strange accent... like me, no doubt.

After our meal I chatted to the owner.

"We have been here seven years. The first Thai restaurant in Galicia," he added proudly.

"And it does well?" I asked. "Is it mainly English customers?"

"And German, and Dutch too," he replied. "We are very international in Coruña."

Back on the pavement, I held my stomach. "I'm full!"

"Me too," agreed S. "Let's walk off dinner."

We strolled along the harbour, eyeing up the huge passenger liner docked there, and in to the old town.

In contrast to the wide *paseo*, the old town is all alleyways and stone buildings - though many of the roads are surprisingly wide for an old city. Lugo's streets are much narrower, suitable only for two horses to pass - or one determined car driver.

We found our hotel and, as it was now three o'clock, checked in.

"We have upgraded your room. You are on the fifth floor," said the pretty girl behind the reception desk. "Help yourself to the complimentary water in the fridge over there, and there is a coffee machine too."

"Nice!" I said, admiringly. She also, had spoken to us in English. The differences of being in a big city.

I'd booked a budget room. We only need a comfy bed, a working shower, and our trusty kettle to be happy. This was a much bigger room with a little seating area in the window, a fancy black and white tiled bathroom with a rain storm shower head, and a huge bed. I was going to struggle to find my beloved that night.

8 Return to A Coruña – walking the City of Glass

"Right. A wee first, then let's carry on round the headland."

In short order we were back outside and walking through María Pita square. The large statue to the Galician heroine, who in 1589 allegedly repelled 12,000 English under Sir Francis Drake with only 4,000 peasants after seeing her husband slain, mocked us as we walked past. I felt no guilt. We English rescued the Coruñés from the French only a couple of centuries or so later, so I considered the debt paid.

From the old town we cut on to the part of the Paseo Maritima around which we had driven with SatGirl some hours earlier, passing the imposing but boxily-ugly maritime traffic control office. The office watched over the incoming vessels from its stilt like legs. It reminded me of one of the Martian fighting machines from War of the Worlds and I began to hum, very softly, Jeff Wayne's haunting music.

On a headland sat the castle of San Antón. It was also a museum and I needed a break from the sunshine.

"I'm sure my neck's burning. I didn't think to put any sun cream on," I said. "Does it look red?"

"You look okay to me," replied my observant hubby.

Note to reader about observant husbands: it was only as I stripped for a shower later that S remarked, "Your neck looks red. I think you're burnt." Thanks!

San Antón castle is built on an island (although it doesn't appear so). The narrow land bridge to the island was not completed until the middle of the last century; prior to that, it was necessary to take a ferry service from the castle pier. The castle itself has undergone a number of different guises over its 450-year history.

Originally conceived by Carlos I in 1522, construction of the fortress didn't begin until 1588 during the reign of Carlos' son, Felipe II. Previously, the island was used as a quarantine station for those suffering from St. Anthony's fire, a disease associated with ergotism (from ingesting grain contaminated with the ergot fungus) or erysipelas (an acute and painful skin infection). The chapel there was dedicated to St. Anthony, which gave rise to the name of the fortress itself. Building was finally completed in the 17th century. The fortress buildings were added to over the years with new structures such as the Governor's House on the first floor.

In the late 17th century, St. Anthony's Castle became a prison, later being used extensively for political prisoners during the Franco dictatorship. Looking around the museum, now housed in the building, I thought it must have been a gloomy place to be incarcerated. I wondered if the prisoners were allowed into the pretty garden on the first floor. I concluded they probably weren't – though jumping into the Atlantic Ocean to escape was not a promising option.

I enjoyed wandering around the exhibits, and dreamt of unearthing some Roman coins or a gold Celtic torc somewhere. On the first floor the sentry boxes offered a rectangular view of the sea on three sides from their lookout slits whilst the cannon, looking out to sea, seemed incredibly small against the backdrop of the huge passenger liner in the harbour.

"That was good value for two euros," said S, as we walked back into the sunshine.

"One euro for you," I replied.

"He didn't ask for proof, did he?" asked S.

"Nope. In fact, he said if we were over 65 it was half price. I'm sure if I'd asked, he'd have charged me half too. I'm not sure I like that idea," I added. "Do I look 65?"

S laughed and walked on. He knows my paranoias.

The Paseo Maritima de Alcalde Francisco Vasquez is a lovely walking route, if a bit of a mouthful for poor SatGirl.

"He must have been a very popular mayor," I said, "to have thirteen kilometres of sea-front walkway dedicated to him."

8 Return to A Coruña – walking the City of Glass

"Or a rich one," said S.

With the sea to our right, we happily strolled along, occasionally skirting around long carbon-fibre fishing rods lying on the pathway, their tips quivering above the sea.

"If they get a heavy fish, they'll be gone. They're not anchored to anything," observed S as we dodged another line.

"I'm wondering if you could sue if you tripped over one of them. What if you were blind?"

"The fisherman would probably sue for damage to his rod. They're really expensive you know," replied S.

"Humph. He should keep it off the *paseo*," I grumped.

As we continued walking, huge standing stones loomed in front of me.

"Look." I pointed. "Stonehenge."

"It's the sculpture park, near the *torre*," said S. "Quite a way off yet, I think."

As we rounded the corner there was a small, south-facing beach to our right and an outdoor swimming pool to our left.

"I can smell the chlorine from here. I wouldn't want to swim in there."

"Yes, but look at the sea."

Below us was a small jetty. Waves were hitting the edges obliquely then rushing across the jetty in a fury to create a short but powerful waterfall at the far end. Each time the sea receded, the jetty stood proud and dry, only to be flooded again and again.

In front of us an older-looking woman, complete with wet-suit and dragging a luminous pink buoy, waded into the sea. She dived under the waves and set off with powerful strokes out of the bay, her pink float bobbing along behind her.

I shivered involuntarily at the thought of swimming in the cold Atlantic Sea. "Ice cream?" I asked.

Beyond the beach a tiny kiosk was selling magazines and drinks. A board advertised ice creams.

"*Dos cornetos de vainilla, por favor,*" I said.

"Two euros with forty," he replied.

I give up. I must just look and sound so English.

S was busy scrabbling through his change. He handed me some coins which I passed to the man. He in turn stared at the coins.

"Forty," he said, showing me the twenty-cent coin I'd given him.

"Oh, sorry. We need twenty more," I said to S, who was still scrabbling in the depths of his wallet.

"Is okay, is okay," said the ice-cream man, waving his hand and passing me two extremely battered looking Cornetos.

"*No, no. Tenemos,*" I replied, looking over at hubby as he miraculously found two five-cent coins and an assortment of tiddlers.

"Mind you," I said, when we were out of hearing, "He should've knocked some off for the dents!"

By now we were within a few hundred metres of the sculpture park at the far northern tip of the peninsula. Set in a parkland devoid of buildings other than the Torre de Hércules, the sculpture park occupies most of the western bulge of the peninsula. Work began on this outdoor museum and living landscape in 1992 as part of the bicentennial celebrations of the reconstruction of the Hercules Tower. Both the tower and its surrounding park is a UNESCO World Heritage Site.

The park is a collection of twenty sculptures designed by an eclectic mix of artists. Many depict Hercules and his legendary labours. The vision of a giant stone Hercules, kneeling in a boat patently too small for his torso, made me giggle. Further on, S attempted a photograph of me below a huge rusted steel seashell. The House of Words sculpture, built on the site of a Muslim civil war cemetery, was bleak; the vegetation within its locked gates was brown, and as dead as the bodies which were repatriated in 1957. The Monument to the Executed, the Stonehenge I'd seen

8 Return to A Coruña – walking the City of Glass

from the walkway, was the most poignant sculpture by far.

A set of henges sits in the area known as Campo da Rata, where many people were executed by firing squad during and after the civil war. One huge standing stone has the names of the fallen etched in a never-ending list, whilst others bear splashes of bright scarlet paint in memory of the blood shed here.

By the time we had passed and discussed each of the twenty sculptures, and stood a while, watching the Atlantic Ocean battering the cliffs below, the sun was beginning to set in the autumn sky. The Hercules Tower was backlit in shining gold. It made for some good sunset photographs.

"Are we going to leave the car here and walk back, or try and find parking nearer?" I asked.

"The receptionist said there was plenty of free parking on the *paseo*. We could try and get a bit closer if you like."

I was beginning to feel my legs after walking the circumference of the bulge, so readily agreed. As it happens, we easily found a spot in front of the university building, Pablo Picasso, and collected our rucksacks (and trusty kettle) from the car.

"Boy do my legs ache," I said, collapsing on the bed while S made tea.

"Mine too. We're just not used to walking so much."

I was sitting in the chair writing up my diary after a much needed, and much enjoyed, shower when I heard music drifting up from the street below.

"We're being serenaded," I said. "John Lennon's Imagine, I think."

The saxophone carried on through an exhaustive repertoire until around 8.30pm when he packed up, to no doubt head to a bar and spend his earnings. Or he might just have been going home to his family. I'd enjoyed our musical interlude and was sad that I couldn't open a window to throw some money down to the busker.

That evening we hit the streets of Coruña looking for a *tapas* bar or two.

Now, as I have mentioned on numerous occasions, in Lugo, you get a free *tapita*, or small *tapa*, with every drink you order from a circulating tray. Not only that but you also have the choice of a second free *tapa* from the kitchen. And the wine is generally around a euro to a euro fifty a glass. I expected the prices to be higher in a big international city like Coruña but...

"Two sixty for a glass of albariño? Wow!"

"What about *tapas*?" asked S.

"Meatballs, two seventy. Chips and salsa, one ninety. *Tequeixo*, one ninety."

"What's *tequeixo*?"

"No idea. *Hola. ¿Dos albariños y que es tequeixo?*"

"*Es un rollo frito con jamón y queso.*"

At last, someone who didn't reply in English.

"Okay. *Uno.*"

"*¿Uno?*" the barman replied, putting rather too much surprise into one word.

"*Si.*"

"At one ninety I'm not buying two unless we like it," I muttered as he left.

A *tequeixo* turned out to be a twist of sweet, soft, deep-fried bread the length of two fingers, with molten cheese and soft ham inside it. I handed S a finger's length, quickly deciding *tequeixo* came under 'tried once' on my things to eat list.

At seven euros ten for two wines and a finger of bread it was going to be an expensive night. Luckily, three wines are our limit and the following two bars, although around the same price, served better albariños and decent sized wedges of rich *tortilla*. By the end of the evening though, I was 'tortilla'd' out and dropped gratefully into our king-sized bed.

And yes, I did struggle to find my beloved in that wide bed.

9 Ramón's city of Ourense

I wanted to include a chapter in here on our second closest city, the titular provincial capital of Ourense. I asked our friend, Ramón – a born and bred Ourensano, for his help. I loved Ramón's witty, informative style so much that I have included his information here as it was written. I hope you will enjoy learning a little of Ramón's city of Ourense.

§

With a little more than 105,000 inhabitants, Ourense is the third biggest city in Galicia, and it might be the least well-known. Crowned as Galicia's Thermal Capital, and with more than 3 million litres of thermal water running from its sources every day, many visitors come to Ourense due to its thermal baths. So, if you go to Ourense, don't forget your bathing suit, flipflops and towel.

Each bath is composed of small open-air pools with warm water; there are few more pleasant and healthy options that cost so little, in fact some are even free!! Available all the year round, visiting them on a rainy or cold day is an extraordinary delight. And, as well as the nice warmth and low prices, they have relaxing and healthy properties. Though little scientific research has yet been made, tradition gives these waters healing powers for skin, teeth, breathing problems, and many other diseases... Recent research from Vigo University has shown the benefits of As Burgas water for fibromyalgia.

There are two main thermal areas in Ourense: As Burgas and the Thermal Promenade alongside the Miño river.

As Burgas is located near the Praza Maior, the City Hall square. Its most iconic image is a monumental fountain with water at over 60 degrees centigrade. The fountain has become the most famous landmark of Ourense, and touching the waters and taking a picture showing the 'burnt' fingers are a must for visitors.

It is said that if you are able to pray a whole *Our Father* with your hand under the Burgas waters, you might go to Heaven. Sorry, we could not get any official confirmation yet, but it is quite possible that you will lose your hand. Not sure if it is worth trying...

As Burgas waters have been used throughout the city's history. Even in the Middle Ages, when the public baths were banned by the pudic Christian kings of Spain, the local bishops kept As Burgas open for the citizens (and of course for themselves). The importance of these sources comes not only from the many uses of its water throughout the city's history (washing clothes, making bread, plucking chickens...), but also because it was around these sources that a Roman camp was settled, giving birth to what was to become the city of Ourense.

In As Burgas there is also a thermal pool, open year-round and free to visitors (don't worry the water here is 'only' at about 40 degrees!). Changing rooms, lockers and even a sauna are available in these facilities. This pool was built in 2010, though thermal tourism goes back at least to the second century.

Calpurnia Abana, a Roman lady living about fifty kilometres south of the modern-day city, has the honour of being the first known rheumatic tourist to visit Ourense. Her name appears in one of the Roman altars found in this area. In fact, behind the pool there is a small garden which hides the archaeological remains of the former Roman baths and also a shrine pool built by the Romans in the 1st century. Even though the oldest remains are from Roman times, this space was certainly used as a sacred place by the previous inhabitants of the area. Many altars related to Celtic gods have been found

9 Ramón's city of Ourense

here, which has the largest number of altars related to the Celtic god Reve.

Some people believe that the warm waters of Ourense come from a volcano beneath the city, others that the healing properties of the waters come from the icon of Santo Cristo within the city's cathedral.

Well, neither of them is totally wrong.

There is a thermal spring in the chapel of Santo Cristo, and the thermal waters are heated by the warmth inside the Earth's core... but, do not worry, there is not a volcano under Ourense!! Instead, due to the special characteristics of Ourense's ground materials, the water is able to retain its temperature without mixing with any other superficial water streams before reaching the surface.

Besides As Burgas, the other thermal area in Ourense is the Thermal Promenade, a four kilometre walk along the banks of the Miño river, starting two kilometres from the Praza Maior.

The oldest facilities might be O Tinteiro fountain, which is very popular for mouth problems and skin treatments. It is popular among locals of any age (there is always someone soaking their feet in plastic tubs). But most tourists come for the thermal baths. There are three main areas for these baths: A Chavasqueira, Muíño da Veiga and Outariz. Here, Japanese and local thermal traditions meet. The pools are inspired by the Japanese *onsen* tradition (though not totally as they are unisex and bathing suits are required).

A Chavasqueira is the closest to the city centre, not far from the Millennium bridge which stands out for the rollercoaster-like staircase that is used as a viewpoint of the riverbanks. A Chavasqueira was the first thermal bath opened in the city back in 2001. Here I shall distinguish between the free and the paying baths – well, the rest of the paying ones, because these baths, completely built of wood according to the Japanese tradition, were totally destroyed by fire in 2019. Quite funny as it burnt on a rainy day and it is located at less than 200 metres from the city's fire station!!

The free baths here, as well as at O Muíño da Veiga, Outariz and Burga de Canedo are open all year around as is the biggest baths, at Outariz, (which costs 5,70€ to enter).

As this is a pedestrian promenade there is a small road train which departs from the Praza Maior and runs along the Thermal Promenade, stopping by all the baths. Even though it is not very fast, it is handy and the price is very nice (0,85€). Besides, it is the only transport which crosses the Roman bridge.

If you are a train lover, do not miss the scale train collection, Fernández Pacheco, located at the cultural centre Marcos Valcarcel, which is a beautiful building from the early 20th century with several temporary exhibitions and cultural activities. On Sundays you can also take a ride in the *Carrileiros* railroad park, a 500-metre train rail loop that will take you back to your childhood!!

In the monumental area or zona vella of Ourense, you should stroll around the stone streets and small squares, and enjoy the ambience and peaceful lifestyle of this city. If you come on a Sunday afternoon, it might look quite deserted, as many citizens go to the rural areas to visit their relatives. But, if you come on any other day, you will be amazed by the ambience of this town; the shops and cafeterias are lively from early in the morning to quite late in the evening. (Author's note: by 'quite late', Ramón undoubtedly means around 3 or 4am rather than 11pm ;)).

When in Ourense, do not miss the cathedral, the viños area, the San Francisco cloister and the charming streets around the city hall.

The cathedral is the main monument in Ourense, and the only paying one. Inside, the Portico do Paraiso and

9 Ramón's city of Ourense

the Santo Cristo chapel stand out, but it holds many other beautiful delights, such as the small museum with San Rosendo's treasure, including one of the oldest chess pieces in Spain.

Santo Cristo chapel is an overdose of gold-like decoration. Every inch of this chapel is decorated with many works from different art periods. In the centre is the Santo Cristo, a very realistic image of Christ on the cross. It is so realistic that when touched, it resembles the feel of real skin. And what a sight!! You can almost feel the suffering of this dying image. It is easy to understand why it holds such a huge devotion in the city. It was brought from Fisterra by the bishop Pérez Mariño, who asked to be buried looking at the Santo Cristo. Unfortunately, the image was moved a few centuries later, so at the moment the bishop might have a terrible neck pain.

It is said that the Santo's beard and hair grow miraculously – though you might have to wait until they take the wig to be washed (and change it for the other) to appreciate the growth miracle :).

The other must-see is the Portico do Paraiso, the cathedral's main gate. This portico was the sculptural equivalent to comic books in the Middle Ages. Built in the 13th century, it tries to teach the Christians how their destination after death might depend on their behaviour on Earth. Sinners are depicted suffering in Hell while good souls are welcomed in Heaven. Even though some building work slightly changed the composition, it preserves its wonderful beauty and, unlike Santiago's portico, the original polychromy from the Middle Ages.

Bishops' sermons in the Middle Ages might not have been much fun, as many board games were carved in the lateral stone benches of the cathedral.

The cathedral is named after Martin of Tours, a 4th century Hungarian saint who, according to tradition, became the patron saint of Ourense after miraculously healing King Carriarico's son of leprosy (a couple of centuries after St. Martin's death). Curiously, even though Martin of Tours was never in either Ourense nor Galicia, he took part in the prosecution of one of the most controversial historical figures of this region - Prisciliano. In fact, Saint Martin was one of the few bishops who was publicly against Prisciliano's murder.

Prisciliano was a Christian bishop who was popular in Europe in the 4th century, especially in Galicia. He led a very simple lifestyle, far from the opulence of the Roman Church. The success of his ideals made the other Christian authorities very angry, so he was charged with sorcery and executed.

Prisciliano's life was erased from the history books, but his asceticism was rooted deeply in Galician society. Priscillianism remained for several centuries after his death (some say that it remains even today, and the name of the cathedral is one proof of this). In fact, many historians claim that it is the remains of Prisciliano, not those of the apostle James, which reside in Santiago Cathedral.

Os viños: Until the beginning of the 20th century the economic activity in Ourense was based on the wine industry. In the Middle Ages, the quality of Ourense's wines was praised by kings such as Alfonso X, The Wise, and the bishops of the city controlled and promoted the wine production to be exported abroad. Nowadays, some parishes of the municipality are under the Ribeiro (the oldest Designation of Origin in Spain), but it is difficult to find any remains of this industry in the city, and only experts can recognise where the multiple wineries were situated, because of the type of gates used in the caves. Nowadays the streets around the cathedral are known as 'os viños' (the wines), as it was here where the wine was brewed and stored. This area has become the place to go for *tapas* and traditional cuisine as these streets hold the biggest concentration of bars and restaurants in the city. Usually, locals go for *tapas* in the

9 Ramón's city of Ourense

evening (they are usually charged for) and go from one bar to another enjoying the speciality of each one. Now, Galician cuisine meets the gastronomy from several countries, and some nouvelle cuisine restaurants can be found here. Some even have a Michelin star, such as Restaurante Nova, which is said to be the cheapest Michelin-starred restaurant in Europe.

Another must-see in the city is the San Francisco cloister, the remains of a former gothic monastery. It is a wonderful piece of art, where each of its 63 arches offers a different decoration. Real and imaginary beings join in this particular universe. Take your time to appreciate each tiny detail, and the perfection of the work in the granite stone, and try to find an elephant!!

Praza Maior: the main square is the centre of the monumental area. Here are the town hall and the former bishop's palace (now a museum), as well as the Art Nouveau building of Casa Fermín. One of the most beautiful pictures of Ourense can be taken in one corner of the square, the Santa María Nai staircase. This church might be the oldest in the city, even though the current building is from the 18th century. The marble capitals preserved in the façade are probably from a Roman temple or a construction of the first Christians in the area.

Some other nice visits are the Liceo Palace, a small Gothic-Renaissance palace which holds the oldest cultural association in the city. And the Belén de Baltar, a nativity scene with more than a hundred clay figures, which mixes the nativity theme with cultural elements of Ourense and its surroundings.

Nature is very present in Ourense, as all the river banks have pedestrian walks, used for sport and leisure activities. Along the river Miño, there is a circular route of more than twelve kilometres, but there are also walks along the rivers Loña, Barbaña and Barbañica. Following the Loña, you can reach the archaeological site of Santome, a beautiful forest with remains of the inhabitants from the 1st to the 5th century. And walking along the Barbañica you can reach Seixalbo, a medieval structured village.

The biggest green area in Ourense is Montealegre, a fifteen-hectare park, with a wonderful viewpoint over the city.

Fun facts of Galicia

Place names: Galicia has more than a half of the place names in Spain. Every tiny hamlet has its own name, even if it is composed of only one house. There are many curious names such as Sol (sun) and Melón (melon).

During Franco's time, the traditional names (in the Galician language) were changed to more 'Spanish standard' words, which make very funny and nonsense names. With democracy, the traditional names became the official ones, but as the Galician language is very rich and there are many variations depending on the area, the spelling is sometimes very different. The official Galician names are quite bizarre – and many official names do not coincide with those the locals use!

A million-languages language and All-in-one expressions: The Galician language is very rich and there are some specific and wise expressions (for example there are over a hundred words for the verb, to rain). As there are so many differences between the regions, and also a very heavy influence from the Castilian language, it is quite common to hear conversations where people speak Galician but don't use the same words.

A friend of mine says that you can make up any word in Galician, and locals will understand it because of the

9 Ramón's city of Ourense

way it sounds. If not, there are some quite useful neutral words and verbs that can be used for almost every situation, such as *aquelar* (literally, to that) or *cousar* (literally, to thing). For example, my grandfather used to say: *O couso de cousar*, which means "the thing of to thing" and can be used in almost any context!

SECTION FIVE - CRUMBLING CASTLES

10 Castro Caldelas – castles and CLOPso

"You're good at word puzzles."

"Oh?" answered hubby, rather warily, I felt.

"I need an acronym using the initials of the four provinces for this new group. But there's only one vowel, so it's ploc or clop. What do you think?"

"Do I know about this new group?" S asked.

"You remember the social outings we went on with the AGA group? They were a great way to see places outside our own area. I thought I'd try and organise something similar."

The AGA, or Anglo-Galician Association, had been an interesting but short-lived group started by a Liverpudlian living in Pontevedra. The group was a lively, mixed bunch of foreigners and locals. We'd enjoyed the get-togethers which had introduced us to places we'd never visited before. I was sure something similar, based just on social outings with none of that association stuff, would be fun and a way to discover more about our beautiful region. I explained this to S.

"Clopso then," he responded. "Coruña, Lugo, Ourense and Pontevedra Social Outings."

"I love it! And you've cleverly used the letters in a clockwise manner from the regional capital. You're a genius."

S wisely kept quiet.

§

The very first CLOPso meeting was in Lugo, organised by yours truly. I'd arranged for us to congregate outside the cathedral plaza before heading off to the Domus museum, one of my favourites in Lugo, and a fascinating history lesson. Then there was to be coffee in the Plaza Mayor and a walk around the Roman Walls before lunch.

My last experience in organising large groups had been as a Brownie Guide leader in England, many moons earlier. Thinking about it, that had almost been a disaster too.

On that occasion, Brown Owl and I had arranged a three-kilometre walk for the Brownies' walking badge. We'd scoped out the route and it was easily doable in an hour, even with tiny legs.

Things did not go to plan.

The first tots wanted to stop for a drink after only ten minutes. An electric fence had been put across part of the public right of way in the previous two days. We were chased by bullocks which had definitely *not* been there two days earlier. And we were caught in gloopy mud in a newly ploughed field, with one Brownie losing her wellington boot. Dusk began to fall before we were anywhere near the finish and I had never been so pleased to see Brown Owl's husband coming to rescue us, industrial-sized torch in hand.

I should have learnt my lesson.

The CLOPso group of twenty plus people arrived in dribs and drabs after the appointed 11am start time. I hadn't expected the Spanish to be on time exactly, but by noon we were still a few short. I'd pushed on, attempting to get everyone into the museum, but by then groups had formed, their members in earnest chats about goodness knows what. I couldn't break them up, no matter how I tried.

By the time I had everyone together, we were in danger of missing lunch.

"Can we go for coffee?" asked someone.

"Good idea. I need the loo."

Before I knew it, my group had scattered to the four corners of the Plaza Mayor. At that point I gave up. We did manage to reconvene for lunch, and everyone said what a lovely time they'd had. For me it was an

10 Castro Caldelas – castles and CLOPso

table experience. It was, as my friend Debs put :inctly, 'like herding cats'.

ebs who volunteered to organise a day trip to ule medieval town of Castro Caldelas, near to their house in Ourense province, together with a walk along the Pasarela do Río Mao and lunch at a converted electricity power station.

Debs has far more experience herding cats than me, having four of her own at home. Our day began with coffee at the Casa Grande de Cristosende. This stone-built country hotel was originally the bishop of Ourense's summer palace. Built in the 1750s, it was transformed into a *casa rural* in the 2000s with a restaurant, stunning bedrooms and a café-bar. People were sitting in groups inside the restored building and outside on a sunny terrace. Debs was busy organising transport for our walk, arranging for some people to park their cars at the far end of the *pasarela* as transport for those people who couldn't manage to walk both ways.

She seemed to have it all in hand so I relaxed, chatting to friends we hadn't met up with for a while and enjoying the beautiful scenery down the Sil valley from our spot on the terrace. I was pleased and impressed that people had made the effort to join us from all four provinces, some travelling two or more hours.

This was one of the reasons the AGA had folded; few people wanted to travel long distances just for lunch. I'd hoped that by combining lunch and an interesting tour, this group would thrive. I already had people lining up to do 'outings' and had a couple more ideas of my own, cats notwithstanding.

"Okay, get your cars. Al's leading with the Landie, so follow us."

Debs' voice carried far more authority than mine had in Lugo. People began to collect their bags and move out like a military campaign. We had Mum's sister, my Aunty

Jan, visiting at the time so we bundled the ladies into the car and joined the long crocodile exiting the village.

The short drive to the beginnings of the *pasarela* was along narrow roads through vineyards with spectacular views of the Sil Canyon. Some of the lanes were barely wide enough for a vehicle; the tiny bridge over the river Mao narrower still. The entrance to the car park for the beginning of the walk was a 180-degree turn, steep and narrow, with a sheer drop on one side. Cars were already parking up at the side of the road rather than risk the turn. With two older ladies to look after, S decided to go for it. I can't tell you how close to the edge we were as I closed my eyes, but we obviously made it.

Unlike my miserable efforts, Debs had the group together in short order and we set off walking along a newly-built tree-lined track.

The Circuito do Natureza da Pasarela do Río Mao, in addition to being a mouthful to say, is a pleasant two-kilometre walk along boardwalks which hug the side of the narrow canyon as they follow the river Mao on its journey towards the much larger Sil.

The walk meandered in a general downhill direction, with lots of steps both up and down to test our leg muscles. The hillsides were clothed in greens of all shades and I thought I could hear the water splashing, a hundred metres below us.

The group was jolly and good humoured. My aunty even wore sensible (for her) shoes. This is a lady who has been known to pick spiky chestnuts in the woods near our home wearing gold lamé sandals. I kid you not. Mum managed well despite her 87 years, chatting to friends along the way.

"Oh, look at the view!"

We'd stopped at a wide balcony, with views across the narrow canyon towards the hills beyond.

"Up there, in the hills, is the Necropolis," said Debs, pointing. "There are tombs and a medieval chapel. The longer *paseo* passes those."

10 Castro Caldelas – castles and CLOPso

"Wow! We'll have to do that one day."

The necropolis itself consists of a set of fifty graves next to the chapel. Remains from the graves were analysed and dated to the 10th and 11th centuries. Roman artefacts have also been discovered there, so that high, wild spot has probably held religious significance for over 2,000 years.

The Ruta do Cañon do Río Mao, of which the *pasarela* we were on forms a tiny part, is sixteen kilometres. We've still not done the whole route, but it's the PR-G 177 if you're interested.

The climate along the *pasarela* is Mediterranean in places; strawberry trees (madroño) and sweet chestnuts give way to gorse, heather and broom at the highest spots. In May, these were in full bloom, scenting our way and sending butterflies fluttering across our paths.

From the viewpoint, we could look both forwards and back at the undulating route we'd taken. The wooden walkway was a work of engineering, and of art. At a distance, it looked remarkably like a matchstick mosaic of struts and angled beams.

At the far end of the *pasarela*, we reached a disappointingly unattractive bridge over the river. Here, at Barxacova, the river Mao forms a quiet backwater where there are stones down to the water.

"Not warm enough for me, thanks. But do carry on," I replied to a question about bathing in the river.

"Lots of people do in summer," added Debs.

It was just the dogs who enjoyed it that day.

Transport awaited those who wanted it, on the narrow road above, but a large group of us retraced our steps along the river and up, up, up the side of the canyon. Basking lizards darted out of our way and the sun shone on our little group. The walk back took in the whole route from a new and different angle. The shade of the overhanging trees was a delight in places. The sun beat down and the dogs ran ahead, panting. By the time we arrived back at the Fabrica da Luz, the rest of the group were sitting on benches below the trees, drinks in hand.

A Fabrica de Luz, or 'the electricity factory', was one of the first hydroelectric power stations in Galicia. It was built between 1914 and 1916 to channel water from the Mao utilising the *canle vella*, or old canal. It continued in use until a new canal (*canle nova*) was built. In 2011 the Parada do Sil council rescued the old power station. It was renovated by the renowned architect, Isabel Aguirre, and converted into a *hostal*, café and restaurant with meeting rooms in the lower part.

The Fabrica da Luz was a special place for our well-deserved lunch. It serves meals outdoors on sunny days or upstairs in a small, mezzanine dining room. Debs had arranged for our group to take over the dining room that day. The menu was short but well-presented, and huge quantities of roast beef and vegetable lasagne were dished out. The starters were lined up along the centre of the tables and included such un-Galician delicacies as beetroot hummus.

After a long and lively lunch, a few energetic souls followed Debs and Al into Castro Caldelas.

This medieval town sits high above the Sil river, its 14th century castle dominating the skyline. The castle was converted into a palace for the counts of Lemos in the 16th century but retained its keep and clocktower. It's also possible to go inside and run around the fortified walls. What more excuse did a group of aging children need?

The Castillo Castro Caldelas cost a whole two euros to enter. Inside there was a central stone-flagged courtyard, overlooked by thick stone walls and the castle keep. There was a museum display, labyrinthine corridors, staircases and statues. An open-air walkway circled the walls, up and down narrow stone staircases, past circular turrets and through a restored wooden tower. There were cannons lined up, and from the top of the walls there were the most magnificent 360-degree views down to Castro Caldelas town and all the way to the Sil.

"What a brilliant place to play king of the castle!"

"And what a brilliant day. Thank you, Debs."

11 Ferrol – el Castillo de San Felipe

The history of the castle of San Felipe, dates back to the 16th century. A massive, stone-built fortress near to the ship-building port of Ferrol on the northwest coast of Galicia, it is still imposing, some 500 years later.

The city of Ferrol is north of A Coruña, along the *ría* of the Xuvia river. Built on the northern shore, Ferrol lies in a natural and well protected harbour. It used to be an important Naval base, and in later years a large ship-building area which employed many workers.

We first visited Ferrol in the early years of our living in Galicia, searching for a DIY store. At least, we drove round and round Ferrol attempting to find the elusive new shopping centre where the DIY store allegedly was.

"We've been here before."

"I know," I groaned, looking down at the map on my lap once more. (This was in pre-Google days.) "I think it's off that way, but everywhere looks the same."

"You'd think a big new building store would have an advert somewhere."

"They did, remember? It was on the hoardings in Lugo."

"Great help."

"Hold on! Here! Here!" I yelled, as I spotted a tiny arrow indicating the new '*parque commercial*'.

That trip involved mooching around the large (and not that well-stocked) DIY store, visiting a sports shop chain for a new swimsuit, and eating lunch at a strange 'eco' restaurant in the shopping centre. We couldn't truthfully say we'd visited Ferrol.

On this occasion, a friend had invited us to try their local Mexican restaurant in Narón, near to Ferrol. Never one to turn down the taste of a new cuisine (for Galicia), we jumped at the chance. It also fitted very well with our weekend plans.

11 Ferrol – el Castillo de San Felipe

The restaurant, Azteca Tasting, was every bit as good as our friends had promised. A tiny place of thirty covers, and only open at weekends, the owner was a genial fellow who acquiesced to my requests for something without spice for my sweet but not spicy husband, and something hot hot hot for me.

"My husband doesn't like spicy food," I explained. "He likes flavour but not *piquante*."

"And you?"

"I love spice. In fact, I love everything Mexican."

"Good, good."

My platter of chicken in a chocolate mole sauce (pronounced molay, and having nothing at all to do with the insectivorous mammal which leaves hillocks all over my garden) came with a pickled jalapeño pepper and a bowl of spicy, smoked chipotle sauce.

S had opted for a large (for large, read humungous) burrito stuffed with chicken, cheese, lettuce and a special green sauce made with pumpkin seeds. He also had a, not very, spicy sauce on the side, which I finished off, along with my jalapeño and my chipotle sauce. As we had also ordered totopos (nachos) and guacamole for a starter, and had more nachos with dipping sauces brought to the table for free, we were struggling to finish our meals.

"The jalapeño, it is gone," our friendly waiter said on his return.

"Very tasty it was too," I said, smiling.

I had hoped to try the Montezuma chocolate cake for dessert but didn't have space. No space for chocolate pudding? Now, that is full.

As S pointed out, we had also begun the day with *chocolate con churros*, thick hot chocolate and the Spanish stick-doughnuts, so didn't strictly speaking need more chocolate (though there are those who would argue that one can't truly ever have too much chocolate. Hands up!).

PULPO, PIG & PEPPERS

After lunch, we all decided to visit the castle of San Felipe, some eleven kilometres outside of Ferrol, at the mouth of the estuary.

Following the colonisation of the Americas, the port and naval base at Ferrol was of great strategic importance to the Spanish. In order to protect the base, King Felipe II ordered the building of a massive fortress to protect the mouth of the bay. The original castle of San Felipe, named after the king's patron saint, was completed around 1589. On the opposite shore, two mirror castles – those of Nuestra Señora de la Palma and San Martín, the latter named after the then captain-general of Castile, Martín de Padilla, were built. The three castles provided a deadly triangle of fire power against any invaders. Between the castles of San Felipe and San Martín, it was also possible to run an iron chain, effectively blocking the *ría* to approaching ships.

The castle at San Felipe is open to the public and free to enter, but the road there was a little daunting to say the least.

We set off, this time with SatGirl to assist or hinder. Other than wishing to take us in the opposite direction in order to pick up the toll road from A Coruña, and sulking when I declined her suggestion, she was fairly well behaved. As ever, her Spanish pronunciation of road names gave me the giggles.

"Take the fee fifteen."

"That's the F E fifteen."

"Continue through Aldaya Brian."

"Brian?" asked S.

"Mmm, that's Brión, the little village we're passing through. BREE ON," I yelled at SatGirl, who stoically ignored me and continued to call the famous village by the name of a cartoon snail.

Brión was the town which, in August 1800, helped to repel an attack by English forces under General Pulteney. The English came ashore on the nearby beaches of Doniños and San Jorge to destroy the naval

11 Ferrol – el Castillo de San Felipe

arsenal at Ferrol. After being pushed back to the heights of Brión, they were defeated – a success which the locals celebrate each year with a re-enactment of the battle. Luckily the Galicians don't hold grudges, and the English did support the Spanish troops fighting the French under Napoleon in the battle of Coruña (battle of Elviña) a few years later. I wonder if the English troops called the village Brian too?

Anyway, back to our short but winding journey to the castle of San Felipe.

The route was straightforward, until we reached successively tighter roads through tiny villages with houses clinging to the side of a precipice.

"Are you sure?" asked S, driving along another narrow lane of parked cars.

I sat with my fingers tightly crossed. "She thinks so!"

At last, we popped out on to a leaf-littered track beneath chestnut trees.

"You have arrived," sang SatGirl.

"What? Oh!" I looked at the huge gates before us. "I guess we have."

Our friends arrived a few minutes later and together we entered the archway into the citadel.

El Castillo de San Felipe was reformed between 1731 and 1775. Larger triangular bulwarks were added to the land side of the structure together with artillery emplacements which allowed defenders to repel attacks from any direction.

Unlike the renovated castle at San Antón in A Coruña, which we'd recently visited, this one looked as if it had simply been abandoned, and in a hurry. The cell-like rooms were musty and damp. The walls were covered in green moss, their paintwork peeling, the plaster crumbling. Jetsam littered the floors; torn pieces of rag and old blankets were scattered about. I could imagine soldiers lying in the rooms, their cots in pairs along the high stone walls, tiny square windows high overhead, awaiting the morning and their orders for the day.

"It must've been a cold and lonely existence," I said, shivering.

In one room, there was an old *lareira*, or open fire, along one wall; ashes still lay in its hearth, the chimney hood above blackened with soot.

As we entered the castle grounds, the first thing I spotted was a loaded orange tree.

"Look! They're all over the floor," I exclaimed, diving in to grab some of the tiny but intensely sweet fruits. "They're delicious. Oh! I'd love to pickle some. Or candy them."

The men shook their heads and wandered off while I filled my bumbag (fanny pack to my American readers) with fruit.

"Don't you eat them?" I asked the security guard as he wandered past.

"No, I don't like them. My brother does," he added, ignoring my thieving.

Inside the inner courtyard I happily ran around, climbing staircases, gazing over the parapets to the intensely blue sea below and peering across the *ría* to the crumbled castle of San Martín on the opposite bank. Alongside one wall we came across a narrow arch in a round tower, and a set of spiral stairs leading into the dark.

"A dungeon?" I asked, turning on the tiny torch which hangs from my bumbag. For something the size of my thumbnail it has a powerful beam, and I led the way confidently into the gloom.

Part way around the first turn, there was a slit in the wall allowing sunlight to shine in. I turned off the torch.

"I can see daylight. It's not a dungeon."

Around a second bend, we exited on to a bright green lawn. In front of us the sea lapped at the edges of a stone jetty. It was peaceful and surprisingly pretty. I took a photo of S, leaning out precariously around the

11 Ferrol – el Castillo de San Felipe

edge of the castle walls, and we stared into the clear water at the outline, still visible, of one of the massive anchors which were used to hold the heavy chain in place across the *ría*.

It was warm in the sunshine but I could see fog out to sea, already turning the mouth of the river hazy. I shivered again.

"Let's go back up."

Back on the parapets I was astounded that already the castle of San Martín, on the opposite bank, had vanished into the gloom. The fog was quickly working its way up the *ría*.

"Invaders would just have to wait for the fog to roll in and they could take Ferrol unobserved," I commented.

"Except they wouldn't be able to see either," remarked S.

"Good point! We'd better go, I don't fancy driving back in the mist on some of those roads."

I'd booked to stay in Ferrol itself that night – at least I thought I had.

We drove the quick route back (via the main road) ahead of the swirling mist, and bounced along the cobblestone streets of Ferrol looking for somewhere to park. Unsuccessful, I had S drop me near to the hotel so I could check in whilst he headed for the underground parking.

"I cannot find your booking," said the friendly receptionist.

The hotel I'd booked was a sister hotel to the one in which we'd stayed in Coruña, but the Hotel Suiza was a complete contrast to that modern edifice. This was an historic building, the lobby all polished brass and wood. I imagined Victorian-era ladies alighting from carriages and porters carrying their baggage across the marble floors. Those floors gleamed whilst the lifts, we found, creaked and groaned alarmingly.

"But I booked this afternoon, on Booking.com," I said.

"Ah! I have you." As I smiled, she added; "But it is for next week."

How the heck had I managed that? In my defence the sun had been in my eyes while I tried to book, but even so.

"You can change the booking," the receptionist said.

"I can't. It was a cheap rate deal, no changes allowed."

The girl frowned. She thought a while, then smiled. "This is what you need to do…"

After more than a little typing on both our parts, I cancelled my booking, Booking.com requested a refund from the hotel, the receptionist agreed the refund, and then I rebooked directly with her for a ten percent discount. Sorted.

Despite our protracted negotiations, S had still to appear.

"I need to find my husband. If he comes here, please hold him," I said to the receptionist in strangled Spanish. No wonder she grinned at me!

I thought it unlikely he would turn up as he didn't know the name of the hotel, only its general vicinity, and had no mobile phone. Something I still need to remedy one day!

I speed-walked out of the lobby, down the steep street and along to the underground parking. As I descended to the lower level, I realised the futility of my search. The car park was vast, dark, and full. It was like looking for the proverbial needle. I climbed back into the sunshine and returned to the hotel. As I stood on the corner pondering my next move, a heavily laden man came puffing down the street. S was carrying both my and his own rucksacks. Neither had much in them, although his contained our kettle, mugs and tea, but he looked overloaded.

"Sorry, I didn't know where you were," I began.

"I've been standing on the corner for ages."

"I didn't see you. I've been down to the car park. Where were you?"

11 Ferrol – el Castillo de San Felipe

S pointed uphill – one street up from the hotel. Oops.

Once settled in, we followed the route advised by our friendly receptionist to best see her city. The lady's enthusiasm was much greater, to my mind, than the reality justified. The views across the *ría* to the shipbuilding docks opposite, their giant derricks silent, were pretty in the setting sun, but along the streets were many derelict buildings, graffitied and crumbling. I edged into one house for a photograph. It was a mess of collapsed roofing beams and elder at ground level, the walls slowly disappearing back into the landscape.

We arrived at the harbour just in time to watch the sun set over the hills to our right.

"Oh! Look at the fog!" I exclaimed.

The mist which we had left behind at the castle was now filling the *ría* from side to side, rolling in waves towards the town. Close to shore the sky was clear, but out to sea was a towering fog bank. I was mesmerised.

"Look how it's heading this way," I said. "It's like a slow-moving avalanche."

S was less than impressed. "We'd better go back."

I was rooted to the spot, fascinated at this natural phenomenon.

"Look! The mountains are disappearing."

Even as we stood there, the fog bank had obliterated the hills on both sides of the *ría*. It now loomed over the town. My fertile imagination was anthropomorphising the fog – giving it devilish characteristics as it moved ever closer.

"You and your imagination. Come on, it's getting cold."

"Maybe the fog will eat the whole town before morning," I said, in what I thought was a sinister tone.

S looked at me pityingly before leading me back to the hotel for a shower, followed by a couple of drinks in town.

"Funny the fog didn't get into the town," I said as we sat outside one of the bars lining the pedestrianised, cobbled side streets. It was a mild and clear evening. I longed to head back to the harbour to see if the fog bank was still there, but knew I wouldn't be able to see anything if I did.

"Maybe," I mused, "the castles at the mouth of the river have repelled the marauding fog too."

SECTION SIX - MASSIVE MOUNTAINS

12 Cabeza de Manzaneda - top of the world

Cabeza de Manzaneda is the second highest peak in Galicia, part of the Macizo Central Ourensán. The highest Galician peak, Peña Trevinca, is on the exact border with Castilla y León so I'm not counting that one, plus Manzaneda has the only ski resort in Galicia.

"I need a mountain for my blog," I said to S one day.

If my hubby rolled his eyes then he did so discreetly. He knows well my oddities.

"Let's go to Manzaneda." If he needed more persuasion, I added, "We can go and see the oldest chestnut tree in Galicia too. And the local *pazo* is doing a special offer on bed and breakfast. I've never stayed in a *pazo*."

Of course, S said yes. Why wouldn't he? The chance to stay in a palace and see the oldest sweet chestnut tree in the region. I spoil him.

It always tickles me that Spain is the second highest country in Europe after Switzerland. It's odd, because Spain doesn't have that many really high peaks. The Sierra Nevada are the highest mountain chain on the mainland with Mulhacén the highest peak at 3,479m (11,414ft), some 4,000 metres below Switzerland's Dufourspitze. But almost the whole of central Spain, with Madrid at its centre, is the *meseta*, the high flat tablelands or plateau which are the oldest geological formation in the peninsula. Worn down mountains, the *meseta* has an area of 210,000 square kilometres (81,000 square miles). With an average height of 660m (2,165ft) above sea level on the *meseta* and only really the coastal areas low-lying, Spain is a high flyer.

The highest Galician mountain reaches just over 2,000m high. We don't have any of the highest peaks in Spain, and we only have one ski station - the one at Manzaneda. A reason to visit if ever there was one.

Our hotel for the night was the Pazo de Pena. I'd already received a collection of emails from them with everything from how to operate the doorbell, to things to see in the area, local restaurants, and even two takeaway menus to peruse. I had high hopes. Once we arrived, via a narrow road which wound its way up the hillsides, the restored *pazo* was everything I'd hoped for and more. We parked up as instructed by the large blue doors – a colour I always think of as Galician Blue as it is ubiquitous in almost every rural house. Our own two houses had more than enough Galician Blue doors and shutters to last me a lifetime.

I digress.

Once I found the bell, which had been the subject of a whole email of its own (I'm not sure why; it wasn't that complicated), we were ushered into an internal cobbled courtyard. I immediately imagined horses' hooves ringing on the stones as our carriage pulled to a halt. I shook myself as I realised our hostess was speaking.

"This door is always open but you have to lift the handle like this."

It was an old brace and ledge door with a huge metal latch, just like the ones we have at home. I could manage that one perfectly, thank you.

As we entered the ground floor and turned towards the reception area, the only modern looking part of the place with glass doors opening onto the courtyard, I tried to take everything in.

Our lovely hostess included a thorough tour of the public rooms before taking us to our bedroom. By the time she had walked us from the reception, via the dining room, the small lounge, the library, the large lounge, and the living room, we were both totally disorientated. She handed us the keycard and left.

"Right, we just need to get the bags up then."

"Which way is out, though?"

We turned around and pondered. We walked to the end of the corridor and pondered again. We walked

12 Cabeza de Manzaneda – top of the world

down the stairs and into the courtyard, found the big blue doors and the car.

"She said the car park was round the corner."

"I saw it on the way in," replied S, jumping behind the wheel.

"I'll walk. I want to examine the *pazo* a bit more," I said as my hubby drove away, leaving me on the roadside.

The granite blocks of the *pazo* on this side were large, neat and squared off, but around the corner, they sat on top of what could only be the bedrock; a rounded ginormous rock was topped by two ornate pedestals and more granite blocks. That's how to save on building costs!

"The lady said the easiest way back in is via the library."

"That makes sense. We'll be on the upper floor then."

No, we weren't.

At least we weren't on our upper floor. We entered the blue (of course) door and I had another peek into the library room. Glass cupboards at the rear of the room housed ancient looking tomes in calligraphed script, whilst modern novels lay on bookcases next to the door. Two huge sideboards filled the remaining space.

We walked out into the corridor. A wide space of beautifully polished ancient chestnut flooring around a *galería*, or glass-enclosed patio, this area was beautifully renovated. The old grandfather's clock next to the wall looked as if it could have been there since the *pazo* was built, whilst discreet signs pointed to bedrooms one and two, and three through to eight.

"Hmm, what number are we?" asked S.

"I don't know," I admitted. "Fourteen, maybe?"

We walked towards bedrooms one and two, and came to a dead end. We walked towards bedrooms three through eight, and came to a halt.

"I think we came in that door," said S, pointing at a matching chestnut door which had no ornamentation.

We opened the door and walked past the small lounge our friendly receptionist had shown us before. I wandered in. It was a cosy room with comfortable looking armchairs pulled up in the centre below a domed skylight. Around the inside of the dome was a painted frieze of a map of the world; above, figures and astrology symbols led to the glass skylight itself. In one corner was another old dresser with some photographs of the *pazo* as it was. But this wasn't helping to find our room.

"This way just leads to reception," I said. "I remember passing this room."

I turned and walked back through the chestnut door.

"This is ridiculous! I know we're on the first floor, so where's the room?"

I turned again and stomped back towards reception. No way would I admit to being lost. I am my father's child. And S is as bad.

"We'll just have to go outside and back up from there," I said, leading us out of the brace and ledge door into the cobbled courtyard once more.

Climbing the outside steps, we found ourselves in the correct corridor. We even found the correct door. It seemed the two halves of the building didn't link up on the upper floor. I really should have taken the kindly-provided map with us!

"I like these keycard readers. They're very discreet, aren't they?" I said, waving the card in front of the narrow black reader. The handle below was a proper, black iron door handle and the whole blended in with the old chestnut floor boards perfectly.

Inside, our room was small but beautifully decorated with a Chinese style, papered red and black wall behind the double bed, which had a red throw over the end. The bathroom was also painted in red above the modern fitted wash basin. Our hostess had offered us the choice of two rooms. The one next door had been almost identical but in shades of blue. No contest.

12 Cabeza de Manzaneda – top of the world

Once I'd had a quick shower it was time for the free organised tour of the private rooms of the *pazo*. I was itching to see more, but S was still showering. (Why do men take so much longer to get ready?)

I went down to reception by myself to ask about the tour.

"Yes, it is every day at seven," said our hostess.

"And where do we wait? In reception?"

"No, I can start whenever you are ready."

"Ah!" A lightbulb moment. "It's you?"

"Yes, of course."

Despite my assuring her that we could start without my elusive husband the girl insisted on waiting for him, so I dashed back upstairs.

"Hurry up," I shouted into the steam-filled bathroom. "We're waiting for you."

S grumbled but dressed quickly. We walked back down to our receptionist-come-hostess-come-tourguide. Another couple were waiting patiently. This is Spain after all. No one expects anyone to be on time.

First, we were shown the public rooms again. This time, a fire had been lit in the *lareira*, a huge open fireplace much in evidence in old Galician homes. Our guide demonstrated how the giant witches' cauldron swung across the fireplace using a wooden derrick arm. Next to the fire was a wooden settle with a table which came down over it. It looked like a grown-up version of a child's high chair. Once down, the occupants were locked in place.

"It's like the one in the museum in Lugo," I whispered.

"But this one doesn't have the chickens underneath," replied S, ducking his head to check under the bench.

I remembered now that the settle in Lugo's Provincial Museum had a wooden frame beneath it with small cut-outs at the front. A couple of (pretend) chickens and a bag of eggs told the story of its use: the chickens kept warm, and were no doubt fed scraps from the table, whilst providing the homeowners with fresh eggs without the need to walk outdoors in a cold Galician winter.

Next to the *lareira* was a wooden hatch and a chute leading down to the floor below.

"The waste food was tipped here for the animals."

All very clever and time efficient. Pigs fed without leaving the kitchen.

The tour was comprehensive. We saw a small workshop dominated by an old hand loom and the paraphernalia of weaving, which our guide said was still in use. The *bodega*, housed in a separate building, was also still used.

"It is only small, maybe 500 bottles of wine in a year are made," said our guide.

I wasn't really listening. The most gorgeous table I have ever seen had caught my eye as I walked in the door. Sitting on two old 225-litre wine barrels, the table top was fully eight feet long by four feet wide and made of one single piece of sweet chestnut. I couldn't comprehend the girth of the tree which had been able to make such a top. I coveted that table like mad and didn't want to leave it.

The tour ended, appropriately enough, in the crypts down below the laundry room. Coming from a warm, clean-washing scented laundry to damp, low-ceilinged, musty caves, made the underground crypts seem even more spooky and claustrophobic.

The next morning, after a filling self-service buffet breakfast, and still having an hour or two to kill before check out, we decided to go in search of the oldest sweet chestnut tree in Galicia. The map the hotel gave us seemed to indicate a straightforward circular route.

"Okay, it's right at this junction then we just carry on 'til we see a turning on the left," I said confidently.

"Are you sure?" asked S.

"Yep. Look it's easy. This is the fork on the map and that's right, into the village."

12 Cabeza de Manzaneda – top of the world

We set off through a muddle of houses and barking but tail-wagging dogs, all eager to join our adventure.

"I should have pinched some ham for them. This mastiff is such a cute fella," I said, talking partly to the dogs and partly to S, who of course wasn't really listening. The dogs were more attentive by far!

Once out of the village, we walked along a surprisingly busy road. Three cars passed by as we walked. The sun began to warm us and I removed a layer, wrapping my jumper around my waist.

"Cool in the shade though," I said, unnecessarily.

Just then S spotted a sign which said 'Castañeiro de Pombeiro'.

"Is this it?"

It was off to the right.

"No. It can't be," I said, turning the map around. "It should be on the left, unless we came up the left-hand fork. I can't see how we could've though."

Meanwhile, S had wandered down the track indicated. I followed, still puzzling over the map in my hand.

A little way into the woodland was a hugely-girthed sweet chestnut tree, surrounded by wooden fencing. The notice board said the tree was 1,000 years old.

"The girth is twelve metres," I said, reading the board.

It was incredible to think what changes had gone on around this tree over the millennium it had been growing, but I was more concerned about the map. It was puzzling me and giving me a headache.

"We must've somehow come up the left-hand fork, though I can't see how," I repeated. "Anyway, the track should loop round the tree and almost double back but heading downhill over there." I pointed to an untrampled expanse of damp green meadow.

I turned around. "But the only track is that way."

We set off, on a continuation of the track we had entered by.

"We're getting further away from the village. This can't be right." I stopped and looked around.

"There's a chap walking up there," said S.

"Right, it must be that way then."

I set off towards the lone walker, as S said; "But that's the road again."

In a few moments we were once more on the road, less than a hundred metres from where we'd entered.

"Shall we try again?" I asked, hating to retrace my steps (or admit failure).

"No!" came the answer.

As we walked back, I continued to turn the map around.

"If we actually took the left fork then there must've been a right hand turn soon after, so look for a left turn on the way back."

We walked along but no turnings sprung out at us.

"There! Oh, it's a driveway."

"That one? No, it's a dead end."

Finally, near to our hotel, I spotted a narrow track heading off to the left. I turned to S. "We have an hour still before check out. Shall we go look?"

"Okay."

The narrow roadway became steeper as we walked.

"I don't know about this," I said. "It's uphill all the way back."

"We can walk for half an hour and then turn back if we don't see anything," replied clever clogs.

Just then we came to a junction. On the corner was an old water fountain, and next to it a sign saying; 'Castañeiro de Pombeiro' pointing to the left.

"Humph. All signs point to the chestnut tree, but none away from it. I don't suppose you…"

"Not really," replied S.

"No, you're right. It says one and a half kilometres and it looks a bit soggy. I would like to know where it comes out though," I grumbled, as we continued onward towards a medieval village – according to my map.

The village had the remains of an ancient-looking wall and a single stone archway. A steep path led to a ruined

12 Cabeza de Manzaneda – top of the world

castle wall and views down into the valley. We needed to get back to check out but maybe we'll return one day and find that elusive loop.

The road from the Pazo de Pena to the ski resort at Manzaneda was slightly over a car's width, steep and twisting. At times there were barriers to prevent cars falling off the mountainside. At other times, there were none.

"I wouldn't like to meet one of those tour buses coming the other way," I said, gripping the wheel. "At least it's quiet at this time of year."

I let the lone other car on the road overtake me by pulling onto the verge, then got out to take a few photographs. The silence was complete. There was not a rustle of leaves nor a breath of birdsong up here. The air was fresh and clear, and just a touch cool. The view was 360 degrees and there was hardly a habitation in sight.

"I can't see any ski lifts though," I said.

"You won't 'til we get there. They're probably the ones you put between your legs and perch on, anyway," replied S.

I didn't like the sound of that!

As we drove in to a large car park, our peace was shattered. I'd thought the ski resort would be deserted in the pre-ski season, but hadn't taken into account the mountain bikers. They were collecting their bikes from the backs of camper vans and padding themselves up like motorcyclists. They even had full face helmets on.

"I s'pose coming off one of those is as dangerous as a motorbike. They must get some speed up coming down the runs."

We wandered over to the ticket office, which was of course closed in autumn, and I looked up the steep, snow-free, slope.

"Not much of a view from down here," I grumbled. "I thought we'd be able to see for miles."

"You probably can from the top," replied S.

The ski resort sits at 1,400m (4,600ft), and the information board said the highest lift climbed to 1,770m (5,800ft) – almost vertically looking at it.

"I'm not keen on walking up there in my sandals. It looks pretty rocky." I eyed the terrain warily. My knees still ached from a steep downhill walk the previous day. Up, I don't mind, but that steep slope looked agony coming down.

"Probably get run over by cyclists anyway," added S.

The mountain bikers were beginning to fly down the slope back towards the car parking area. I couldn't imagine they'd be able to manoeuvre around us should we get in the way.

"Maybe I'll come back when it's snowing," I said. "Though I can't imagine how people get up here when it snows. That road must be impassable."

"They probably have a snow plough, pushing the snow off the edges."

"You'd think there'd be a better road up to a ski resort though. I sort of imagined it like the European resorts you see pictures of."

"You'd be surprised. Not all of those have good access either," replied S, who has actually been skiing. "We'll have to come back and get you on some skis," he added.

"No way! I can't skate, and I fall on my bum walking. I can't see me staying upright on skis."

I drove out of the car park and decided, on a whim, to take the other road down – the one opposite where we'd entered. It was wide, with a white line down the middle, and we were soon back below 1,000 metres.

"Well, what d'you know! I said there'd be a quicker way down."

I looked around as we drove through woodland.

"Not as amazing as the road up though. I'm glad we came up the other way. I can say it now…" I put on my best Jimmy Cagney gangster voice. "I made it, Ma! Top of the world!"

13 O Courel part I - two feet in the past

I was unsure where to put this chapter. O Courel, in the far east of Galicia, has *castros* and castles, ancient woodlands, and massive mountains. In the end, I've spilt our trip into two because the area just has so much to offer.

No planes fly overhead here, many of the roads are narrow and winding. It's easy to imagine life 1,000 years ago. Remote, and hours from the nearest 'big' town, O Courel really does have two feet in the past.

"It says here that O Folgoso do Courel is the biggest town in the Courel region," I said, doubtfully.

We'd parked up in what I thought of as the main street. There was a medical centre next to us, and a bank and an information centre opposite. We stepped out of the car and wandered over to the noticeboard.

"This shows some of the walking routes in the area."

"The information centre's closed though," I said, trying the door. "It says it opens 'til three but it's only two minutes to two."

"It's just closed for lunch then," joked S.

I saw a lady walking back from dumping her rubbish in the municipal bin.

"*¿Hay un restaurante en Folgoso?*" I asked.

She pointed down the road, "*Al final del pueblo.*"

"There's a restaurant at the end of the village. Singular!" I said to S, after she'd left. "I thought this was the major town in O Courel!"

We walked past a *panadería* and a shop selling chestnut products, before reaching a hairpin bend. Beyond, the narrow road continued through pristine countryside.

"Must be down there. I think we've reached the end of the village," I said, stating the obvious.

The Restaurant and Hotel O Mirador had a sunny terrace overlooking the hills beyond, but the dining room was on the floor below. Although we didn't get a view, we did have a good, and rather filling, *menú del día*. At thirteen euros, it was more expensive than usual, but the risotto was tasty, the steak huge, and the coffee flavoured *crème caramel*, sweet and rich.

We'd left home at around 11am that day and reached Quiroga, the gateway to O Courel, a little after 12.30pm. The road towards O Folgoso looked like a 'proper' road on our map. That it actually wound round mountain after mountain was not quite so clear. As we climbed higher and higher, I struggled to concentrate and not to gawp at the scenery. Luckily, the council had thought to install plenty of *miradores*, or viewpoints, for awe-struck tourists.

The 45-minutes our temperamental satnav, SatGirl, had announced the journey would take, was far longer. I continually pulled off the road to stare at the mountains.

We were at an average height of 1,200 metres (3,940 feet) here but the mountains were, in the main, rounded and green. To me, they looked as if someone had thrown a roll of green baize over craggy hillsides, smoothing the lines and making them soft and comfortable. The air here was crisp, but the temperature was rising even as I watched an eagle steal a thermal in front of my eyes.

A little further on, we passed through a narrow defile in a hillside, popping out on the sunny side of the mountain with a view down to a small town.

Just before we arrived at O Folgoso we saw a sign for a waterfall pointing to the right. There was no parking place but I managed to pull in to the side of the road. We grabbed water and my camera-phone, and set off.

The hike to the waterfall was not long, though it was almost vertically up shale rocks and I felt a burn in my chest.

13 O Courel part I – two feet in the past

"I thought we were getting fit with all this walking," I puffed.

"I think it's the altitude," replied S. "We're at almost fourteen hundred metres here, that's higher than a Munro."

"Quite a bit higher. A Munro's one thousand metres, isn't it?"

"Three thousand feet, so yes, more or less."

"Wow! And this whole area is higher than that!"

The waterfall itself was a bit of a disappointment, being little more than a trickle down the rockface.

"I guess coming after summer, and in an especially dry autumn, probably isn't the best idea. Oh well, I've worked up an appetite anyway."

After our filling lunch, I suggested heading for a *casa rural*, or country house hotel, that I'd seen on Google.

"One of the circular walks heads out from there, and Google says it's only four K away."

After driving along impossibly narrow roads for four kilometres, SatGirl still said our destination was five kilometres away. Something was off somewhere.

At Vilamor, where I thought the hotel was, I jumped out of the car to explore. The village was completely deserted and every single house looked ruinous.

"Ah, but there'll be someone living in them," said S, when I reported back.

"Half of them don't have roofs!" I replied. Still, he had a point; in our early house-hunting trips to Galicia, we'd been continually caught out staring at a ruinous house, only for someone to emerge from it. One can never tell.

Just then an old woman, dressed in black, came to the municipal bin. It seemed to be 'catch a local with her hands full day', so I approached.

"*¿Cómo?*" she screeched, when I asked if she knew where the *casa rural* was.

I repeated my question and she gestured back the way we'd come.

"*¿Casa Aira?*" I confirmed.

"*Si. Si,*" said the elderly woman, before wandering off.

"Either she's batty, or SatGirl is lost," I said, getting back in the car.

"Let's see," replied S, turning the car round.

We travelled about ten metres before SatGirl beeped.

"Re-routing," I said.

"Follow the road for nineteen kilometres," chirruped SatGirl.

"I think not."

S did a second three-point turn.

Beep, beep. "Re-routing. Follow the road for four kilometres."

I sighed, but we both agreed to trust SatGirl over dotty old woman. Possibly a mistake.

After what seemed more like a dozen kilometres, SatGirl turned us past a field full of the biggest multi-coloured pumpkins I've ever seen.

"Wow! They're huge! Why don't mine grow that size?" I asked, thinking about my hand-sized crop this year.

"Not enough cow poo," replied S.

"Turn left," replied SatGirl.

S swung the wheel and somehow managed to get the car around the 180-degree bend in one go and without us sailing over the edge.

"Oh! Well done," I said, as SatGirl told us to take another left.

"Here?"

The turn was nothing more than a gateway. I shrugged. "Looks like it."

We parked next to a curved stone wall – a renovated but empty cottage to our left and a couple of derelict barns to our right.

"I think I'll go explore," I said. The village didn't look wide enough to take a car further, and I didn't fancy us getting stuck.

13 O Courel part I – two feet in the past

Unlike Vilamor, many of the houses here looked as if they'd been renovated, and by the same hand judging by the finishes to the stonework.

I wandered through narrow lanes between the crowded stone houses then popped out into an open plaza. There was another large house to the right and beyond, a recreation area. A board announced the walking route we wanted. Opposite, the village *lavadoiro*, or washing place, had a commemorative plaque on it.

Unable to see the hotel which SatGirl assured me I had reached, I rang the number.

My conversation was rather surreal.

"*¿Hola, es la casa rural?*"

"*¿Cómo?*"

I know my Spanish is '*mal*' but people don't usually spend so much time saying 'what?' at me. After a couple of attempts, the phone was put down whilst someone else was located. The renewed conversation didn't start wonderfully.

"*¿Hola, es la casa rural?*"

"*¿Cómo?*"

"*¿Está el número para la casa rural? ¿Casa Aira?*" I pronounced, slowly.

"*Aira, sí.*"

Hallelujah!

My delight was short lived though.

"*Está cerrado.*"

So why didn't you say it was closed on your website, I muttered to myself after saying a carefully friendly, "*gracias*".

S had joined me, no doubt wondering if I'd been taken by aliens.

"It's closed," I said, as a child poked its head out of the door of the large building opposite me. It peeked at us, then quickly closed the door again.

"Is that the *casa rural?*" asked S.

"I think so, yes. I suppose having a sign saying 'casa rural' would be too much to ask? Oh well. Look, the board shows the hiking route. Shall we go for a walk anyway while we're here. We can either try Folgoso later or Quiroga even. There's bound to be a hotel open there."

"Okay. Which way?" asked S.

Good question. The yellow and white flashes showed the walk going in two directions from the village, but we wouldn't now have time to do the full eighteen kilometre circuit. We walked up to the road.

"Just tell me if that green lane is wet," I said. "My trainers are no good in the wet. I'm going to photograph these pumpkins."

As I got to the field, which was full of large multi-coloured pumpkins, I had a *déjà vu* moment.

S wandered up.

"Didn't we pass these on the way?" I asked.

"Yes. Right before the double hairpin bend and the narrow gateway."

"So why didn't she direct us through this nice wide gateway and in to what looks remarkably like a large car parking area next to the hotel?"

"Devilment!"

The green lane was soddened, so we headed off through the well-preserved village, high above the river Lor and below a canopy of trees.

"All the rivers seem to be the Lor," I said. "Odd that."

"Maybe it meanders a lot."

I could hear the river, leaping over rocks below us, but the birds were surprisingly quiet. The trees here were predominantly oak.

"Is that cork oak?" I asked, feeling the rough flexible bark on a sapling. "I didn't know it grew here."

"We're not that far from northern Portugal," S replied.

There was a little wooden bridge over the river. The water was still some ten metres below us but it looked deep and clear as it thundered over the rocks.

"I bet kids jump off here in summer," I observed.

S was dismissive. "I shouldn't think so!"

"Well, it's quite high."

13 O Courel part I – two feet in the past

"And the river's full of rocks."

"True," I replied.

The opposite bank of the river was an entirely different ecosystem. Few trees grew here and the shale-strewn path was in the full sun. We were also climbing rapidly. I guzzled at my water bottle, and gasped.

"I'm definitely not feeling fit and healthy today!"

"It is hot," said S.

"Who'd think it for almost November?"

We huffed and puffed a bit further, the sounds of the river fading away below us, our only companions the few pine trees next to the path and a white painted house on the opposite side, hidden in the vegetation.

"Five o'clock. That's an hour. It'll be six when we get back. Shall we turn round?"

"Fine by me."

"Just to that corner then. See what we can see."

At the corner, the view along the river was stunning.

"Is that Folgoso in the distance?" I asked. "It's the only place big enough, I think."

"Probably."

Above us, the track continued to wind uphill, ever onwards, but we wanted to be somewhere flat, and preferably parked up, before nightfall. I didn't fancy negotiating those bends in the dark.

"Can we drive through the village and come out on this road d'you think?" I asked as we got back to the unaccommodating, *casa rural*.

"It looks wide enough. And it's probably easier than that hairpin again."

S did a masterful negotiation of the narrow tracks through the village and didn't even need me to assist with directions. We turned right and headed back towards Folgoso.

"I've been thinking."

"Oh dear," was my hubby's normal response to this oft repeated line.

"Well, if we drive all the way to Quiroga, we won't want to drive all the way back tomorrow. B...ut if we stay in Folgoso, we can try another of the walking routes in the morning. The information centre might even be open."

I'm a born optimist, S a realist. We fit well together.

"You think so?"

"Well, it might be. And the restaurant was good."

"The waitress was a misery though."

"She smiled when I said the risotto was *muy rico.*"

Decision made, we drove back into the metropolis of Folgoso and parked up under a tree, rather closer to the edge of the road than I'd have liked. I popped into the bar again and the same chap came over.

"Do you have a room?" I asked in my best Spanish.

"For two?" He replied, holding up two fingers.

I nodded.

"One night?"

"Yes."

"Okay. But not two nights." He shook his head at this idea, suggesting they were full. In late October?

The room he showed us was basic, but clean, and had a view down the valley. There were two beds.

"He probably thought we weren't married," said S.

"They're big singles though, we could share. D'you want a shower first? You can be guinea pig for the shower hose for once!"

I always have first shower, and consequently always have to be the one to battle with different controls. It's either too hot or too cold, and I never get the cascade force versus barely discernible dribble quite right. This one was simple enough, though S came out of the bathroom shaking his head.

"I knew it would do that. The bathmat's soaked, I had to use it to mop the floor."

"Doesn't the shower curtain work?"

"There's a gap one end where the towel rail is, and the other end where the soap dish is."

13 O Courel part I – two feet in the past

I successfully had a shower, without adding to the saturated bathmat or the puddled floor, by the simple expedient of using the shower as a hand-held and turning it off between rinses.

"I want to watch the sunset from the terrace. Are you ready?" I asked a few minutes later, my still damp hair tousled. "Can I borrow your yellow fleece? It's warmer than mine."

S sighed, handing over the fleece which, in the nineteen years we've known each other, has been worn by him twice and by me dozens of times. I maintain yellow suits me better. S maintains he never gets a choice. I don't know why he doesn't just do the decent thing and donate the jumper to me.

We settled at a table on the elevated terrace just as the sun began its display of fire. I sipped at my red wine and bit off a piece of the ham on bread which came alongside our drinks.

"Nice," I said appreciatively. "The ham's a bit garlicky. I think it's the tomato paste. Lovely."

"The wine's pretty good too. I wonder how much it'll be?"

"Probably dearer than home, but hopefully cheaper than A Coruña," I replied, watching the soft yellows and blues turn to fiery oranges and reds as the sun gave its magnificent show for us.

Our second wine came with hot, tuna-filled *empanadillas* – a small, deep-fried pastry on which I warmed my hands before popping it in my mouth.

"It gets cold once that sun goes down," I said.

"Do you want your jacket?" asked S, the gentleman.

"I'll survive. I'll tuck my hands up my sleeves. I want to see the last of the sunset. What a lovely day," I sighed.

SECTION SEVEN - FORBIDDEN FORESTS

14 O Courel part II – *castros*, castles, and a forest

"I still can't believe the price of the wine last night," I said, as we drove along a road impossibly narrower than those of the previous day. "Four twenty for six wines and six *tapas*."

"Nice wine too," said S. "We should've bought a bottle."

"I love how when I double-checked the price, she asked if it was too little or too much."

"It was their own wine."

"Yeah, but it is at home. And it was good quality. And the information centre was open this morning. It's going to be a good day!"

S laughed at my enthusiasm, but agreed that it was a good day.

Earlier that morning we'd wandered up to the bakery to buy some *pan chocolate* or fresh cakes for breakfast. I was disappointed to find the *panadería* was just a general store, which sold fresh bread but no cakes. My disappointment was assuaged by S finding four ready-packaged chocolate chip muffins for a euro sixty. With a cuppa from our trusty kettle, breakfast was sorted!

After we'd paid up at the hotel, we stopped by the notice board outside the information office to check the routes we wanted to do.

"It's open!" I'd said in astonishment. "It was closed when we got our breakfast."

"It must open at ten."

"Yes, but the door says nine," I said, pedantically.

"It said it closed at three too," S reminded me, as we entered the large space.

The lady was most friendly and suggested a drive and walking route which took in many of the region's sights; waterfalls, mountain views, *castros*, castles and a forest.

"Should be easy," I said as we drove away. "Straight to Seoane and look for the 'camping' sign."

Seoane do Courel was the next 'biggest' town in O Courel. It had a supermarket and no less than four cafés, which I felt was greedy.

"Should we get some bread in case we don't make it to Quiroga in time for lunch?" I asked, looking at the dash clock. "It's twelve now. We can have a picnic."

"And if we don't eat it, we can have it for tea."

Shopping concluded, S took over the wheel so I could navigate.

"I think it's this road," I said, pointing right.

We turned on to the (obviously) narrow road and eventually passed a sign saying 'camping'.

"We carry on through Esperante, which is another hairpin, then up to the *castro*."

I was following our little blue roundel on Google maps, having given up with SatGirl, who claimed she 'couldn't find a way there' when I asked her for directions!

At Esperante, S was reluctant to turn into the tiny village even though I said we had to pass through it. He got out to recce on foot and came back laughing.

"Someone has felt-tipped a sign which says; '*No hay salida*'."

"Ha! Brilliant. No through road. I bet they're fed up of tourists trying to drive through the village. Onwards, then."

When we eventually found it, the Iron Age hillfort, or *castro*, was perched on the top of a steep, shaley mount. A narrow slate strewn track led us there. Again, we'd parked the car on the grass verge, hopeful that it wouldn't slide down the hillside while we were gone.

"The Castro da Torre was a mining town constructed around the first century of our era for those involved in extracting the newly-found gold deposits in the area," I read.

"So, it's Roman?"

14 O Courel part II – castros, castles, and a forest

"Looks like it. Probably built on top of a Celtic settlement. It says here it's built on a spur of slate 300 metres above the Río Lor. It's a great view, that's for sure."

S stood next to the knee-high slate walls which had formed the rectangular houses, and gazed off towards the mountains on all sides.

"That makes a great photo. You look very pensive!"

"I'm thinking how quiet it is here."

"Except for me, talking." I grinned.

The spur on which the settlement perched was apparently 150 metres by 45 metres in size (492 feet by 148 feet). It seemed a tiny and remote spot to live. Even in 2021, I could see only one house from our all-round view, and not a single electricity pylon crossed the green countryside. We walked back to the car as the sun began to warm the dark slate. I heard a tinkling sound coming from the valley.

"I can hear cow bells."

"I can't hear anything. Is the car at more of an angle than when we left it?" asked S.

"Very funny. Next turn is to Mostaz. There's a cave there."

As we rounded the first bend, a flock of around thirty goats meandered along the road in front of us. They were all colours, from black through caramel to blond, and the largest of them had a bell around its neck.

"Goat bells!"

Mostaz turned out to be a tiny village, on another spur above the valley floor, with a mix of derelict and renovated houses. We couldn't find a signpost to the cave, nor anyone to ask. Instead, we wandered around for a while, pondering on the pros and cons of living somewhere so remote.

"It's so peaceful," I said.

"With Covid, it's ideal. And I guess most people here are self-sufficient."

"There's a good crop down there on that little flat bit. Probably sheltered too. I can't imagine going into Monforte shopping though."

"You could go once a month."

"More like once a year, I reckon! With a big store room, you could buy most things yearly if you grew your own veg. We don't buy much fresh stuff."

"As long as you had electric."

"What for?"

"The freezers!"

"Ha! But if you grew your own chickens, rabbits, and even goats, you could kill one as needed. Maybe share with a neighbour."

"Be perfect if you wanted to be a hermit."

"Or a writer," I added, smiling. "No distractions here."

"Okay, next right. It's a steep turn."

"I hope that wasn't it," said S, as we passed a grassy, almost vertical track on the right.

"Oops, yes it was! I think maybe the lady in the information office was being optimistic there. Time to rethink."

The track was literally that: a green lane, just wide enough for a narrow vehicle or a quad bike, which seemed to be the transport of choice hereabouts – with good reason.

We carried on the 'real' road.

We wound upwards through the most incredible mountain ranges. We twisted and turned; the river would be on our right, then we would cross over a tiny bridge and it would be on our left. We went up and up. We went over a mountain pass and continued onwards and upwards.

"There's a viewpoint here somewhere," I said as we drove around a left-hand bend with no barrier on our side, just a sheer drop of who knew how many hundreds of feet. I love heights but I'm not keen on narrow roads, even without the added bonus of no railings and crazy

14 O Courel part II - castros, castles, and a forest

Galician drivers haring around the bend on our side of the road.

We passed a wooden viewpoint and as I looked over to my right, I gave an involuntary shout. "Stop!"

S did a perfectly controlled emergency stop and looked at me.

"Reverse, reverse! Look over there!"

Sitting on a pinnacle about a hundred metres off the road was a magnificent ruined castle. The round tower was still in evidence, as were the high stone walls on one side. It sat on a rounded mound of bedrock, looking down on the surrounding meadow, and at a level with most of the hills around, in glorious isolation.

"What a place to build a castle," S said, as we walked back to the viewpoint and information board. We'd decided to leave the car where it was, again overhanging the verge and a long, long, drop, rather than try to reverse along the road.

"The Order of Santiago was a religious and military order founded in 1179, which disappeared in 1836."

"Like the Knights Templar."

"I guess. Their objective was the defence of Christianity, specifically against the Moors, and they answered directly to the Pope. The earliest record of this castle, Castelo de Carbedo, is in a letter to the Order of Santiago in 1181."

"Shall we go down?" asked S.

"Can we get?"

"There's a track. Look." S pointed to a steep narrow track down the hill from the road which then wound back up to the base of the castle walls. How could I resist?

"Let's go."

When we got to the base of the fortress, I looked up, and up some more.

"I didn't realise it was so high from the road."

"There's no door," added S, before wandering up the track and around the edge of the castle walls.

The dry, earth ledge was only a foot or so in width and in one place had collapsed leaving an interesting sideways jump above a rather high tumble, down the side of the hill. I bet the grass wasn't as soft as it looked.

Around the far side of the tower, we gazed up at the solid wall above us.

"Still no door then?" I said. "Can we get all the way round?"

"May as well now we're here."

Around the far side, the walls were more tumbled down and some rocks were hollow beneath.

"I think this might have been a tunnel." S pointed at a rock with writing carved into it. "It's like something out of Game of Thrones."

"The Wall! Mmm, it is. And they probably had an entrance at ground level too."

As I walked downhill to try and get a photo from the edge of the tumble-down walls, S headed upwards towards the round tower. We both exclaimed at the same time.

"Whoa! I didn't expect that drop!" I said, peering down at the nothingness beneath my feet.

"Same up here," replied S.

I climbed over the scattered rocks to his position. We were now above the level of the road with a vertical drop of over a hundred metres below us.

"We're not going to get down this way, are we?" I said, unnecessarily.

"Not unless you have a rope."

"Upwards then." I scrambled the last couple of feet to the highest point. I had a perfect view of the landscape all around now. The flat grassy top of the round tower was about ten feet across; the circular, lawn-like patch was edged with the stones of the tower wall but lacked a parapet. I pivoted slowly, taking my 360-degree photos whilst trying not to lose my balance.

"It's weird seeing the hills over there on a level. The trees look so small, like toy trees. What a strange feeling.

14 O Courel part II – castros, castles, and a forest

I feel dizzy looking out there yet not looking downwards."

"It's because you have no point of reference," said S.

We had to retrace our steps around the castle to the track and scramble back up the slippery rock to the car, but we both agreed it had been worth it. And the car hadn't slid into the abyss either, which was a bonus.

I took over driving and almost immediately came upon a cow, grazing at the side of the road.

"Why is it always when I'm driving?"

"There's a donkey too," S pointed out.

The biggest donkey I've ever seen decided to wander over to investigate us. It stood right in front of the car, looking down on us before leaning its neck over the bonnet and pushing its nose onto the front windscreen. I tried to grab my phone but by the time I'd got it onto camera mode, the donkey-giant had got bored and wandered off. A shame as it was the photo of a lifetime.

"It must be watching the cows," said S, as we carried on.

"Boy, these roads are hard work," I replied. "You can't lose concentration for a second, can you?"

We came to a narrow defile in the road and topped out with another magnificent view. It was 1.30pm. We had been driving for three hours and had covered hardly any distance at all – in a straight line that is. We had covered many kilometres in twists and turns, and hairpin bends.

The walk we had been shown was along a ridge and I was looking forward to more fabulous views. We kitted up and S took charge of our picnic lunch.

The first part of the track sloped down in the sunshine, until we entered a woodland. It was surprisingly cool out of the sun, even though our temperature gauge in the car had read 26 degrees centigrade.

"I should've brought my thicker fleece."

"I've got a waterproof if you're cold," offered S.

"S'okay, ta. I'll be too warm when we reach the next sunny bit."

The walk was pleasant, through woodland described as humid-Mediterranean. The forest grows on the north side of an old glacial cirque, explaining the bowl-like shape below us. This unusual formation keeps the air humidity high, but the soil humidity relatively low, allowing species such as holly, beech, holm oak, and birch to thrive.

"Shall we stop at the next bit of sun for lunch?"

"There's a rock there." I pointed at a narrow ledge overhanging the canyon.

"Bit narrow, you'd be poking me."

"Ha ha."

My knee, which had been giving me some grief with all our recent walking expeditions, made itself felt.

"Ow, those downhills are killers."

"Here's a flat rock, shall we have our picnic?"

"Plan."

I unwrapped the bread we'd bought from Seoane and handed it to S to cut in half with his penknife. I opened the 'butty' box and handed out a big chunk of cheese, also from Seoane, and an apple each from our own tree.

"Glad I thought of that steak I had left from yesterday's lunch," I said, ripping the flattened fillet steak in half. "Quite a picnic really!"

"Very Galician," agreed S. "Hunk of bread, hunk of cheese, and meat."

"And an apple," I added.

It was a tasty lunch, perched on our rock, but I was getting chilled beneath the trees and my knee was still hurting despite the rest stop. When we arrived at a steep incline I'd had enough.

"Sorry. I don't mind going up but we'll have to come back this way and I don't think my knee will take the downhill. I'm getting cold too."

"It is chilly in here, isn't it?" said S as we turned around and headed back.

14 O Courel part II - castros, castles, and a forest

"I do love woodlands, but I have to admit I prefer the openness of the mountain views."

"I know what you mean. I prefer the sun!"

"It would be lovely under here in summer; the air is so cool."

"It's not damp like the Fragas do Eume though, is it?"

"No, totally different biome."

As soon as we reached the sunlight again, I stopped and held out my arms, feeling the warmth seeping in to me.

"Oh, that's better! I'm glad you parked the car in the sun," I quipped.

"I didn't; I moved it!"

"I know!"

15 Fragas do Eume – flipflopping through the forest

The Fragas do Eume natural park is situated in the northwest of Galicia, inland between Ferrol and A Coruña. The 9,000 hectare (22,240 acre) nature reserve is a rare and well-kept example of a disappearing biome – the Atlantic forest or temperate rainforest. Home to native species of trees such as oak, sweet chestnut, and silver birch; high humidity and a mild climate create a green paradise for ferns and mosses, lichens, birds, insects, and woodland fauna. *Fraga*, in Galego, is a natural woodland; everywhere you walk in the natural woodland of the Eume river there's the fresh smell of damp earth, the sound of running water, and the feel of being close to nature.

We first visited the Fragas do Eume in 2018 as one of our cross-province meets. I had initiated CLOPso (Coruña, Lugo, Ourense and Pontevedra Social Outings, my hubby's clever acronym) as a way for those of us living in Galicia to experience areas we may not otherwise visit. We had some lovely outings in Lugo, Castro Caldelas, the Fragas do Eume, and Monforte, before Covid ended our further travels.

This particular trip had been an August picnic by the banks of the river Eume followed by a walk to the Monastery of San Caaveiro, perched high above the forest floor. On that occasion there were some fifteen of us picnicking under the trees and jumping in the river to cool off. I had been impressed that Mum, then a sprightly 87-year-old, had managed the walk along the river bank and up to the monastery. She was out of breath by the top, but enjoyed her walk. S, meanwhile, had seen a longer hiking route which followed the river back through the woodland on the opposite bank. He vowed we would return one day to walk it.

15 Fragas do Eume - flipflopping through the forest

Our opportunity came in October 2021 when Mum went to France with my brother, leaving us with empty days and oceans of sunshine. Walking weather.

The road to the visitor's centre of the forest park is a single track, twisting and narrow but without turn offs. This didn't prevent SatGirl from telling us to; "Turn right" every few metres as the road wound around and around.

"It's a bend, not a turning," I yelled at her.

S, driving, sensibly kept quiet whilst I ranted at the immovable and dim machine.

"Why does she insist on telling us the name of every road?" I asked. "You can't see the road names in town and out here in the country, who knows what the road name is. In fact, who cares? Just tell me the name of the place we're heading for," I shouted again, as SatGirl told us to follow Avenida Coruña - the third such Avenida in two days. All roads lead to A Coruña it seems.

At long last we passed the place where we'd had our picnic lunch some three years earlier and bumped to a halt in front of the visitors' centre.

"*Buenos días,*" I said to the girl behind the Plexiglas screen as she hurried to put her mask back on. "*Hay un mapa de las rutas de senderismo por favor?*"

"No maps, sorry," she replied. "You can use the QR reader here."

S butted in quickly to prevent my going nuclear over yet another blasted QR code reader, by saying, "It's easy enough. Look, we just follow the river to the bridge then up to the monastery and back along the river on the other side."

The girl was obviously following this conversation, and nodded. "It is six point five kilometres circle. You can park there." She pointed to a smudged spot on the battered map stuck firmly to the desk. In case anyone wished to steal it, I presume.

Grumbling at the lack of paper maps nowadays, I returned to the car.

"I'm just going to have a wee before we set off," I said, pointing to the café next door.

No, I wasn't. 'Patrons only', said the conspicuous notice on the door. Oh well, there were plenty of woods around this time.

We parked the car at the designated parking area a couple of kilometres down the road from the visitor centre, and began to walk.

"Hold on. I'm going to wear my sandals today, at least on the road. They're more comfy and if I end up with wet feet, at least they'll dry quick."

S kindly volunteered to carry my trainers in case of emergencies. With our picnic lunch and one of the bottles of water, he was suitably laden.

We set off at a good pace along the tarmac road. Despite it being little more than a track there were a succession of cars whizzing past every few minutes, often seemingly in convoy.

"I thought it was residents only past here?" I grumped.

"Maybe they own houses down here. It is the weekend."

I'd forgotten that. I hadn't expected it would be so busy in October, even if it was 24 degrees centigrade.

I dashed into a secluded area for a quick wee, thankfully without being bitten on the behind, and we carried on walking and dodging cars.

"Why don't people walk facing the traffic?" I asked as we skirted round another group of people taking up the entire roadway.

"I think some do. That car's had to stop for that lot, look."

I laughed as a car edged carefully round the large group of people we had just passed.

"I can't believe Mum managed to walk this far," I said a few minutes later. "How far do you think the bridge is?"

15 Fragas do Eume – flipflopping through the forest

"I think the first suspension bridge is coming up now," replied S, as a second parking area came in to view, with picnic benches scattered around.

"Ah! We must've parked here last time!"

We carried on walking as the traffic thinned out, both vehicular and human. After another thirty minutes, we reached the second suspension bridge. I looked at my watch.

"I'm thinking the six and a half kilometres starts at the final bridge, in which case we'll have done another four and a half by the time we get there!"

"We have plenty of time," said S, nonchalantly.

Cars still passed us on a rather more regular basis than I'd have liked, but the light filtered beautifully through the green leaves above and reflected from the water, making it sparkle emerald-like.

I stopped to photograph a small waterfall and the river, seen through the canopy of trees. "Ouch!"

"The chestnuts are attacking us," laughed S. Another large, green, and very spiky bomb dropped to the ground in front of us.

After an hour's walking, we reached the bridge leading to the monastery. There were cars parked all about in various attitudes of abandonment, which the Spanish seem to do so well.

"Lazy lot!"

"You only wish you'd thought of it," said S.

"True. But still. If we had to walk all this way!"

The road up to the monastery of San Caaveiro is steep and cobbled, so it was with amazement that I saw a car hurtling down the slope towards us.

"Crikey," I yelled, diving to one side.

"I thought there were steps on this bit," said S.

"Hope not, or she's in for a shock! Oh, look, we're here already."

I'd thought the route to the monastery was much longer, but the walking we'd being doing over the last few days must have paid off. I was barely out of breath by the time we reached the little café at the top.

"Lunchtime."

We commandeered a slate-topped bench to sit on and unwrapped our left-over burrito. Strictly speaking it was half a burrito and it was S' left-overs, but he'd kindly agreed to share.

The previous day we'd met friends at a Mexican restaurant in Narón. We had, as usual, over-ordered and struggled to finish our meals. When S started to rewrap half his burrito the owner came and removed it.

"I prepare to take away for you," he'd said.

He returned the leftovers in a neat cardboard box, together with napkins. All it needed was a penknife to halve our impromptu picnic meal – sitting on a slate bench, next to a medieval monastery at the top of a hill, in a nature reserve of ancient Atlantic forest. And delicious it was too.

The monastery of San Caaveiro was originally built in the 10th century and was declared a monument of historical interest in 1975. The monastery was abandoned during the 18th century Spanish reformation, before being taken over and renovated by the provincial council in 1986. It sits at the pinnacle of the hill on five levels, in keeping with the steepness of its surrounds. We had thoroughly inspected the monastery previously with Mum, clambering up stone steps to preserved gatehouses, through low doorways into chapels, down modern metal staircases and around glass-fronted displays. This time we had more walking to do.

A couple of slices of homemade cake, an orange I'd purloined from our trip to the castle of San Felipe the day before, and a glug of water, set us up for the descent.

"Are you sure it's that way?" I queried.

"Yes. I went down a bit last time to see. But it wasn't any good for Mum so we went back the other way."

"But that says to the Sesín river."

15 Fragas do Eume – flipflopping through the forest

"Yes. We get to that first, then cross it to the Eume. It's a tributary."

Unconvinced I headed to the information desk.

"Yes, it is that way. You walk here to the Sesín, then across to the Eume. It is very beautiful and peaceful this side. No sorry, I don't have a paper map but you can photograph this one if you wish," the friendly young man replied to my query.

"Why no paper now?" I asked.

"It is Covid," he replied.

"Happy now?" asked S, as we made our way to the footpath my clever clogs husband had pointed out previously.

"Yeah, but better safe than walk miles in the wrong direction. Look, this map says the red route goes way up there to the north, and that's the colour on these marker posts."

"But we're not following that route. We're following the green route."

"The post doesn't show the green route," I whined, frustrated. "It shows the red route, which we don't want."

I am a very logical person and cannot cope with things which are not. Galician maps are one of my bugbears; unlike 'normal' maps where north is at the top, Galician maps often have the zero-degree compass point either at the bottom or off to one side. Very confusing. And SatGirl turns the map that I'm following around as we drive – that really gives me a headache.

Luckily, S has an excellent sense of direction so on this occasion I bowed to his internal compass, whilst still whining about the markers.

The first part of the route was steep but beautiful as we wound down through the chestnut and oak trees, each competing to throw nuts at us. A little way along we reached a marker. 'Monasterio Caaveiro' it said on the right-hand arrow. 'Monasterio Caaveiro' it said on the arrow pointing back the way we'd come.

"See what I mean! What help is that?" I spluttered. "And it doesn't say anything the way we're going."

"Well, we don't want to go back to the monastery so we go down here," S said, helpfully.

We carried on through dense woodland until we suddenly approached a bridge.

"That's quicker than I expected," said S. "This is the Sesín."

"Are you sure?"

"Yes." He smiled. "The Eume is just down here."

We crossed the tiny bridge, looking incongruous in the middle of a forest, and continued downhill.

"Oh! I think we'll have to jump this bit."

"No, you can get across here easily," said S, at the exact moment that I leapt across the tiny rivulet. "Or you can jump it!" he added.

"Not even a damp toe," I crowed.

We had almost descended to the Eume river when the path suddenly turned away and began to climb. And I mean climb. As I clambered over rocks and boulders, using tree roots as handles, I puffed, "Why are we going up? I thought this was a meander along the river."

"Mmm. I remember seeing a cliff here somewhere, we'll have to go around it."

Great! Still, I enjoy clambering and my cheap five-euro sandals have a good grip and plenty of flexibility. So long as I don't stub a toe on the rocks.

"Ouch!"

"What's the matter?"

"I just stubbed my toe on that rock," I replied, hopping up and down a bit.

As we continued upwards, we met a group of people descending towards us. With them were two dogs. A golden retriever calmly stepped to one side to let us pass, looking on and smiling down at us. The other, a smaller mongrel, was yapping and pulling on its lead. As we passed, it dived off the tree root on which it was perched dragging its owner behind it. I could see an

15 Fragas do Eume – flipflopping through the forest

accident waiting to happen. The owner was pulled off balance and attempted to half jump, half clamber down the tree roots one handed, clutching the lead tightly in her other hand.

"She should let the dog go free," S observed.

"It's obviously not to be trusted, though. Look at the other one."

The retriever was happily jumping down the slope, checking every now and again that its humans were following.

"They're such different personalities, aren't they?"

Of course, what goes up must come down and the slope on the other side of the rocky outcrop was even more precarious, being mainly gnarled tree roots and occasional huge boulders.

"My little legs aren't designed for this," I said, sitting on a boulder so I could swing my legs over. "Though having little feet helps when the ledges are so narrow."

"You have to jump downhill. Go sideways," said S, the mountain climber.

"Ha! I remember going the whole way down from Abraham's Cave in the Peak District on my behind when I was little. I'd been for a day out with friends. The uphill was okay but I was terrified coming down."

Back at river level I clomped happily along in my cheap sandals.

"*¡Hola!*" I cried at a couple coming towards us.

"*Hola*," they replied, before the man asked S how far it was to the monastery.

"*Media hora*," replied S, as I said; "It's taken us fifty minutes."

The man laughed and pointed behind them. "This way. Two days!"

"Very funny," I said, after they had gone. "And you, you do exaggerate," I scolded my hubby.

"I was encouraging them."

"Mmm. I think 'two days' was more encouragement. It'll be a pleasant surprise when we arrive."

Our next encounter was with a family of four. The man carried a, not so small, girl in a carrier on his back as his partner held an older child by the hand.

"D'you think he'd give me a lift if I asked nicely?"

I was tiring now and slipped for the first time, crossing a muddy patch of ground, when the rock I was using as a stepping stone overturned.

"Ugh!"

My sandals squelched as I pulled my foot out of the gloopy mud, but at least they'd dry.

There were more boulders to negotiate before we reached the first of the two suspension bridges that we'd passed on the way in. There were a few more people here, wandering along the mainly level and root-free earth track. A mature lady with an elderly dog was bending every few metres to pick chestnuts and pop them in her pocket.

"Dinner," said S.

"Cheaper than buying them!"

I pointed out a well-dressed couple looking more suited to an afternoon in church. "They'll have a shock when they reach the rocks."

"They're probably only going between the two bridges."

"Mmm. My legs are going rubbery!" I exclaimed. "And I feel dizzy when I move my head quickly."

"Let's sit on that rock and have our peaches," suggested S.

We sat, side by side on a mossy rock near to the river, eating sweet soft peaches from our garden and throwing the stones in the water.

"That's a peach tree on the bank," I said.

"That one's heading for the sea," replied S, throwing his into the current.

We drank some of our water and I attempted to scramble back to my feet.

"Sitting was easier than standing again," I said, offering up a hand for S to help me.

15 Fragas do Eume – flipflopping through the forest

By the time we finally reached the second suspension bridge, my legs were not obeying me at all and I knew my energy had nearly gone. Across the bridge, there was a small picnic area.

"Emergency break!"

We sat and munched on the box of trail mix I'd brought along, and finished our water.

"That's better," I said, as we ate. "I like the honey-coated nuts."

"Sweet and savoury."

"Like me!"

"I can get the car while you wait here if you like," said my beloved.

"Naw, that's not fair. I'm not making you walk on your own. I'm okay after my trail mix. It's not far now. Or maybe someone'll give us a lift if I stick out my thumb," I joked.

No one did, and I didn't try sticking out my thumb in these post-Covid times, but we reached the car park in a remarkably short time.

Where before there had been empty spaces, there were now cars queuing for each vacant spot. As I pinged the door unlocked, another car stopped next to us, his indicators on.

"He's going t'have a wait," I said. "I've got to change my shoes and get SatGirl going yet."

"I don't think he minds," replied S.

"It should be straightforward getting out. Shall I drive?" I asked. "Just hold onto SatGirl and tell me if anything important occurs."

I fiddled with the Satnav. "No, you stupid woman, I do not want the AP9. I think she has shares in the AP9," I added. "We'll be back in Coruña if she has her way. I just want to get on to the A6. Hold on, I'll try inputting that village. Right. That looks better. Ready?"

S held onto my phone as I backed out, waving to the patient driver waiting for our parking space.

"I can't believe how many people are coming in at this time," I said, glancing at the dashboard clock. "Five o'clock. I suppose that's not late for Spain. Just in time for tea!"

"Turn right," said SatGirl, as we wound through the narrow lane again.

"Shut up, you idiot," I replied.

"At the roundabout, take the third exit."

"Really? She's taking us back on ourselves."

"It's okay, it says Betanzos. Look," replied S.

"Oh. I know where we're going now then. We came this way before. We can pick up the A6 at Betanzos."

"Rerouting…At the next opportunity turn around."

"Nope, I know where I'm going now. I don't need you anymore. Better turn her off or she'll sulk," I added to S, leaning across slightly to click the cross on the maps route.

"No wonder she sulks. You always turn her off before she gets you to your destination. She'd probably appreciate a thank you occasionally."

"True. Thank you SatGirl. And thank you, darling, for suggesting our walk. It's been a lovely day."

SECTION EIGHT - CROSSING BORDERS

16 Las Médulas – gold diggers

"You must visit Las Médulas, it's amazing. And a lovely walk," our friend Mike would tell us at least every few months, but we never had…

"Where shall we go next?" I asked, one crisp sunny October day.

"What about those gold mines Mike's always talking about?"

"Las Médulas? Great idea. It's only a couple of hours if we set off early. Mike says it's a nice walk up to the mine workings."

"Knowing Mike, it'll be miles."

"He probably ran it!"

Mike was the same age as S, but a long-distance runner. He had won his age group in the local fun run a couple of times when they lived in Galicia. We were no runners but we did enjoy a good walk, especially with the promise of stunning views. And then there was the lure of gold…

We set the alarm the following day for 8am. (Don't laugh, those of you who regularly arise well before daybreak, the Galician day begins later than most. At least, ours does!) We had fed ourselves and the animals and were out of the door by nine.

Las Médulas was declared a UNESCO World Heritage Site in 1997 for its incredible Roman gold mining heritage. The village of that name, and the mines, are situated in El Bierzo province, just over the border in Castilla y León. We were leaving Galicia behind.

Other than the closure of a large section of the CG2.1 near to home, and a rather steep and snaking road up to the actual village of Las Médulas, which sits below the most vivid orange-rind coloured rock pinnacles, we arrived in good time and without any major arguments.

The N120 towards Ponferrada hugs the banks of the Sil and closely follows the railway line to that Leonese city, though sadly there were no stations where we were going.

"It's very lumpy country, isn't it?" commented S, as we drove along.

"What a perfect description! It is! Wild and lumpy."

The hills we passed through, round, over, and at times, beneath, were indeed lumpy. Not pointed or craggy, in the main they were dark-green clad high rolling meadows and forests. There were rounded pom-pom firs, each having a poodle tail top, and pointy Christmas tree firs. In other places, the landscape had an abundance of deciduous trees. The birches shone a bronzed yellow, whilst the fruit trees glowed deep red in the autumn sunshine.

Through our wild and lumpy landscape, we crisscrossed rivers and railway lines, tunnelled through mountains, and gazed at churches and castellated buildings. We passed a large lake, which I made a note of for our return journey.

"What a gorgeous landscape. I'm confused with these rivers though. We keep crossing them."

"And the railway line. We've just crossed it again."

"Oh! I thought that was the river."

"No. We crossed the river first, then the railway."

"Oh heck!"

The peaks we passed through were of granite rock, like at home in the Lugo hills. The occasional bare, rocky outcrops were grey and craggy, thrusting through the forest. As we drove up towards Las Médulas though, the main geology changed from igneous to sedimentary rocks. Instead of being forged in the fires of ancient volcanoes these rocks were formed from alluvial soils, washed down by meltwater some six million years ago at the end of the Miocene period. Great pressure over millions of years compressed the sediment to form sandstones,

16 Las Médulas – gold diggers

limestones and grit. Instead of granite-grey, these rocks were sandy-yellow.

At times, further upheavals in the Earth's crust had twisted and buckled the rocks, so that in places the layers were no longer horizontal. We were now walking through this landscape, from the car park, towards the mountains

"Oh look! You can see where the shale's been pushed up here. It's lying sideways. Not very comfortable to walk on, but I bet there're fossils in here if we look."

For an amateur geology buff, the landscape was endlessly engaging.

S was more pragmatic. "I'd rather look for gold than fossils."

"Ha! I bet that's long since gone, though you never know. Look for something glittering! We can be real life gold diggers."

Gold was mined in the northwest of the Iberian Peninsula well before the Romans arrived. It may have been the beauty of the tribal gold ornamentation which first alerted the Roman conquerors to its presence, or maybe the acquisition of the Gallaecian and Asturian territories was a deliberate measure to allow the Roman Empire access to this treasure.

"What does Las Médulas mean anyway? The Medals?"

"Maybe. I s'pose all coins were originally medals. Or vice versa."

In the early first century of our era, the Roman emperor, Augustus, was busy regulating the monetary system; gold became the metal of choice for minting the new Aureus coin.

Early Celtic tribes would have panned for gold from the auriferous rivers of the area, but this was too slow and too inefficient for the Romans. They simply destroyed the very mountains themselves.

"So, how did they get the gold then?" I asked, as we walked uphill through heather, holly (or holm) oak, and heavenly-scented lavender.

"They literally flooded the mountain via galleries cut into the sides until the whole thing collapsed."

"Wow!"

As we walked along, the autumn sunshine now surprisingly hot at this altitude, I pondered on the Roman destruction of the landscape.

By the time the Romans arrived in the peninsula, the remaining gold at Las Médulas was too deep to mine easily, so the Romans created the biggest open-cast mine in the northwest of Hispania as the Romans called the peninsula. The easiest way to expose the deep gold-bearing seams was to remove the entire upper layers – all at once.

As S had explained, a network of galleries was dug into the mountain but not all the way through – there was no exit hole. These tunnels were then flooded until the lower rock layer became saturated. Unable to hold the pressure of water building up within, there was a slippage and the entire side of the mountain collapsed. The Romans called this method of extraction '*Ruina Montium*', which needs no translation! I couldn't help wondering how many people had died during that hazardous operation.

As we rounded a bend, the beautiful golden-orange sedimentary mountains were aligned in front of us. Sharply pointed now, protruding above the flora on the hillsides, their sides bare of vegetation, their flanks exposed to the erosion of wind, rain, and time; they were beautiful.

"That ugly quarry opposite is spoiling my photos," I grumbled. Then, I realised what I'd said and laughed. "I suppose that's what the ancients said about the Roman mines! It's sort of the old and the new methods of quarrying side by side, isn't it?"

"Don't forget the Romans did more than just blast away the mountainside, though."

"That's true. They changed the entire landscape round here."

16 Las Médulas – gold diggers

One of our first stops had been at a viewpoint overlooking the valley and the village we'd hiked from, way below us. That valley was crisscrossed with gullies. These were not natural gullies but man-made water channels created by the Romans. Flooding a mountain to the point of saturation takes a lot of water and the Romans created reservoirs and a network of canals to move the water to where it was needed.

At one point there was a sign at the side of the track. S was immediately off to investigate.

"It's one of the old canals. Look!"

Sure enough, the interpretation board explained that part of the canal had been excavated to give us, the visitor, an idea of the scale of the operation. The channels were two metres in width and around sixty centimetres deep (six feet six wide by two feet deep). In the diagram, the channels looked like nothing so much as a very shallow helter-skelter or water flume, carved as they were into the mountainside.

"Hey! They used T-bars for levelling, like you did for our sewerage pipes." I pointed at a diagram of a man sighting along a wooden stick with a cross piece on the top. In the distance was a second man, also holding a T-bar.

"That's where I got it from," replied S.

"Hmm. What did the Romans ever do for us?" I said, laughing. "They really did change everything, didn't they?"

"Even our lunch stop was man-made."

"What? That lovely field with the picnic tables?"

We'd stopped near the very top of the mountain track at a flower-strewn shorn meadow, dotted with open, stone barns – perfect for a shady rest stop. We'd enjoyed our peanut butter, marmite and banana butties, listening to the birds crying high overhead and examining the delicate, pale mauve *Colchicums* pushing through the dried grass.

"It used to be a big tank for collecting the water."

"Wow! That's why it was so flat compared to everywhere else! But how do you get water from there?" I mused.

"Using the canals. But later, as they got higher up, they had another big water deposit at the top of the hill. Look." S pointed at the portion of the board he'd been reading.

"It's amazing how good the Romans were at engineering isn't it? I can imagine a project like that now would take years to get through the architects' department."

"Now they'd just blast it all," said S, never the romantic.

"Haha. I meant with the technology they had. It's incredible what they achieved. Though having access to thousands of slaves helped, I guess."

Although in the early years the work was done by slaves, later, free men (and women and children) worked at the mines. Often, these workers owed 'days' to the Roman Empire in lieu of taxes; at other times they would be paid a pitiful wage for their hard labour. Maybe they weren't slaves, but they were wage slaves. Not much changes for the poor, I thought.

Once the mountain had been 'ruined', the fine work of sifting began. Firstly, all the large river-washed boulders were removed from the workings and piled to one side. The hillside opposite us glittered with huge mounds of rounded black rocks which the Romans called *murias*. I shuddered as I looked across the valley.

"I wouldn't want to live below those piles; it reminds me too much of Aberfan, the Welsh mining disaster."

"That was coal shale though. Because the heavy rains soaked the heap, the shale slipped against itself and caused an avalanche effect. I think these might be more stable being round. They can settle into the hollows, like a ball in a cup."

16 Las Médulas – gold diggers

S might well have been right, but looking at the huge mounds of glistening coal-black boulders sitting above the villages in the valley made me shudder again.

"It's the 55th anniversary of the Aberfan disaster this week," I said. "The Coal Board never did admit liability, you know. I suppose those piles of stones have been there a long, long time, but even so. One loose boulder and it would be like a mass of giant ball bearings, rattling down the mountain."

As I tried to photograph the *murias* against a bright sun, I counted. There were at least twelve huge circular mounds marching down the hillside. I'd seen one close up, at the beginning of our walk, and wondered how such obviously river-washed stones had arrived halfway up a mountain. Now I knew. Each of those stones had been around twenty or thirty centimetres in diameter, and way too heavy for me to lift (yes, I tried). They reminded me of old cannon balls, and looked just as deadly.

Once the larger boulders had been removed from the river beds the gold, suspended in the remaining sediment, was filtered out by panning. The channels constructed for washing the auriferous mud were called *agagae*. The bottom of these channels was lined with heather cuttings to help filter the sediment.

"Maybe that's why there's so much heather along the pathways."

"It says here that there was so much waste sand, rock, and mud that it altered the course of some of the waterways."

The lake we could see below, Carucedo, was created after some of this waste blocked the river Isorga, producing a huge reservoir.

"So, the whole of this gorgeous landscape is basically man-made or man-altered," I mused.

Everything we'd seen, from the glowing umber-gold pinnacles to our sunny picnic meadow, and from the ancient water channels carved into the green hills to the glistening black mounds of boulder rocks, even the blue lakes below us, were all man-made some 2,000 years earlier.

The Romans extracted over 230,000 kilogrammes of gold from the northwest of Hispania. Of that, around 10,000 kilogrammes were extracted from the El Bierzo region. The consequence for Las Médulas was a complete alteration of the landscape. Two thousand years later, that man-made landscape attracts tourists all year round. In fact, the village of Las Médulas is one big tourist trap, with hostels and cafes, and people offering guided tours.

What *did* the Romans ever do for us? I pondered, as we wandered past shops selling local honey and stuffed, full-size toy sheep, whilst restaurants with 13€ *menús del día* and cafes served a horde of tourists – even in autumn. And I wondered what the Romans or the ancient Celts would have thought of modern commercialism.

Some things don't change in Spain though; even in a tourist haven, lunchtime is sacrosanct.

The Orellan Galleries were open to the public, and I was eager to have a look at the remains of some of the Roman excavations. The open mouth of one of these caves gaped across the valley at us as we stared at this human-created scene. The galleries though, were closed for lunch.

"Daft idea expecting a tourist attraction to be open at lunchtime, I suppose?"

"Well, no one would visit then, would they?" said S.

"Because it's lunchtime!" we chorused, laughing. After so long in Galicia, we had low expectations *vis à vis* opening hours.

"Not sure sandals were such a good idea through chestnut woods," I said, a little later, hopping about as another chestnut husk embedded itself into my foot.

We were descending through a deep forest to the valley below, heading for another cave, El Cuevon, or The Cave. When we arrived, the entrance was firmly blocked with a notice warning of the dangers of rock slippages. Beyond the notice, a couple came towards us offering a smiling '*buenas tardes*' as they climbed over the rope and passed by.

I looked at S and grinned. This is Spain. No words were necessary.

"Well, I don't know what the Romans did for Spain, but Mike was right about this being a worthwhile trip."

"And a good walk," added S.

17 Caminha – and why we can't return to Portugal

It was summer 2017. Mum was due to visit my brother in France and we were trying to sort out the easiest route for her. Unfortunately, our closest airport, Santiago de Compostela, flew only to Paris in France, rather a long journey for my brother. However, Oporto in northern Portugal had started to run flights to smaller northern French airports. Combine a road trip to Portugal and we were set.

We left home on a scorching June morning, having watered all our many tomato plants and fed the animals in the expectation they would all survive a day alone.

As is our wont, S and I shared the driving, turn and turn about. Our first stop of the day was in the small town of Porriño for morning tea. Sitting at a small table outside one of the many cafes along the main street, it felt like we were already on holiday.

We were surprised to cross the border so quickly – so surprised that I almost missed the turn off for our first destination of Caminha.

Caminha is a Portuguese town on the south bank of the river Miño/Minho opposite A Guarda on the Spanish side, another favourite destination of ours. Caminha is a small town, with a long walkway along the river front and many tiny houses decorated in the Portuguese style – with brightly coloured ceramic tiles on the outside walls. One house had a doorway so low, even I would need to duck to enter.

In a weed-strewn square sat a statue of a man on a bench, his bronze dog watching him intently. Below, washing itself nonchalantly, was a real, grey cat which looked entirely bored with its surroundings. Nearby, a house had been demolished; the only remains, a rusted *cocina* at second floor level, was attached to a small part of the floor twenty metres in the air.

17 Caminha – and why we can't return to Portugal

Having wandered the streets to our hearts' content and investigated the tourist information office, the church and the plaza, we were ready to eat. Checking my phone, I was disappointed to find it was still only 1pm. Then I remembered – we were an hour behind in Portugal. My phone had automatically updated the time. Luckily, Portugal also eats earlier than Spain so we were just in time for lunch.

The main square in Caminha was dotted with eateries of varying prices. One stood out. It was a Sports Club, called O Clube, with a hand-scribbled board outside.

"*Prato do día*. Bread, soup, plate, erm main I guess, and drink, five euros," I read.

"Sounds good to me."

"What is it?" asked Mum.

"I'm not entirely sure. I think there's salmon and a beefsteak on the list. And soup of the day. Shall we try it?"

"Yes, please."

"We can't go wrong for five euros," added S.

Inside the wide entrance was a stone staircase rising up to the floor above. Here there were a maze of rooms: a trophy room, a store room for canoes, a couple of locked doors, a small lounge and, eventually, a restaurant.

The room was small but clean and brightly lit from the many windows, open to the gentle breeze outside. A young waitress showed us to a table and reeled off, somewhat too quickly, the choices in rapid Portuguese. Now, Galego, the local language in our adopted home, is very similar to Portuguese in many ways but that doesn't mean I understand either well. Thankfully our waitress spoke both Spanish and a smattering of English, as do most of the Portuguese we've met. I'm told it's because their films are subtitled rather than dubbed, giving them an ear for the English language early on.

"Do you want the soup? It is leek with vegetable?"

"Oh, yes please," came three replies.

A good choice, the soup was served in a huge bowl with crusty bread.

I'd guessed both mains correctly, to my surprise, and we were further surprised to find that both came with real-life vegetables – an unheard-of luxury in the meat and potato land of Galicia.

Dessert wasn't included, but the coffee was a measly fifty cents extra. I struggled to order mine and Mum's espressos, which instead of being a *solo* are simply a *café* in Portugal. S wanted tea with lemon.

"*¿Té con limón?*"

"Okay!"

What arrived was a cup of boiling water with a lemon slice alongside. After a bit of pointless searching for a tea bag, I called to our friendly waitress and asked if they had forgotten the tea.

She laughed. "Ah! Lemon tea in Portugal is lemon and water. You need *cha preto,* black tea."

What is it they say about a little knowledge being a dangerous thing?

After lunch, we set off for our home for the night, Viana do Castelo, near to Oporto where Mum's flight was leaving from the following day. Being us, we'd decided to avoid the toll motorways by taking the scenic coastal route to Viana.

It was the slowest journey I have ever taken by car!

Most of the roads had fifty kilometre per hour speed limits. On the odd occasion that the limit rose to seventy, I would just have time to accelerate before the next sign would have me back at fifty. It was frustrating, and not particularly scenic as trees and undergrowth screened the views of the Atlantic coast for much of the way. Although we passed through some pretty villages, I just wanted to arrive at our destination.

We stopped at the free car park, near the harbour at Viana, and walked the short distance to our

17 Caminha – and why we can't return to Portugal

accommodation. The hotel was centrally located in a pedestrian area; the staff were once more friendly and obliging, though I felt warning potential guests on the website that the bedrooms were on the third floor without benefit of a lift might have been useful.

Poor Mum puffed her way up to her room but soon forgot her discomfort at the strange and interesting artwork along the walls. There were masks staring down at her from all around while our room had gaudy figurines in papier-mâché. It was most bizarre.

In the evening we went to look for a bar. The second place we found was called The Cave, and was exactly that – a cave-like room in the basement of an old stone building. Inside was dim, but a large table in the corner beckoned us. Drinking Portuguese wine and eating *tapas* we watched a stage being set up.

"Is there live music?" I asked the barman.

"¡*Sim!* Ten of the clock." Checking my phone, I saw it was already 9.30pm. As we had front row seats, we decided to stay put.

The three-piece band were called The Sons of Morpheus, and probably one of the best rock bands I've heard for a while. The lead singer and guitarist was a Johnny Depp lookalike, with a huge top hat and fingers which blurred on the strings. The drummer was Animal, from The Muppet Show. He began wearing trousers and a T-shirt and ended the set in shorts – bare chested, dripping sweat and flinging his hair out of his eyes every few seconds. His playing was wild, loud, and brilliant. The bassist was a quiet, unassuming chap with an excellent sense of rhythm who held the band together.

The Sons played mainly rock covers until after 12.30am, and I think our collective ages were ten times the average of the other patrons.

The following morning, we began the day with an excellent breakfast at our hotel before setting off for the airport. Again, the road had a fifty kilometre per hour speed limit the whole way.

We arrived in plenty of time to book Mum in for her flight. Unlike Santiago, our local airport, where we go directly to the special assistance office on arrival, we could not collect a wheelchair at Oporto until after we'd checked Mum in. This meant Mum would have to queue for half an hour at the check-in desk before being able to sit down. Needless to say I queued for her, but if she'd been alone it would have been a nightmare. Once checked in, Ryanair themselves called the wheelchair people. This took some time as they appeared to be understaffed, but eventually they came to wheel mother away and we breathed a sigh of relief that all had gone to plan so far.

"But I'm not driving back the long way," I protested. "Let's find out how we pay for the toll roads."

Portugal has an odd system for its toll roads. Instead of booths such as in Spain or France where one throws the money into a box, or pays an attendant, Portuguese motorways have electronic tolls. Cameras photograph car number plates and determine the cost of the journey as one travels. The choice for tourists is to pay in advance at a post office or to pay online afterwards. The airport had a post office where we were told we could pay for our ticket.

"¡Ola!" I called to the grumpy looking woman on the post office counter in Portuguese, before switching to Spanish. "¿Hablas Inglés?".

"¡Não!" Was the curt reply.

"Ah! ¿Hablas Español?"

"¡Não! ¡Português!" She replied.

Now, forgive me being blunt, but to work at a post office in an international airport I sort of assumed the staff might at least speak the language of their nearest, and much larger, neighbour. As my Portuguese is non-existent, I continued speaking in Spanish; despite her negative assurances, the woman understood.

17 Caminha – and why we can't return to Portugal

"We need to pay for the toll," I began.

"Which motorway?" snarled the assistant (a misnomer if ever there was one).

"Oh, I don't know. The one towards Tui, I guess."

"Which motorway?" she repeated.

"I don't know the motorway numbers, which one goes to Spain, please?"

A shrug.

"Do you have a map I can look at?"

She shrugged again and pointed to the shop opposite. I didn't want to buy a blasted map, only to look at one. S ran down to our car in the parking garage and came back with our Spain-Portugal map. We checked the road numbers and I told the woman.

"Registration."

I gave her our car registration number. She paused. "This is a Spanish number."

"Yes, we live in Spain."

"When are you coming back?"

"I'm not if I can help it," I mumbled under my breath. Out loud I said, "We are driving home, we only need the toll one way."

"Impossible! I cannot do the paperwork for a foreign car."

That was an interesting concept. So only Portuguese cars could drive on the Portuguese motorways? Mmm.

Eventually, by some means I wore her down and we were issued with the elusive piece of paper saying we'd paid our toll. Our foreign registration was in the system for when we whizzed past the cameras en route home.

Except it wasn't.

It was only after we returned home that I realised that in my annoyance and distress (my excuse), I had inadvertently given the old hag, sorry, assistant, the letters from our new Spanish registration but the numerals from our old car. This of course meant we were illegal all the way home.

Mum was away for two weeks, returning on S' birthday, the 18th of July. As a treat I decided I would book us into a hotel in Caminha for the night. We had Workawayers staying on that occasion, so the animals and plants were in good hands as we set off at 10.30am for our return drive to Portugal.

Mum wasn't due back until 5.30pm so we had all day to get to Caminha. We repeated our previous trip by stopping for tea at O Porriño and arriving in Caminha in time for lunch at O Clube once more. The soup this time was vegetable; the meat was a type of Portuguese sausage which was rather strongly flavoured, and possibly included offaly bits. Sometimes not understanding a menu is a bonus.

The Hotel Muralha de Caminha had the most gorgeous rooms, set against the town's old walls. We inspected both and decided to give Mum the one with the huge walk-in rainforest shower, though not before testing it ourselves. I decided to go online this time to pay for the toll road. I set up my laptop and signed into the Portuguese roads site, sitting on our comfortable double bed.

"Hmm. It says I can't pre-pay. I have to do it afterwards. I guess they don't know where you're going until you've arrived!"

"Didn't CJ say there was a toll booth at the beginning of the motorway near to Caminha?"

"I think he did."

The friendly lady in the tourist information office confirmed there was indeed a toll booth, whilst collecting S' reading glasses which he'd left on her counter on our previous trip. Now there's service.

We set off in good time for the airport and easily found the toll booth. It was an unstaffed, card machine. Our debit card was, I remembered too late, sitting on the side in our hotel room where I had left it after trying and failing to pay online. No one answered my frantic

17 Caminha – and why we can't return to Portugal

beeping of the 'help' button, and I decided the word obviously didn't translate.

Once more then, we hared down the motorway illegally to collect Mum from Oporto. The plane was late, and when she appeared Mum was hobbling and out of breath. The wheelchair assistant told me they had no wheelchairs available. I was furious. What was the point of booking wheelchair assistance if they don't then provide it?

I had, I think, already decided I didn't like Oporto airport.

This is a shame as every other person and place in Portugal was delightful.

We showed Mum to her room, which had a view of the medieval castle – its parapets draped with flags from a recent fiesta. We decided on a quiet dinner at the hotel, which seemed to have a grand and well-appointed dining room. No one had taken any money for our rooms nor even glanced at our passports by that point, which amused me. After all, we had already had a shower and driven away once; only our consciences stopped us from doing so again.

Dinner began with bread and those peculiarly Portuguese tin foil packets of fish paste which are charged for per opened pack.

Ordering the Bacalhau (cod), we waited, and waited, and waited. Eventually our meal arrived. It was tasty but once finished, again we sat and waited. I asked a waiter for the dessert menu which he kindly brought, leaving our dirty plates on the table when he left.

Eventually we stacked the plates in a toppling tower to one side, but still no one came. S and I wandered over to the dessert fridge, peering in and trying to catch the eye of a waiter, or anyone who might help. No one came. Eventually, realising we were not going to get served that night, we gave up and left.

Around the corner from the hotel was a street full of bars and cafes doing a decent trade. S had already spotted one selling artisan beers so that became our home for the evening.

On arrival we were brought a plate of *tapas* without being asked. Having just finished dinner we were hardly hungry, but my mother taught me it's rude to leave food so we chomped our way through the offerings. It was only when we paid at the end of the evening that I found the unrequested *tapas* had been charged for. Another Portuguese predilection I would be wary of in future. It also made me realise how spoilt we are in Spain.

The following morning, we awoke early but heading towards the dining room found our way barred by a locked and rather solid-looking door. On the door was a note in English, Spanish, and Portuguese saying breakfast commenced at 10am.

"To exit the hotel before 10 o'clock, please use the side door," I read.

Given that we had still to pay for our rooms, and our meal the evening before, I was again intrigued by the level of honesty which must exist in north Portugal.

We wandered around the deserted streets, scoring me a new pair of five-euro sandals from a beach shop, before returning for a delicious and filling, if rather later than expected breakfast.

"Since Portugal eats lunch at one instead of Spain's two o'clock, a 10am breakfast doesn't leave much time in between meals, does it?" I mused, as we drove away.

As it was Wednesday, we had a treat in store for Mum on the way home. Wednesday is market day in Valença, a Portuguese town near the Spanish border. The market here is legendary both for its size and for its bargains. Despite the fact that it was raining for most of our trip, Mum managed to go on a wild shopping spree – buying unneeded tea towels (for which she has an odd fetish), smart new dinner plates (which were also totally unnecessary, though rather swish in kiln-fired dark-red and incredibly cheap), a new lacy red-bordered

17 Caminha – and why we can't return to Portugal

tablecloth, a green bedspread for her spare room, and an orthopaedic pillow. The car was filling rapidly as S and I traipsed back and forth piling in each item the *jefa* (boss lady) bought.

There were stalls full of shoes, piled into higgledy piggledy heaps. I imagined someone trying to find a matching pair, like some kind of manic game show. There were also stalls of designer handbags – which were obviously not so designer as the police did a raid whilst we were there, taking away black bin bags full of Calvin Klein and Chanel whilst the stallholders looked on piteously.

As the rain came down more heavily, we sheltered under an inadequate parasol drinking hot chocolate surrounded by damp clothing and damper shoppers. We walked down yet another aisle towards what I hoped was the car park. Then, I spotted a furniture stall.

Wooden furniture is my weakness and this stall had something I'd long coveted – a set of library steps. For anyone who doesn't know, this clever piece of furniture folds up to make a comfortable chair and unfolds to a two rung step ladder. I'd seen them at our local market in Monterroso for around 40€. I was amazed that here they were being sold for only 25€. The chap even admitted that he drove regularly to Spain to sell them on at a better price. I wanted one but would the chair fit in the car?

We walked back to the car park, installing Mum in her seat before dropping the other part of the back seat. A quick measure from S' trusty tape and the verdict was… S says yes! The car was really rather full on the way home.

§

So that was a nice story, but why can't we return to Portugal?

Having failed entirely to pay for our tolls again on our return trip, I revisited the Portuguese road website on the Thursday. No ticket was showing as due for our car. I checked again on the following Monday. The system had finally updated and I entered our card details to pay. The screen told me the card needed authorising via our mobile. I waited but no message came through on my phone. I gave it a while longer then walked up to the bank.

"*Hola, Cris.* You have our phone number, don't you?" I asked.

"I think so, hold on. Yes, here it is."

I explained the problem and Cris said she would double check our number was in the system, but to give it a few days. I did so.

The following week I tried again with the same result. The week after was the same. I returned to the bank.

"Let me see the card," said Cris. "Ah! It is in your husband's name."

She was correct. We only had one debit card between us. Spanish banks charged a fee per card and we were rarely apart when shopping, so it had never been an issue.

"But it's a joint account," I replied.

"Yes, but the card is only valid for the person named on it. Who is the mobile registered to?"

That was an easy one. "Me!"

S doesn't use a mobile and is a technophobe of the highest order.

"Then that is the problem," said Cris, triumphant at finding the cause.

I was still lost.

Seeing my confusion, she continued; "We can only use a mobile number registered to the card holder to authorise a payment."

Ah! Now that *was* a problem.

"You must buy the phone for your husband, or you can order a second debit card for you," Cris said.

I didn't want to do either. With no other option in sight we have still, to this day, not paid our tolls. We have also never dared return to Portugal in case we are instantly arrested and thrown into jail!!

18 A trip to Salamanca – bonus chapter

"Those ones have little chimney pots on them. And there's smoke coming out too. Oh, there's washing by that one!"

Over the years, for the sake of safe driving, and my sanity, I have learnt to tune out Mum's backseat monologues. She tends to give a running commentary on every single thing she sees; "There's a tree." "There's an aeroplane." "There's a cloud." This particular commentary, however, was strange enough to filter through to my ears.

"What?"

"The hills over there," replied Mum, pleased to get a response. "They have chimneys on them."

This was a weirdness too far, so I risked a quick glance over my left shoulder. Sure enough, the hillside sprouted dozens of metal chimney stacks glinting in the sunshine. And, yes, there were indeed washing lines dotted here and there across the rolling expanse of green. Clothes danced in the breeze to an invisible choreographer, looking like marionettes escaped from their shackles. Besides the incongruity of the chimneys and lines of washing, the hillsides were bare, with no other signs of life.

I looked at the dashboard clock. "It's nearly lunchtime, shall we turn off and explore?"

§

It had been a lovely mid-week, spring break. It was the end of March 2016, and a week earlier I'd been looking at the weather.

"It's Mother's Day coming up. Where shall we go?" I asked.

"How about Salamanca? Mum's always going on about visiting," S suggested.

18 A trip to Salamanca – bonus chapter

"Oh, yeah. They did it at school or something. I'll see what I can find out."

I checked Booking.com and found a *hostal*, or guest house, right in the centre of Salamanca with good reviews, good prices, and car parking included – all bonuses in a big city. We packed overnight bags, fed the animals and set off on a misty Monday morning in March (the alliteration being entirely coincidental).

Salamanca is known as The City of Learning, possessing one of the oldest universities in Europe. The origins of the university of Salamanca go back to 1130 CE with the building of early cathedral schools. In 1218, Alfonso IX granted the Studii Salmantini the status of general school. This was upgraded to university in 1254, during the reign of Alfonso X. At this time, the first university public library in Europe was also created there. By the 16th century there were more than 7,500 students in Salamanca.

Mum had been fascinated by the city ever since they had a talk about it in school back in the 1930s. For whatever reason, the place had stuck in her head and become an obsession. Always happy to indulge obsessions if it involves a road trip, we set off that drizzly Monday morning via Ourense.

For once I had the directions ready, printed out and on my lap. This was in the days before we owned a smart phone or Satnav, but I'd found the RAC (Royal Automobile Club) site online and printed off their directions. How very organised of me!

The first thing I discovered was that there was a speed camera on the way into Ourense – who knew? We successfully negotiated it and, safely on to the A52, I took over and set off at a good clip – slowing down to a much gentler clip as I found the main east-west corridor Autovia had the deepest potholes I'd seen in years. The journey turned into a slalom race; swerving the worst holes and bouncing through the ones we couldn't avoid, whilst cursing Spanish governments and hoping the new car didn't get too battered. By the time we reached our magical 2pm lunchtime, both S and I were exhausted from the concentration needed to avoid the potholes. Luckily, there was a village signposted off the main road. Vila de Ciervos, or Town of the Deer, sounded interesting enough for a look.

We turned off the main road and drove, and drove. We crossed over a river, then seemed to cross it again before paralleling the same river on a tiny road built on a raised bank high above the water. I later discovered that we had crossed two of the many tributaries to the reservoirs which are scattered around this area. This one was the Valparaíso reservoir, also used as a river beach in the summer months. The road is built up to alleviate flooding. That road was narrow and ran straight through empty countryside, but the arrows still pointed ahead so we continued on our lonely way.

The actual town, when we finally arrived, was quite small. There was one main street with a few bars and cafes dotted about – all empty. In fact, the town seemed pretty empty, but then again so does our own town of Taboada at most times of the day. The buildings were mainly of stone; golden sandstone rather than the granite of our own house, with wooden balconies overlooking the deserted road. The sky had turned grey as we got out to wander down the street looking for a promising restaurant, and the wind was fierce as it chased across the empty, flat landscape. In my photographs Mum looks frozen, wrapped in her woolly jacket. Eventually we simply got back in the car and drove to a restaurant towards the end of town with large glass windows. There were a few vehicles parked outside and chatter coming from within.

The restaurant turned out to be a pleasant surprise. One part was filled with greenery and light came in through a glass roof. The other side featured stone walls and a cosy ambience. Despite the town's name, there was no venison on the menu but the meal was good,

18 A trip to Salamanca – bonus chapter

tasty and filling. And, of course, cheap, at ten euros a head. On the way out we spotted a statue of a stag, sitting on a plinth and surveying his town. I bade him a fond farewell as we drove away.

Suitably fed and watered, we carried on to Salamanca through scenery so flat we could have been in the Low Countries – except that this flatland is at an average height of 660 metres (2,165 feet) above sea level. We were driving through the Spanish *meseta*, or tablelands, the oldest geological landscape in the Iberian Peninsula. The grey sky was touching the bare brown fields; there were virtually no trees and the wind howled around the car. It looked a very barren place to live compared to our hilly, green and forested Galicia.

We made good time to Salamanca once we got off the A52, with its dire need for road repairs, and arrived in the city by 5pm. Finding the *hostal* I'd booked was not quite so simple; the roads all appeared to be one way or pedestrian. Eventually, having exhausted almost every route I got out of the car, leaving S and Mum, to walk to the Hostal Sara. The lady on reception was delightfully friendly and came with me to help us find the car parking we'd booked. This turned out to be a single narrow space reserved for the hotel in a tiny underground car park.

Most Spanish underground car parks seem to be built with scooters in mind rather than cars. The turns are so tight as to need nerves of steel and excellent all-round awareness. This one involved heading down a ramp, almost running into the car parked opposite, then reversing into a space between two pillars – the width of which was only slightly bigger than the car reversing in. I dreaded to think how we were going to get out again. S managed the manoeuvre wonderfully and I gave him a hearty round of applause.

Our room at the *hostal* was spacious. There was a tiny galley area with a hob, and an en suite bathroom. Mum's room was similar, though without the kitchenette. My first job was to plug in our kettle and make three well-deserved mugs of tea whilst we had showers and changed. A quick relax to watch the US *Tiny Homes* series, which I am addicted to, and then it was out to explore the city.

Stone buildings soared above the cobbled streets in the old town. The cathedral was magnificent with its anthropomorphic carvings, and the Plaza Mayor gleamed in the damp. The lights around the buildings reflected off the golden stonework all around us. We all fell in love with Salamanca that evening.

The first known record of the place that was to become Salamanca, was in 220 BCE when Hannibal (he of the elephants) laid siege, taking the Celtic settlement there. The Romans took the town (and the peninsula) after Carthage fell. They named it Salmantica and set about reinforcing the existing Celtic fortifications. The ford over the river Tormes (one of the tributaries of the river Duero, or Douro in Portuguese) became a bridge and Salmantica became part of the Via de la Plata or Silver route: a Roman road between Emerita Augusta (Mérida) and Asturica Augusta (Astorga) and now one of the routes of the Camino de Santiago long-distance pilgrimage.

Salmantica became urbanised, with a grid structure, fortified defences and the trappings of prosperity; inns, Roman bathing houses and merchants' buildings.

The first bar we went into that evening was called Erasmus. It was near the *hostal* and recommended on TripAdvisor. I have no idea why. It was noisy, expensive and lacking in any decent *tapas*. Three wines somehow cost us 18€ which was outrageous, even for a big city. Luckily, the night improved as we bar crawled our way around the old town. The '4 Gatos' bar was friendly, and three wines were only 6.60€. The Tentazion was lovely, and the wines the same price. I couldn't help but think we were swizzed at the Erasmus. Still, we wouldn't ever be back there so it didn't matter.

18 A trip to Salamanca - bonus chapter

I popped into the tourist information office in the Plaza Mayor to see what needed to be on our itinerary for the following day. I ended up with tickets for the Motor Museum and the Art Deco Museum, Casa Lis, in a sort of two for one offer. We also booked a cathedral tour for Mum, while S and I were going up the Ironimus towers.

The cathedral in Salamanca is, in actual fact, two cathedrals. The old cathedral was begun in 1085 under Alfonso VI, after Christians took the city. It is Romanesque and was originally laid out in a cross. Next to, and built partly into, the old cathedral, is the new one. A monstrous gothic magnificence, the new cathedral is almost Gaudí-looking with its many curlicues, turrets and sculptured reliefs of scenes from the nativity and epiphany. Some of the sculptures are a surprise, with restored reliefs featuring an astronaut and a monkey or griffon eating an ice cream cone... go look!

When it was decided to build a new cathedral in Salamanca, the old Romanesque cathedral was retained to allow the congregation a place of worship during the rebuilding. This has led to an intriguing and bizarre state of affairs, with the two cathedrals melding in an orgy of competing yet somehow sympathetic styles. Both cathedrals are built in warm Villamayor sandstone, the old cathedral less ornate both inside and out and, to my uneducated mind, more beautiful because of it.

The following morning we ambled down to the Roman bridge over the river Tormes at the lower end of the town, then across it to the Motor Museum.

Whether a motor freak or not, this museum kept us enthralled. From the earliest internal combustion-engine car ever made by Mr Benz to the most modern sports cars and from penny farthing bicycles to top of the range motorcycles, the place was a joy over three floors. Had it also had a café we would have stayed longer but our stomachs said it was tea time. We made our slow, meandering way back up the hill into the old town, stopping for a welcome cuppa on the way.

Back in the Plaza Mayor, we could better appreciate its beauty as the sunshine transformed the plaza and buildings alike. The Plaza Mayor was declared a National Monument in 1935 as the 'most decorated, best proportioned and most harmonious of all those of its historical period'. It is based on the Madrid model, with open-arched arcades and balconies around the golden Villamayor stone buildings. The plaza was originally proposed as a perfect square, but in fact none of its façades are the same width making it look much more 'natural' and interesting (to me). On each column holding up the arches, there are sculptured roundels. On one side, these depict various Spanish kings (and the dictator General Francisco Franco who was added in 1936 and has not yet been removed). On another side are Spanish heroes and conquistadores. In 1967 various artists were commissioned to continue sculpting the remaining roundels, resulting in depictions of Cervantes, the Duke of Wellington, and Saint Teresa. It was great fun wandering the square and trying to guess each face without cheating.

Once we'd had another walk around the centre of Salamanca, and eased our aching necks from staring upwards too often, it was time for lunch. I'd spotted a likely looking restaurant on our travels, not too far from the main square.

The Mariseca was everything I'd hoped for, with its delicious *menú* and quirky seating. In addition to the 'normal' tables and chairs, there was a large round table made from a cable drum. Around this table were some of the oddest chairs I've seen in a bar. One was a reclining chair from a dentist, or possibly a hairdresser, whilst another looked remarkably like an adult high chair!

18 A trip to Salamanca – bonus chapter

After perusing the menu and changing my mind numerous times, Mum and I started with a salad of goat's cheese and baby tomatoes in a berry sauce whilst S opted for the chicken Cesar salad. Mains were varied, and all slightly different to our usual fare at home in Galicia. I couldn't resist the *cochinillo* or suckling pig – a local speciality, the friendly waiter told me. Mum had cod with roasted vegetables, and S chose a burger – but what a burger! The meat patty was in a huge bun, smothered with Ibérico ham and local Zamoran cheese and served with a generous helping of chips (fries). Yoghurt with honey and fresh berries rounded off a delicious meal, perfectly.

After lunch, Mum did her tour of the new cathedral. S and I burnt some calories climbing to the very top of the Ironimus cathedral towers, standing amongst the pigeons with views across the city. Back inside we peered down on the tiny figure of Mum with her two walking poles, far below us in the cathedral. I didn't dare shout to her, and S vetoed me dropping something on her head, so we had to wait until we all came out into the sunshine on the Patio Chico, where the new and old cathedrals meet, to tell of our discoveries and she of hers.

Although the décor inside the cathedral was as ornate as most Catholic churches seem to be, to us the architecture itself, with soaring stone buttresses and domed archways, was the most interesting part. Since reading Ken Follett's *Pillars of the Earth* many moons ago, I've been fascinated by cathedral architecture and masonry. One section of stonework was badly cracked; the keystone above an archway was out of position and a fist-sized gap opened up next to it. S and I stood examining this feature far longer than the guidebook would probably suggest. I didn't bother to mention to Mum that the building may be falling down.

PULPO, PIG & PEPPERS

We were a bit late starting out for the Casa de Lis that afternoon, but the information leaflet which came with my tickets said it was open until 8pm so I thought we had plenty of time.

This art noveau building was built for the Salamancan industrialist Miguel de Lis in 1905 to the design of architect Joaquín de Vargas. In stone, glass, and wrought iron, it is a magnificent edifice. The stained glass windows on the upper storeys filter through light in a range of vivid colours to an atrium with chairs around.

After exploring happily for an hour we found the museum's very excellent café, set amidst stained glass windows and with an old but beautifully maintained burnished copper coffee machine.

The Casa de Lis was expropriated by the city council in the 1980s, abandoned and derelict. Then, in 1990, the house was turned into a stunning and well-stocked museum after a Salamancan antiquarian, Manuel Ramos Andrade, donated his vast collection of art deco and art nouveau pieces to the city, together with his large collection of dolls.

Mum had just found that particular room in the museum, her favourite – the one full of dolls of all sizes and descriptions – when a security guard told us the place was closing. I looked at my phone – 6.55pm. I rechecked the information leaflet – 8pm closing, it said. The guard was unimpressed by my leaflet, iterating that they closed at 7pm. Feeling we were being cheated, especially poor Mum who was gazing adoringly at the dolls in glass cabinets, I decided to ignore the guard and carry on looking around.

We did a fabulous job of avoiding the poor man for almost fifteen minutes until he finally caught up with us and escorted us out through the gift shop, which surprisingly remained open much longer!

Early closing apart, it had been another lovely day full of new and interesting sights.

18 A trip to Salamanca - bonus chapter

After a quick shower and change we headed out for more bar hopping, ending in the restaurant where we had eaten lunch, the Mariseca. It turned out to be our favourite bar in the whole of Salamanca and we toasted our road trip with red wine and delicious *tortilla de patatas* with the kindly barman.

The next morning, our last in Salamanca, saw us eating *churros* with Spanish hot chocolate at the café Valor. Valor is the premier chocolate company in Spain so we knew it would be good. Mum, not a fan of the Spanish thick hot chocolate, breakfasted on toast and coffee. Our *churros* were fresh and crisp and the *chocolate* as thick and delicious as we expected. In a totally unnecessary but perfect addition, each cup came with a handmade chocolate on the side. It was probably the best hot chocolate I've had in Spain (and I've had a few!).

Breakfast over, we wandered the old town again for a while before bidding the beautiful city a fond *hasta luego* and setting off home by a different route. We dislike covering old ground on our road trips if we can help it so opted to take the road north this time, towards Lugo, thus completing a circle.

It was whilst I was driving along the A66 that Mum's commentary about hillsides sprouting chimney pots had popped my defences. The village, when we arrived, was called Pobladura de Valle. At the edge of town was a large and empty car park, suggesting that in summer this was a bit of a tourist haunt. And no wonder - the village was a real life Hobbiton.

Along the main street were houses built into the gently rolling hillside behind. Only their front doors showed; those, and the chimney pots sticking incongruously out of the green hillside. Of the Hobbits, or any other inhabitants, there was no sign. It was a strange and mesmerising place.

PULPO, PIG & PEPPERS

After meandering round snapping photos on deserted streets, we made our way back to the only place that looked like it might sell food. The Bodega La Gruta looked like a lean-to shack, with its brick-built pillars and bright egg-yellow roof. There was no *menú* on display but there was nowhere else to go. I left Mum and S outside in the sunshine and said I'd pop in and ask if they did meals.

I opened the outer wooden door into a small 1960s decorated lobby, with toilets off to the side. Then I opened the inner door – and stopped.

I'm sure my mouth was hanging open as I walked down the sloping quarry-tiled floor into the bowels of the earth. The entire cave-like restaurant was built into the hillside. The entrance was arched and narrow. Beyond was a long bar. I stopped to ask my question but was unable to articulate a thing, my astonishment was so great. The waitress, obviously used to such a reaction, kindly showed me the rest of the underground restaurant.

There were six or seven 'rooms' all chiselled directly out of the living rock. The main hallway soared to thirty feet in a high dome. It was dim inside, the electric sconces on the walls having no pale surface to reflect off as the black rock all around sucked away the light. In each low, domed side room there were wooden tables set for lunch and in the hallway stood a huge wood burner, its chimney disappearing up into the rock and out onto the hillside.

I must have spent fifteen minutes or more wandering around and staring in each and every alcove and cave-room before remembering my family outside. Leaving the waitress to set us a table, I returned to a worried Mother, who thought I'd been kidnapped, and an unconcerned husband. But even my nonchalant hubby let his jaw drop a little as we entered the restaurant.

Although it was my second view of the astonishing place, I was still speechless. The waitress told me the

18 A trip to Salamanca – bonus chapter

'building' was over 400 years old and would have been dug out by hand. The marks of the chisels could still be seen on the walls. I was incredulous, thinking of the time and work taken to dig out these houses.

Inside the cave, the temperature remains constant though the darkness would get to me. Some of the homes apparently have light wells in the roofs now to bring some daylight inside, but many more are lit like this one – using artificial light. Our meal at La Gruta was a tasty *menú* but, to be honest, it could have been almost anything that day as I gazed around the walls at the chisel marks and imagined long-ago miners digging out the rock, piece by laborious piece.

I also vowed to take more notice of Mum's back seat ramblings from that day on.

SECTION NINE - BEAUTIFUL BEACHES

19 Carnota – the longest beach in Galicia

My beautiful niece, Belle, tries to visit us at different times each year. She has been in snow storms in February, heat waves in October, and wearing flip-flops in January, but she rarely gets to visit in the summer. This year, Belle was coming in July so we decided a road trip was in order.

"We can either collect you directly from the airport and head to the coast or, if you prefer, we can go to the coast the day before you go home and go to the airport on the way back. Either way it will save us an extra journey and give us more beach time," I said to her when she confirmed her booking.

"Can we go after you pick me up, Aunty Lisa? I'm not sure about getting the flight if we go on the way back."

It was only the once that we'd been late for Belle's flight home and she had never forgotten. That particular time we'd enjoyed an afternoon in Santiago de Compostela, the capital of Galicia, and a rather excellent 3D exhibition and show. We'd taken part in a virtual race through the streets of Santiago and helped to virtually pull the famous *botafumeiro* in the cathedral before being catapulted into the catacombs beneath the city on an amazing rollercoaster ride. Unfortunately, all the excitement meant we were later setting off for the airport than we would've liked. Our inability to spend money on parking had also meant a hike back to the car and a bit of a to-do getting out of the incredibly tight space on a steep hill with our decidedly dodgy handbrake.

Still, smoking brakes and burnt rubber notwithstanding, we'd made it to the airport and with a little light jogging Belle had caught her flight with a whole five minutes to spare. The girl has no sense of adventure!

"It's your birthday the weekend Belle arrives. How about visiting the longest beach in Galicia for our road trip?"

"Sounds good," replied my ever-accommodating hubby.

"They have the longest *hórreo* too," I teased.

"And how long *is* the longest grain store in Galicia?"

"Ha! I knew you were listening. I'm not telling. You'll have to wait and see."

Summer is a busy time in the garden for us, with endless watering and fruit picking. Belle's visit was a long weekend, so a quick two-day trip with an overnight stay somewhere in between was the perfect short break.

Belle duly arrived at the airport in the afternoon of the 17th of July 2019 and we headed for the west coast beyond Santiago, an area we'd not yet visited in our travels.

The sun was hot as we sat with drinks at a roadside café. The sandy beach opposite was asking to be explored. The steps down to the beach were exactly on a blind bend in the road, which made for an interesting game of chicken with an 88-year-old in tow. Luckily, traffic was light and drivers more than happy to stop for my outstretched hand as we hobbled across the road.

The small beach was adequate compensation for almost getting mowed down. The beach sloped steeply to the sea; the sand was fine and golden, and hot to the touch. Mum and S relaxed on bunched up jackets while Belle and I paddled in the icy Atlantic waters.

"Okay, I've cooled down enough now," said Belle.

I looked down at my blue feet and quickly agreed.

The beach was steeper than I'd thought. We sunk ankle deep in the soft pale sand as we battled uphill to our waiting spectators.

"Oof. You could have given me a pull," I said, collapsing next to my grinning hubby.

"Your choice to go down there."

19 Carnota – the longest beach in Galicia

A little further on, we entered the town of Muros. The seafront was lined with glass-balconied houses and looked prosperous. We had a pleasant wander along the promenade above the large beach before stopping for another drink, in a café in a small square near the front. I enjoyed playing 'which house would I buy' whilst the others chatted and supped their drinks.

I'd booked a hotel in Carnota, the small town known for its long beach. The Pensión Sol e Mar was a handsome building on a quiet road behind the main thoroughfare. The owner was jolly and our rooms overlooked the square below. They were large, airy and tastefully decorated.

"Do you like it, Mum?" I asked my most discerning parent.

"It's lovely," came the inevitable answer.

For dinner we chose a bar just a short amble away, in the direction of the beach, with a delicious, seafood-heavy menu. The Bar O Cuberto had a lovely, partly covered terrace area outside, its tables surrounded by greenery. It was a delightful spot in which to stuff ourselves with *chipirones* (fried baby squid), huge mussels, and for my seafood averse mother, a giant platter of chips, eggs and spiced chunks of pork. All was washed down by a rather good coastal Albariño wine.

The sun was already slipping over the horizon by the time we'd finished supper, painting the sky in a soft palette of pinks and yellows. We were not far from the shore, according to Google, and I decided a west-facing beach would make a fabulous sunset picture. Belle and I set off jogging, leaving Mum and S to make their way back to the hotel bar.

It was much further than it had looked on Google maps when I'd made that silly decision. The sun sank lower, I puffed harder, and the sand dunes which backed the beach seemed as far away as ever. We passed a couple of men outside a lighted shed who grinned at us. They probably couldn't see my redder-than-usual face but could surely hear me wheezing, my trainers slapping the ground with little rhythm but plenty of percussion.

By now, the sunset had ramped up to full glory, lighting the evening sky in deep purple, dusky pink and blazing orange directly ahead of us. The dunes, a dim, dark shadow on the horizon, completely blocked our view of the beach beyond.

A little later, and still no nearer the dunes, a shape materialised from the gloom next to us. It snorted and I nearly fell over.

"It's a pony," laughed Belle, still young enough to have good night vision.

"Hmmm," I snorted back, trying to save my breath.

As we made our final approach to the car park next to the sand dunes, the sky darkened for the final curtain. With no time to climb the dunes, and little enthusiasm for walking bare foot across unseen hazards, we were just too late for that perfect shot. But it had been an interesting way to work off supper.

By the time we got back to the hotel, we were at least two rounds behind Mum and S, and thirsty to boot.

"You'll have to come running with me more often, Aunty Lisa," said Belle.

I looked at her over the rim of my glass and smiled. "Thank you, but I think that was quite enough running for me, darling."

The next morning was S' 70th birthday. I woke my hubby early (for us) at 8.30am to give him my handmade card, before sneaking downstairs to pay for our rooms before Mum or Belle did so.

Breakfast was served in the bar area. It seemed a bit of a mishmash, with various items littering a circular table at one end, but the pastries were fresh, the juice fresher still, and the huge fruit bowl overflowed with apples, pears, bananas and peaches. I was content.

19 Carnota - the longest beach in Galicia

After breakfast, we drove rather than jogged to the beach. It really was quite a way and I was impressed with my stamina the night before, keeping up with my much fitter (and considerably younger) niece.

La Playa de Carnota is seven kilometres long, the longest beach in Galicia. We positioned Mum comfortably near to the sand dunes in the centre of the beach before the three of us set off to walk to one end. As soon as we left the area directly in front of the car park the crowds (of around twelve people) thinned to nothing, and we soon had the beach to ourselves bar a few intrepid walkers. At the far southern end there were huge stones and rock pools, which we investigated thoroughly. I believe there's a bit of youthfulness left in everyone, and rock pools always bring out my inner child - which is admittedly never far away!

We walked back along the wide, deserted white sand, getting a drink and chatting to Mum as we passed by, heading the other way. The north end of the beach was equally deserted, and seemed to continue for miles. By the time we returned to Mum my legs were aching, and I was surprised how far we must have walked.

"Phuf. That's fourteen K," I gasped, plonking myself down next to Mum.

"Is it?" asked Mum, not having any idea what a 'K' was.

"Not quite," interrupted Belle, consulting her Fitbit thingy. "About eleven, I think."

"We didn't quite get the whole way to the north end," added S.

"Well, anyway, it seemed a long way to me," I pouted. It *was* a long way.

Back in town, we still had Carnota's other record breaker to visit.

"Go on then, guess how long it is," I said, pointing at the long, narrow stone building which stood in a field next to a small tourist shop.

Hórreos are designed to keep maize dry and rodent free over the winter months. In central Galicia, where we live, they are usually set on solid stone bases with a deep overhang to prevent mice and rats getting to the harvested corn. They average three to four metres long with stone-built ends and wooden slatted sides for ventilation. On the coast, *hórreos* are more often built on rounded stone pillars, like giant mushrooms, and have granite sides with narrow slits in them for air circulation.

This granite-built structure seemed to disappear into the distance like an art student's study in perspective.

"Thirty-four metres long! That's over a hundred feet, Mum," I added for my pre-decimal parent.

The *hórreo* at Carnota is not actually the longest in Galicia. I discovered while researching this chapter that it is in fact only the third longest. The *hórreo* at Lira, a few kilometres down the coast and completed just a year later in 1884, pips it to second place at 35 metres long. I'm sure that was deliberate! The longest *hórreo* in Galicia is at Araño, and is 37.10 metres in length. The one in Carnota is a national monument though. It is 1.9m wide, 34m long and sits on 22 pairs of stone 'mushrooms'.

The man in the tiny tourist shop was grumpy. Maybe he had an off-day. We declined to buy a miniature *hórreo* or a can of overpriced soda and moved on.

"I'm hungry anyway," I said.

Again, Mr Google helped me out by suggesting a couple of nearby restaurants. I was glad we had Google maps as I don't think we would have found the Casa Fandiño otherwise. Or, if we did, we'd have turned around thinking we'd entered someone's private garden.

My phone directed us up a tiny pedestrian lane off the main road. It ran past allotments full of ripening tomatoes and figs, and the backs of houses. One house

19 Carnota – the longest beach in Galicia

had a laden plum tree overhanging the track – we all agreed the fruits were delicious. At the end of the lane was a gravel turnaround and a two-storey house. There were a couple of plastic chairs outside and the odd beer crate. There was no sign, no indication this could be a restaurant.

The door was a standard glass and aluminium one, and was closed. A gentle shove had it opening into a lobby area. I hesitated, still thinking we'd wandered into someone's home. Luckily, before I had time to run away, coward that I am, a waitress appeared.

"*¿Para comer?*" she asked, smiling.

"Yes please," I replied. "I thought it was a house you see…" I began, but our waitress had wandered off and the family were following her. Oh well.

Beyond a slatted divide were tables and chairs laid out for dinner, and a gaggle of Galicians tucking in to what looked like huge meals. White painted chairs sat at dark topped tables; the walls were slate-faced to window height, and said windows let in a cooling breeze. I surreptitiously eyed diners' plates as I passed, offering a, "*Que aprovecho,*" to each table.

I love the Galician tradition of exhorting everyone to enjoy their meal (or more literally 'take advantage of') as one passes. It feels friendly. The nods I got in return confirmed my happy feeling about this place. By the time we took our seats I'd decided the food here looked excellent, and the smells were definitely enticing.

The menu was short. There were just seven choices which could be combined as one wished for starter and main course. Belle had paella as her starter, S and I had *empanada de pulpo*, a large flat Galician pie filled with octopus, and Mum had spaghetti bolognese. The starter versions of each dish were the same size as the main course ones, resulting in huge platefuls.

Our main course pork ribs were outstanding. Cooked until meltingly soft, they were flavourful and tangy. I tried to guess the marinade.

"*¿Soja?*" I asked the waitress, "*¿Y romero?*"

She was delighted I'd guessed correctly. Soy sauce and rosemary are not common ingredients in Galicia, and the combination was divine.

For ten euros, including dessert and coffee, it was probably the best meal I've ever had in Galicia (though please excuse me if I repeat that assertion elsewhere in this book – I change my mind a lot). It also brought home the old adage of doing a few things well rather than a great many things poorly. The menu had been short, but every single item had been perfectly rendered. There was also the advantage that my decision averse niece didn't have too difficult a choice to make.

"I do wonder, though," I said, as we were climbing back into the car, "whether we could have ordered ribs for a starter *and* a main course. Double helpings!"

After lunch we headed higher up the coast to Ézaro, and a meeting with a waterfall.

In its final drop, the river Xallas, on the west coast of Galicia, falls 40 metres directly into the foaming sea below, as the Fervenza do Ézaro. It is the only waterfall in Spain to do so, and one of only a handful in Europe.

There was work going on to improve access to the waterfall when we visited so we were unable to get close, but the walk to the little market alongside was interesting and the noise from the falls alarmingly loud even from a distance.

The drive home seemed interminable, though we only got lost once – somehow being directed straight into the centre of Santiago's industrial estate from the motorway. Handy if we wanted some paint or gardening tools but, since the signposts instantly disappeared once we were there, not good for getting home. The Satnav, which I'd turned off, mistakenly thinking I knew where we were going, was called back into service and extricated us successfully.

It had been a lovely trip full of superlatives. The longest beach, largest (almost) *hórreo*, highest waterfall and fullest person; the latter was me after that incredible lunch. I was so full that I only managed one drink (and *tapa*) that evening in Taboada. Now that is superlative!

20 Camelle to Laxe – the Walk of Death

Galicia is a wonderful place to discover on foot. Most people have heard of the Way of St. James, or the *Camino de Santiago*, but this region also has many lesser-known unofficial walking routes which are worth taking the time to discover.

One of these is O Camiño dos Faros, which I discovered by accident when we visited Laxe and Camelle, on the Costa da Morte, with Mum back in 2018. At Laxe, where we'd stopped for lunch, I saw a signpost directing walkers along the coast towards Arou.

"That would be a nice walk," I'd said at the time.

For some reason, the idea of walking the 'Coast of Death' stuck with me. In Autumn 2021, with Mum on her holidays and a couple of long walks under our belts, we decided to try one of the sections of the 'two headlights way' as Google kindly translated the Galego name.

O Camiño dos Faros, or The Lighthouse Way, begins at Malpica in the northwest and runs for 200 kilometres along the Costa da Morte, visiting at least one lighthouse on each stage, to the end of the world, Finisterre (Fisterra in Galego).

Finisterre is traditionally the end of the line for walkers on the Camino de Santiago, where pilgrims head to dispose of their old clothes and shoes in the Atlantic – a practice I'm sure the coastal region would prefer ended.

Although the association, *O Camiño dos Faros*, is petitioning the Xunta de Galicia for funding, this particular long-distance walk has yet to be made official. This means the route receives no money and relies on association members keeping the way signposted and clear – a difficult job on a trek which winds around some of the deadliest coastline in Europe.

20 Camelle to Laxe – the Walk of Death

Having Googled and planned extensively, I decided stage four of the route, from Laxe to Camelle was the most easily doable.

"How do we get back to Laxe though?" I asked S.

"We could walk one way on the first day and then back on the second," he replied.

"Mmm. The problem is that the first site I looked at showed the route in miles not kilometres so it's actually eighteen K, not twelve. That might be a bit much back-to-back. Plus, I don't think there's anywhere to stay in Camelle. And we'd have to leave the car somewhere."

I rang Debs, my friend and guru of walking. Debs and Al have done many of the Galician long-distance routes, including the Portuguese Way a number of times.

"What do you do about getting back to your starting point when there's no public transport?" I asked.

"We try to use the train where we can, or just call a taxi."

"I can't see himself wanting to call a taxi," I grumbled. "We need two cars."

"We use taxis all the time. We even skip a bit of the route if we don't fancy it or are too tired," continued Debs.

I gasped at this heresy, then thought, 'why not?'. After all it wasn't a competition. We were only walking for us.

"It puts money back into the local economy. And tell him there are no pockets in a shroud," finished my friend.

Decision made.

S had one concern. "I think we ought to walk from Camelle to Laxe."

"But that's back to front," I said, horrified.

"I know. But think about it: if we walk to Camelle, we then have to phone a taxi to collect us or we have to give a time of arrival before we leave Laxe. Either way we will be sitting around waiting or rushing to finish. If we get a taxi to the start then walk back it won't matter what time we get back to the hotel."

I forced my brain around the idea of going backwards.

"It could be better," I conceded. "And if we're tired at the end, we can miss out the loop around the lighthouse. We could do that the following day. Yeah, it's a good idea. I just hope we can follow the route backwards."

"How difficult can it be? We just keep the sea on our left," replied Mr Clever Clogs.

§

"Which way do we go now?"

It was a warm and sunny day in October. We were standing at a fork in the track on which we were walking, and we were lost.

The previous day we'd fed the animals and locked up the houses before setting off for the coast. It was the 12th of October - National Day in Spain.

"Shall we eat in Rábade? We should be there by two and that restaurant we ate in with Mum had good food."

"The Avenida? Sounds good."

We arrived at the Avenida at 1.43pm. It was closed, the shutters down.

"That's odd. Plan B?"

"I think there's another restaurant up the road," said S.

Off we went. It too was closed, as was the next, and the next. By this time, we were heading out of town.

"Google says there's one on the left. Oh! There! Turn left here!"

The Paz y Ana was off the road on an industrial estate and was definitely open judging by the number of cars parked up. It was packed. Sadly, it was too busy to accommodate two travellers.

"I'm sorry, we don't have enough staff. It will be a very long wait if you haven't reserved," the friendly waitress told us.

Plan C.

20 Camelle to Laxe – the Walk of Death

"A picnic?" asked S. "We have that pasta salad you made."

"But that's for on our walk. There's nowhere to buy food once we set off."

"We can buy something else this evening to take with us."

"No, we can't, the shops are shut. It's National Day! Let's go back onto the A6. There's a services up the road. If they haven't got any food, we'll have a picnic there and rethink lunch tomorrow."

Luckily for us the services at Guitirriz had a decent café-restaurant and our chicken and chips were enough to keep us going to Laxe.

We'd wasted so much time searching for lunch that it was after 4pm when we arrived outside our hotel. Still, it was a hot and sunny day and the dunes glimmered whitely.

"Quick change and wander on the beach?" I asked.

"Sounds good."

I asked the friendly man on reception, at the appropriately named Hotel Playa de Laxe, if he could order us a taxi to Camelle for the next morning.

"Of course. You are walking the faros?"

"Yes, but the other way."

"Ah! *Al revés.*"

In reverse. Yup that's us, I thought, as we ambled the few metres to the beach.

The sand at Laxe is so white, it hurts the eyes to look at it. Nearest the nicely paved walkway are dunes topped with grass and deadly sea holly, which dries up then buries itself in the sand until someone unsuspecting comes along.

"Ouch! Ouch! Ouch!" I yelled, hopping on one leg whilst trying to pull the tiny hooked spikes of sea holly out of my foot. "That stuff is vicious!"

Beyond the dunes, the beach was sea-washed and littered with pretty pebbles. It made walking along the firm, clean sand endlessly fascinating as we each sorted through the different coloured rocks. There were pieces of rose granite, banded gneiss and sugar-like marble. There were malachite greens, turquoise blues, alabaster whites, and obsidian blacks the size and shape of a bird's egg, speckled and striped ones, round and flat ones, large, small and medium sized ones. It was a wonderland for rock enthusiasts and we were soon at the far end of the beach, bumbags overloaded with 'just one more' pebble.

"Better put these in the car in case they search us on the way in to the hotel," I said. "We can get the food out of the car too and put it in the fridge in the room."

We had a pleasant evening wandering the lively streets of Laxe and trying the local Albariño wines at a couple of bars. It seemed that many visitors were down for National Day and the town was buzzing.

The next morning, our taxi driver turned up promptly at ten o'clock and dropped us at Camelle beach.

"That way for the *camino*," he'd said, pointing.

I took the lead, happily stomping up the road away from the beach until I checked Google maps.

"Oops. We should have followed the beach. Never mind. It joins a little way on, I think. Then we follow this road all the way to the next beach at, erm, Señora."

The road was easy to follow and metalled, winding through pine trees and heading inexorably towards a set of hills. I didn't see any of the green arrows the route was supposed to be marked with, but as S pointed out you don't put arrows where they can be seen from the wrong direction.

The beach at Señora was as different from Laxe beach as it was possible to be. A small sea-washed area, it had no sand at all just large boulders. These were not pretty pebbles; these were giant things and they extended on to the path we had to follow.

"Oh, great. A balancing act first off."

20 Camelle to Laxe – the Walk of Death

I held out my arms and tottered across the rounded, wobbling stones until I gained *terra firma* on the other side. S, of course, jumped across without any effort at all. I swear he would have ridden one of the rocks had it started to roll.

Just beyond Boulder Beach, as I renamed Señora, the narrow track began to wind through gorse and brambles.

"Oww! That's spiky on my legs," I said, trying and failing to avoid the thorns. "Ugh, it's soggy underfoot too. I'm squelching!"

At a fork in the track, there was a notice pinned to a bush. 'Adrian's taxis' it read. Someone had good marketing sense, I thought.

"Which way do we go now?" I asked. Both tracks looked well used. "I can't see an arrow."

S wandered around to the right while I explored the left fork.

"Two bunnies round there," he said, appearing from behind a gorse bush. "It's a loop," He added seeing my confusion. "The track comes round and back to here. The bunnies weren't at all bothered by me, they just hopped slowly away."

"They know you're Bunny Man," I said, smiling.

A little while before, one of our does had upped and died, leaving a litter of three orphan kits just three weeks old. S had hand fed them with kitten milk and a dropper until all three were happily hopping about and eating the normal rabbit nuts. They were consequently very tame and came up to S for an ear rub every time he went near them.

As we climbed the hillside, I saw a tiny fishing boat motoring towards the cliffs.

"Dangerous job, especially on this coast," I commented.

The submerged rocks are one of the reasons the Coast of Death got its name. Many unwary sailors have foundered along this stretch of rocky coast. From where we stood, I could see waves breaking around a seemingly open area of ocean – an area hiding a cluster of deadly rocks.

Beneath a small wooded area of pine trees, we enjoyed the last of the morning coolness before hitting the rocky headland. From here on there would be no shade, and the day was surprisingly hot. I was pleased I'd gone with the shorts and sandals option, even if my feet were already filthy from the dusty tracks and my toes had been blue in the cool of the early morning.

The headland was a jumble of ginormous erratic rocks interspersed with short gorse and sea pinks. Looking back, the view was spectacular but we could still see Camelle clearly.

"We haven't come far, have we?" I said. "Had we better speed up?"

"We've got all day. But we can walk a bit faster on this flat bit," replied S.

We did, briefly. But there was too much to see, and to photograph, for me to keep up the pace for long.

"Go and sit by that guinea pig," I instructed S.

He looked at me.

"There, that big stone with four feet and a snout. It looks like a guinea pig. I need you for scale."

S reluctantly obeyed, then proceeded to pull silly faces and spoil my photograph.

"Why can't you ever pose nicely?" I grumped.

A little further along we met our first humans of the walk. Two cyclists came towards us and waved a cheery hello as they sped past.

"They'll have fun at Boulder Beach," I observed.

"I wouldn't want to do this trail on a bike," added S.

The tracks left by our cyclists were perfect to follow, and we soon arrived at our second beach. Long and sandy, it was deserted except for a lone walker – an older man with a walking stick who was hobbling towards us with excruciating slowness.

20 Camelle to Laxe – the Walk of Death

"Must've been hard work cycling through this sand," said S, as we sank into the fine, soft white dunes. The tyre tracks were deep here; with their panniers on cycling must have been very difficult indeed.

A boardwalk ran along the back of the beach and off towards a small recreation area. I washed my filthy, sandy feet at the thoughtfully provided shower before walking barefooted along the boardwalk.

"I'm glad I came in sandals, even if all the walking groups said not to," I crowed, happily clomping along the wooden boards whilst dodging the protruding screws. "My feet are so much more comfortable."

I've had problems with my feet for a while. My hard-soled walking boots made the bottom of my foot feel like I was walking on a bed of nails. Trainers were okay if I took it easy but the most comfortable footwear were my five-euro sandals. The doctor had told me I had something called Morton's Neuroma – a thickening of the nerve tissue under the ball of the foot which is agonising when pressed or squashed. She advised me not to wear narrow fashion shoes, to which I'd laughed. As if! My problem is that I have very short but very wide feet (I maintain they are almost square) so fashion shoes have never really been comfortable. My cheap beach sandals, however, let my feet spread as much as they need. It was luxury. I just wished it was warm enough to wear them all year round.

"My feet would get frostbite in winter," I lamented. "But it's perfect today, even if the gorse is spiky."

After a short stop on a bench at the recreation area to allow my feet to dry, we continued along the village road. I checked Google maps, squinting at the screen in the bright sun.

"Wait a minute. We're too far east. We need to be over there."

A man was washing his van, soapy water trickling along the track we wanted to take. I skipped through the foam and we continued along a wide, closely cropped field.

"Someone's cut the grass here."

"Probably one of the association members. I wonder if they have a patch each to keep clear?" I mused.

Through a short piece of woodland, I at last spotted an arrow. I'd turned back to photograph our route and there it was on a rock, right in front of me. Once we'd seen one, the arrows seemed to proliferate – popping up everywhere.

"They blend in well. They look like blobs of lichen. Oh, hold on. That's the lagoon ahead, we need to be on the left of it. The seaward side."

"Makes sense," said S.

The turn off took us onto another boardwalk through reeds and *Juncus*. Although I stood on tiptoes, I couldn't see anything of the lagoon. There must have been water in there somewhere but the water plants effectively blocked our view.

"I bet it's great for birds in the spring."

The boardwalk took us to yet another huge and empty beach, and a recreation area. We sat and ate bananas, and muesli bars that I'd made from the pressings from my fruit jellies. They were delicious and refreshing.

Sated, we continued along another empty track which passed above a tiny beach with six people on it.

"They must be the green gang," said S, pointing at the group's matching luminous T-shirts.

The track continued straight but we turned left, back towards the clifftops. Coves and steep drops on to rocky outcrops litter this part of the Costa da Morte but we stayed on the sandy track, winding through short scrubby grass, the wild sea to our left, gentle hills to our right.

Just before the next beach, at Soesto, we stopped for lunch. There were a series of perfectly positioned flat rocks on which to perch, and a lovely view down to the beach where a few brave surfers were battling the cold Atlantic waves.

"Nice breeze up here," I said, unpacking our pasta salad boxes. "Watch the forks, they're some cheap plastic ones I found in a drawer so don't put much pressure on them or they might snap. Then you'll have to eat with your fingers."

Despite the breeze, it was hot on the rock and my face was burning.

"Problem with this route is the sun is always to the same side. I'll be striped by the time we get back."

"You could always walk backwards," said S, adding; "To Christmas."

"Haha. Then I would fall over. I hope we don't have to climb that big hill over there," I added, pointing beyond the beach to a tall, squared-off mount, rising above it.

Of course we did!

First, the track took us behind the beach along another boardwalk and past a fleet of campervans bearing French, German and Andorran plates.

"Andorra! Hold on, I wonder if he has any two euros?"

I headed for the tall, tussle-haired young man ferreting in the back of his van.

"*¿Hablas Español?*" I asked.

"*¡Sí!*"

I explained in my best Spanish that we collected two-euro coins and were only short of a few countries. Andorra was one of them. I wondered if he would be willing to swap a coin with us.

"Ah, yes. Andorra is very small. I'm sorry, I haven't been in six months. I have no coins left of there," He replied in perfect English. Of course he would!

"Oh well, thank you anyway."

The boardwalk ended abruptly at a small, brackish lagoon.

"Oh. Should we have been on the roadway the other side d'you think?"

"I'll see if this goes all the way to the sea or if it really is a lagoon. If it is, we can cross the beach," said S, heading off towards the sea.

I peered at Google maps. "It looks like the route goes along the beach," I said as I caught up with my hubby. "Oh! It is a lagoon. How odd."

We walked around the end of the lagoon and waded through the soft, white sand to a track up the hillside.

"We are going to climb that, aren't we?" I said, staring upwards at the hill, which had now gained mountainous proportions before me.

"Probably."

We followed the track up and up. It became steeper, and I stopped to catch my breath on a handy rock. "Good view though."

On we went. The track became steeper yet, and I was clambering up rock steps far too high for my little legs. Each time I thought I was at the top, I made the mistake of looking up. The hill loomed ever higher above me.

"I hope it's not like this going down. I don't mind up but I'm hopeless at down," I puffed. "I'm sure we should have followed that little track round the front of the hill rather than climbing over it."

"Green arrow," pointed out S.

At last, we were on the top, with magnificent views back the way we'd come and forwards to Laxe itself nestling on the opposite side of the peninsula.

"Wow! Great views. But the path goes down towards Laxe. Look!" I pointed straight ahead. "We should be heading that way, further up the coast towards the cemetery."

"I think this route might have been for those who wanted to climb a mountain rather than follow the *camino*," conceded S.

"Well, I don't fancy going all the way back now. Shall we just head in to Laxe? We can do the lighthouse tomorrow."

"Good plan."

20 Camelle to Laxe – the Walk of Death

I felt slightly guilty missing out part of the walk and felt sure we would have been able to complete it had we followed the correct track. Those views from the top of the hill were worth the extra effort, though.

The following morning, after checking out of our hotel (and indulging in their very excellent breakfast), we walked through the sleepy town towards the lighthouse and our missed loop.

The evening before we'd gone into town for a pizza and a drink, to find almost all the bars were closed. Obviously National Day was the last hope of decent business before the winter. I'd mused on the differences between a town like our own Taboada, where business is pretty constant year-round, and a seaside town which relies on tourist dollars to function. Still, the pizza was good and I felt we'd deserved it after our long trek.

Thursday morning dawned bright and sunny, and cool. My bare feet tingled and I shivered in my cotton long-sleeved shirt as we set off on our missed loop. I knew it would be hot once the sun came up and didn't want the extra baggage of jacket or sweater.

Our loop this morning was also part of a local route called 'The Percebes Way.'

Percebes are goose barnacles, a prized and outrageously expensive seafood treat in Galicia. At over fifty euros a kilo, they are a treat best reserved for special occasions. They are also one of the most dangerous shellfish to harvest. *Percebeiros* are killed on the dangerous rocks each year, battling the ferocious sea to collect the barnacles. I shuddered as I watched the waves thunder against the rocks on this coast, over and over. I couldn't imagine having to face those on a daily basis for a living.

The loop was short and fairly easy going. There were wooden posts and rope barriers along some stretches to prevent walkers tumbling down the cliffs. The narrow track we were on though, only wide enough for one foot in front of the other and mere centimetres from the edge of the sheer cliff, had no such safety rail.

"Better not slip!"

"I think it's to stop people climbing down the cliff to pick the flowers," replied S, pointing.

This part of the cliff was carpeted with a low-growing succulent. In summer, *Mesembryanthemum* has pretty pink flowers but it's an introduced species which is decimating native cliff-top flora, as it spreads madly. I did my part to eradicate it by cutting some pieces to plant in pots at home. Not fully hardy, so not a risk to native flora in the central Galician hills, it nevertheless looks attractive in gravel pots over summer, the flowers only opening in full sun.

The 'end' of our loop was the ocean front cemetery I'd seen the previous day from our hilly lookout, and Crystal Beach.

This tiny beach was, at first glance, a disappointment. It was an area, not much bigger than a dining table, of dull greeny-brown shingle squashed between two tall cliffs. The sun had yet to penetrate this sheltered cove and it felt cool and damp.

"Not a place for sunbathing," I said, as we stepped onto the 'beach', crunching our way through seaweed and a long-dead seagull.

Just then, the rising sun cleared the cliff top and hit the shingle; it shone and glittered invitingly. Amongst the usual flotsam and jetsam were thousands of tiny pieces of emerald, nut-brown, and pure white sea-washed glass. There were also pieces of tiles, rounded by the waves but still bearing their glazed faces.

I read that there used to be a glass factory nearby, which of course dumped all its waste offcuts into the sea. These, by some action of the tides, all ended up on this miniscule beach, growing it in height if not in width.

A notice at the top of the beach asked visitors not to remove the '*cristales*' as this would denude the beach (and take away a tourist attraction from the council). We

20 Camelle to Laxe – the Walk of Death

did as we were asked, carefully banging all traces of glass pebbles from our shoes as we climbed back in to town.

It had been a fabulous couple of days, exploring a new part of the coastline on tracks that few people used. We'd seen maybe a dozen other walkers or riders on our hike and most of the time had been spent in glorious isolation, with not even a house in sight. There was just us, the rocks and cliffs, and the never ending but always changing sea. I was happy that I'd seen that sign years before and returned to this area.

"I'm glad we did this walk of death," I joked. "Now. What about doing the next section?"

SECTION TEN - CELTIC CASTROS

21 A Castro da Baroña – a Celtic hillfort

"Why doesn't anything ever go to plan," I screamed.

"Because this is Spain," said S, the voice of reason.

"But we've come all this way and we still can't buy the house. It's so frustrating."

"I know. But look, we have the hire car for the week and it's lovely weather. Why don't we go exploring?"

"I suppose."

"Sitting here won't speed things up at all. We may as well enjoy our holiday."

I smiled. "You're right, as ever. Where shall we go?"

It was autumn 2005. We were in Galicia for the third time – still trying to buy a house we'd first seen some eighteen months earlier following our aborted Camino along Spain's north coast.

The house at Nogueira de Ramuín was set high in the hills above the Sil valley. I had instantly fallen for the charms of the stone building and the wrought iron balcony along the front, S for the straggly oak woodland full of house-sized boulders. The estate agents seemed to be having problems getting the paperwork sorted and, as we'd already paid a hefty deposit to them towards the sale, we'd flown over to try and jolly things along.

We'd spent a few days wandering around the outside of the house in the September sunshine, me making notes, S anxious to run off and climb boulders.

"It's a pity the granite blocks look like concrete ones from a distance, isn't it?"

"They're relatively new, I think. The walls are much thinner than the older ones we've seen."

"True. I'd like to see inside again. D'you think we'll ever be able to finalise the sale?"

That comment turned out to be prophetic.

We'd booked two weeks holiday from work in the hope of finalising the sale but those plans looked to be dashed. Our jollying had failed dismally and we were still no further forward. To say I was frustrated was an understatement. With little else we could do, a break from the house sounded a great idea.

"We've already done that walk along the tops, and we've visited Monforte and that place with the three rivers."

"I enjoyed the walk. Let's just check out from the hotel and head to the coast for our last week. See what we can find."

So, we did.

Our little hire car was a small-engined Peugeot with a big heart, which seemed to run on hot air and clambered up the steep hills around Nogueira like a mountain goat. She would probably enjoy a run to the coast.

The Galician map we had was not particularly detailed, and the odd leaflets I'd managed to pick up from the tourist information centre in Monforte were in Galego. Still, I had a few ideas.

"The coast around Sanxenxo is supposed to be good. And I love the name!"

"San what? It sounds Chinese."

"San-shen-sho. It does, doesn't it?"

"Okay, which way?"

"Head west young man!"

As soon as we were on the road, I felt better. With every mile we moved away from the clinging disappointment, my heart lifted along with the autumn sunshine. I began screeching along to the only CD we had with us – a Meatloaf compilation which S had agreed to buy in a moment of weakness in a local shop, after we discovered the hire car had a CD player.

"Must you sing?"

"Yup!"

21 A Castro da Baroña – a Celtic hillfort

We arrived in the holiday resort of Sanxenxo in the afternoon of a hot, late September day. The town beach, a sweeping arc of golden smooth sand, was backed by a promenade. Facing the shore were large, stately hotels which reminded me of English seaside resorts like Brighton or Scarborough. I expected them to be called 'The Grand' or some such.

"Looks a bit touristy."

"Let's see what the tourist information has for us," I replied, heading for a wooden hut on the beach side.

The lady inside was very friendly but unable to find any accommodation for two English people on a late September afternoon.

"No room at the inn, eh?" I said, as we walked along the front. "How very odd."

"This looks more us," said S, pointing ahead.

We'd been following the promenade westwards, passing round a grove of tall fir trees and leaving the long beachfront of Sanxenxo behind. In front of us was a smaller, quieter beach. Seaweed marred its surface near the sea line and small rowing boats bobbed about at anchor further out. Beyond the beach a higgledy piggledy mess of buildings reared up, the sun setting behind them.

"Yep. Definitely more us!" I agreed, striding out.

Our hotel in Portonovo, as the new resort was called, was perfect. Small, family-run, not at all flashy, and friendly. Our only problem was managing to pay when we checked out two days later.

That evening we walked back into Sanxenxo and enjoyed tasting the local Albariño wines for the first time. A dry, white, slightly tart wine, Albariño is known for its floral and fruit flavours. We know nothing of wine, but we do know what we like – and this hit the spot.

As often happens in Spanish bars, when we asked for a glass of house wine an open bottle was chosen from a bucket on the counter. These bottles were the left-overs from the lunchtime trade or previous customers. Always popular, no bottle lasts long enough to oxidise. Our second glass that evening was our favourite, with honey-sweet peach flavours and a tang of acidity. We had, of course, failed to check the label and by the time we wanted a third, that bottle was gone. In the seventeen years since, despite dedicated efforts, we've never managed to find that particular Albariño again.

The next day was spent enjoying the beach at Portonovo, taking a long walk around the seashore and deciding on our next stop.

"O Grove looks interesting. It's on a spit of land that balloons out at the top. Look! It's like a cartoon head."

"Well, that's settled then," replied S, straight-faced.

"Actually, I remember one of the guide books I got from the library saying O Grove was like Blackpool. You should be right at home. Bet they talk funny and everything." I smiled innocently at my Lancastrian soulmate.

"You've sold it beautifully, as ever."

O Grove was disappointingly unlike Blackpool, with no kiss-me-quick hats or pleasure beach. We found a small *pensión* next to a bridge to a tiny island called A Toxa, or La Toja, depending on which sign you read. Our room overlooked the sandy beach and pine trees of the island, and the sentry boxes which were positioned at the far end of the bridge.

"Do you think it's to keep the riff-raff out?" I asked.

"Or keep the inmates in," replied S.

I hadn't thought of that!

We wandered on to the island without being challenged, and spent a relaxing morning walking along the pine-backed beach. We stared in wonder at the scallop-shell-covered chapel dedicated to La Virgen de Carmen del Mar, patron saint of the sea and fishermen, and peeked at ridiculously fancy (and therefore far too

21 A Castro da Baroña – a Celtic hillfort

posh for us) homes through wrought iron railings, like street urchins looking for scraps.

"It's very fancy here, but I think I prefer O Grove town itself."

"More down to earth you mean?" I said.

"Cheaper!"

We passed the afternoon sunbathing on some convenient rocks down by the seashore on A Toxa, out of sight of everyone except the occasional fishing boat passing by. S even paddled in the sheltered bay, away from the Atlantic waves.

After O Grove, we made our way to yet another deserted and beautiful beach. Here, cliffs framed the white sand and tiny dunes formed along the high tide line as we paddled and wandered through the surf. I felt my house buying troubles ebbing away with the tides.

The Illa de Arousa, further up the coast, didn't arouse any passion in me. It was crowded and noisy. The small plaza in front of our hotel was a playground for teenagers revving motorbikes until the early hours. The restaurant we visited for lunch was not pleased to be asked for a *menú*. The owner offered us no choice and the spaghetti he produced was lack-lustre and tasteless. I was pleased to drive back onto the mainland.

"There's supposed to be a *castro* somewhere up the coast," I said, as we once more motored north.

"Like an Iron Age village?"

"Yeah, I think. A Celtic fortification."

"Sounds good."

"It's supposed to be near to Porto do Son. The map isn't very specific, it just shows a blob! Maybe we'll see a sign."

We didn't.

The small, pretty town of Porto do Son was a working port too. Bougainvillea grew over walls, and a stone-balustraded walkway encircled a small park. The hotel we found near the harbour offered us a discount if we stayed two nights. It wasn't a difficult decision. The manager even told us how to find the *castro* and recommended a local restaurant for dinner.

"I've got a whole chicken here!"

"Well, it is a small chicken."

"It's still a whole one though. Look!" S pointed out the two legs and two wings attached to the butterflied piece of meat threatening to engulf his dinner plate.

"A good recommendation then."

I was on navigation duties when I saw a small sign which said 'dolmen'. There was an arrow pointing off the road.

"What's a dolmen?"

"I think it's a Stone Age burial chamber."

"Ooo. Let's turn off."

The ancient structure turned out to be a cleverly balanced stone 'table' atop three more large stones, forming a chamber below. The whole thing stood as high as me and was set in a parkland of trees. It was unsung and quite astonishing.

"Just imagine people building this 4,000 years ago. In England there'd be an entrance fee."

"And no playing on the monument!"

"Ha! That's true."

A little way on we finally spotted a small sign which said 'castro'. We turned off the road and parked near to a narrow forest track. At the start of the track was a wooden signpost formed into an arrow with, again, the single word 'castro' scribbled on it.

"Not exactly advertising itself, is it?"

In amongst the trees were a jumble of brightly painted campervans. Most had clothes lines strung up nearby. Wetsuits hung from tree branches and sleeping bags reclined over the top of the vans. Kicked over traces of campfires suggested this was a popular hangout for the surfing crowd.

"OH! Wow!" My powers of speech had left me as we rounded the next corner.

21 A Castro da Baroña – a Celtic hillfort

I gazed across a thick sheet of granite to a rocky mound, littered with circular stone structures. The twenty-metre-high mound was surrounded on three sides by the ocean and attached to the mainland on the other side by a thin isthmus. The isthmus passed through a narrow defile in a stone-built rampart. In front of this rampart was the remains of a wide moat. The settlement would have been easily defensible. The circular stone structures within the defences were only waist high, but their purpose as dwelling walls was obvious. I was enthralled.

"Look at the view from up here!" I yelled from the very top of the rocky cliffs above the *castro*. Here, more stone walls suggested homes built on the leeward side of the mound – definitely a good plan in a wild and windy Galician winter, surrounded by the frigid Atlantic Ocean.

S was sitting in one of the Iron Age houses, looking completely at home.

"They were built for folks our size, weren't they?" I yelled down.

"Six-foot-six you mean?" joked my five-foot-four-inch-tall partner.

Celtic hillforts, or Iron Age fortified settlements, are common throughout Europe but there is a particular conglomeration of them in this region of Spain, with over 3,000 listed. A Castro da Baroña is one of the most jaw-dropping of them all.

We spent an enjoyable afternoon, clambering over that 2,000-year-old Iron Age Celtic hillfort, up ancient staircases to rocky hillocks, and finally, relaxing on a warm, windswept beach, backed by dunes and soft mossy hummocks filled with golden-yellow creeping rock roses. It was more picturesque and peaceful than anything I'd ever seen.

The next morning, we headed to a small café in Porto do Son for breakfast.

"D'you think it's a bit dark?" I asked as we rounded the harbour.

"Can't say I've noticed."

It was the 3rd of October 2005.

There was the usual giant-screen TV blaring out above the bar. I watched, hypnotised, whilst we waited for our breakfast doughnuts.

"Oh look!" I said, pointing to the screen. "There's supposed to be an annular eclipse today."

"Really? Where?" said S, suddenly interested.

"Well... here! But I'm not sure what time."

As we left the bar, the day seemed far dimmer than it ought at ten thirty in the morning.

"The eclipse must be coming. Shall we go sit on that bench?" I pointed to a long wooden seat facing the sea. A number of people were already there, wearing those odd-looking sunglasses they gave out for the last eclipse I'd seen in the UK, back in 1999.

"We haven't got any glasses! Don't look at the sun or your eyeballs'll fry!"

S glanced at me before sighing. "I could make you a pinhole camera if you had a shoebox handy."

As we went to sit down on the bench, I noticed the spectators removing their glasses and getting up. Crowds of people were walking away from us.

"Do I smell?" I asked, disconcerted.

"No. But I think we might have missed the action. Look!" S pointed at the sky, which was lightening by the second.

"It's over?"

"Yes."

"Oh!"

On the 3rd of October 2005, northwest Galicia was one of the best places in the world to see the annular eclipse – where the moon passes in front of the sun at such a distance as to leave a thin, annular ring around it like a halo. The arc of the eclipse was directly over where we stood, passing over Spain northwest to southeast. The eclipse began at 08.51 Universal Time, which was 09.51 Spanish time. We had missed it by minutes in favour of a greasy doughnut. What a blow!

We arrived back in Nogueira to the news that the owner of the property could not be located. We could not legally buy the stone-built house, nor its erratic boulder filled woodland.

It was another blow, but in hindsight a fortuitous one. Although we had to walk away from that house overlooking the river, 650 metres up in the mountains, we'd had a delightful week exploring Galicia's coastline. And a year later, in November 2006, we discovered our forever home, *A Casa do Campo*. And that, as they say, is another story altogether!

22 Celtic *castros* – Iron Age settlements

There are Celtic, Iron Age *castros* dotted throughout Galicia. In fact, you'd be unlucky to visit here without seeing one. There's even a *castro* close to our home.

The Castro de Moreda is on a prominent, lumpy hill not a kilometre from our house. When we climbed up there one day, not long after moving to *A Casa do Campo,* we were somewhat disappointed that there was nothing to find. The few rocks scattered about told no story, gave us no clues; they could have been from any old stone wall. But it was still an enjoyable scramble through bracken, gorse and brambles with a good view down from the very top – and it's a landmark, a mound of local history.

Castros (in Spanish) or Celtic hill forts, called *oppida* by the Romans, are found throughout Europe. Built during the Bronze and Iron Ages from 1300 BCE to 50 CE, the Romans subsumed the larger fortified towns whilst the smaller ones were abandoned over time.

Early human populations were nothing more than small, nomadic family groups – a few Neolithic families co-operating to hunt jointly then moving on. Wanderers, looking for food.

As human populations grew, they needed more structure; societies became more complex with social hierarchies and specialised craftsmen. Hundreds of people were now living in close communities, farming animals and crops. The world population grew from an estimated two to five million in the Neolithic (late Stone Age) to over twenty million by the late Iron Age. Many Iron Age settlements had fifty or more people in them, working and living together.

Defensive townships were set up to protect settlers from marauders, and the animals from straying. These defensible villages were often built on hills and

22 Celtic castros – Iron Age settlements

surrounded by earthen banks (later stone ramparts) and ditches or moats. By the time the Romans arrived in the peninsula around 200 BCE, some hillforts had become large, thriving towns of up to 1,000 people.

Many of the 3,000 known Galician *castros* are far better preserved than our local one. The first one we ever visited was A Castro da Baroña in 2005, which I've talked about in the previous chapter. It was quite an experience and is still one of my favourite *castros* for sheer wow! factor.

The second *castro* we visited in Galicia was that of Santa Trega, a hillfort which sits high on a mound overlooking the mouth of the Miño river and the coastal town of A Guarda across from Caminha in Portugal.

We returned to A Guarda with Mum in 2014, before we found a second house to renovate and before Mum moved here to live.

It began one sunny May morning. I know I always say it was sunny, but it usually is if we've decided on a road trip and, to be perfectly honest, it's sunny in Galicia far more often than most people think!

Mum had been staying with us since the end of March. Her visits had become much longer since *A Casa do Campo* had benefitted from such amenities as heating, windows, and floors throughout. It seemed a waste for her to buy a plane ticket only to return two weeks later, so this trip was six whole weeks.

We'd all had a lovely time visiting friends (and having them visit us for lunch), going to fiestas and markets, and working in the garden. Mum had arrived the day after S and I returned home from a weekend trip to Barcelona, which had meant a whirlwind of cleaning and preparation for *La Jefa* (the boss lady). We'd returned home to a record eighteen eggs from our chickens, so eggs featured heavily on the menus in April.

Anyway, back to our sunny May morning and our weekend trip south.

We set off after breakfast, and after feeding the menagerie that was eleven hens, three rabbits, and a wild cat called Clarence.

"Where are we now?"

"Erm, I'm not sure but I think we're in Tui."

Tui was one of the seven ancient provincial capitals of Galicia and an important centre in Celtic times, but not where I'd been hoping to arrive.

"Are we supposed to be in Tui?"

"Er, nope? But it's okay, we can get back on the road up ahead."

Crisis averted, we arrived in A Guarda in plenty of time for lunch.

"Our hotel is down near the harbour," I said, directing S along a steep, narrow lane. "There should be some good restaurants down there too, I reckon."

There may well have been some good restaurants in the harbour, but ninety percent of them were serving seafood and we had my seafood-hating mother along. The meal we ate at the Celtic Harp (yes, the name should have rung alarm bells) was average, but the wine was drinkable and the view across the harbour was a definite plus.

After lunch and a long wander around the harbour area, we checked into our hotel for the night.

El Convento is, as its name suggests, a restored 17th century convent which is now a unique hotel.

The convent of San Benito was hidden behind a stone wall. A wrought iron gate set into a stone arch stood, thankfully, open and the small courtyard in front had a few tables and chairs dotted about. The building was architecturally captivating both outside and in.

"Oh, isn't it beautiful?" breathed Mum, as we entered the stone-arched entrance.

22 Celtic castros – Iron Age settlements

The thick rugs on the floors gave an air of opulence, with their flowered designs. The reception desk was wood panelled and discreetly positioned in the corner of a set of stone stairs; the staircase even had a carved stone balustrade. Opposite was a high arched doorway. Stone seats protruded from the walls, whilst religious paintings peered down on us and saints blessed us from their stone niches.

"It's a bit fancy," I replied, gazing around.

The receptionist was friendly, and happy to show us around the building. We set off down a narrow wooden-ceilinged corridor with tiny high-set windows, and wall sconces. Thankfully the lights were powered by electricity rather than oil, otherwise the place felt as if it hadn't changed since the Middle Ages.

Our bedrooms were pretty, with exposed stone walls. I was concerned Mum's single room had a step up to her bathroom.

"I'll be fine," Mum said, dismissively. "I have my stick."

That evening we went out for dinner down at the harbour, sitting outdoors, listening to the waves and happily exploring the many bars in the area. Our last stop was at the bar next to our hotel.

"Can I have a brandy?" asked Mum.

"*Un cognac, por favor,*" I said to the waiter.

He must have taken the 'cognac' bit literally as he returned with a huge warmed brandy balloon into which he poured a very generous measure of Remy Martín Reserve cognac. Mum was in brandy heaven.

"That was lovely," she said, licking her lips. "You should always warm the glass you know."

"The fumes are more than enough for me, thanks," I replied.

Unfortunately, combined with the couple of wines she'd had with dinner, the warmed cognac went straight to Mum's head.

"You don't think they'll tell the sisters, do you?" she giggled, as we half-dragged her across the carpeted foyer.

"Ssh! This is a fancy hotel you know. They might chuck us out." I was mortified.

S on the other hand thought the whole thing a great joke.

"Do you think she'll be alright?" he asked, as we closed her bedroom door behind us.

"She'll be fine."

I then spent the rest of the night worrying she would fall down that blasted step from the bathroom and crack her head. I have never been so pleased to see a healthy and hangover-free mother the next morning.

Mum had no memory of her embarrassing evening.

"You can't remember shouting about the nuns?"

"Did I? Oh dear! I did wonder why I was fully dressed this morning though," she admitted.

"Can't take you anywhere twice," I mumbled.

"Course you can," replied S. "Second time to apologise."

"Haha! Let's go and explore the *castro*."

The Castro de Santa Trega sits on Mount Santa Trega, 341 metres (1118 feet) above sea level at the very southwest tip of Galicia. Southwards is the Miño/Minho River and beyond, Portugal. To the west is the might of the Atlantic Ocean and to the east, Tui, and Ourense in the distance. It seems a perfect defensive position, though archaeologists argue whether the walls surrounding the mound were for protection or merely to delineate the village boundaries.

The first reference to Santa Trega is the discovery of a bronze sculpture of Hercules found by stonemasons in the 1800s. The site is also mentioned in Manuel Murguía's History of Galicia (Historia de Galicia, 1888). Murguía was a Galician journalist and historian, and the husband of one of Galicia's most famous poets, Rosalia

22 Celtic castros – Iron Age settlements

de Castro. In 1912, the Pro-Monte Society of Santa Tecla was created.

A quick note here about names: These can be incredibly confusing in Galicia where there are two official languages – one of which has many variations in spelling and pronunciation. The mount and its *castro* were known by its Castilian name of Santa Tecla for many years before reverting to the Galician name, Santa Trega. The name Santa Tegra is also often seen on official literature. I asked a good friend of mine, who happens to work in one of Galicia's tourist offices, to help me clarify the correct name.

"I think the official name is Trega, but everyone says Tegra," he replied.

Clear as mud then.

Between 1914 and 1933 there were extensive archaeological excavations on Mount Santa Trega. A link was even suggested to the mythical Mount Medulio where classical writers placed the final Gallaecian resistance against the might of the Roman Empire. In 1931, the site was declared a National Historic and Artistic Monument, and A Place of Cultural Interest. Oddly, then, just two years later all excavations were suspended. Work didn't recommence until the late 1970s.

Only around half of the settlement has been excavated, but it is still one of the largest found in Galicia. Most of the excavations now completed are on the west side of the site where stone roundhouses, huddled in family groups, fill the hillside. Santa Trega is estimated to have been inhabited between 100 BCE and 100 CE, putting it firmly in the Castro-Romano type of settlement. Finds here have included Roman glass and beads in addition to traditional Celtic pottery. Traces of pigment on the plastered internal walls show that these were tinted in a variety of colours, Roman style. Whilst stone blocks, embedded in walls, plinths, and door jambs, were decorated with designs such as Celtic roses, spirals, triskelions, and Celtic knots, suggesting a strong Celtic influence.

Mum has always been interested in archaeology and loved poking around the roundhouses.

"They must have been very crowded," she said, peering into the gloom of one restored house.

"Just right for us!" I replied, squashing in next to her as S took a photo.

The archaeologist Michael Avery stated: "The ultimate defensive weapon of European prehistory was the hillfort of the first millennium BC."

Santa Trega, with its imposing position high on a mountain top, and A Castro da Baroña, on its pinnacle of land surrounded by the ocean, certainly seem to be examples of this type of settlement. But other archaeologists believe the Celtic hillforts to have been primarily assembly places for seasonal farming families.

The *castro* at Viladonga seems to fall more into the latter category.

Another local *castro*, Viladonga sits on a low mound in the Terra Cha area some twenty kilometres north of Lugo. The last time we visited this well-preserved *castro* was with our friends, Dawn and Greg, who live nearby. It was a cold and windy day, the sky a slate-grey threatening imminent rain (see, it's not always sunny!). Although Viladonga isn't on a mountain the hilltop is exposed to the weather, sitting above Lugo's flat but high Terra Cha 550 metres (1,800 feet) above sea level. The wind whipped around the site and the rain, when it came, lashed the stone walls of the Iron Age dwellings.

The path to the settlement, beyond the excellent museum and information office, leads uphill beneath chestnut trees to a narrow gap in a grassy mound. This is part of the settlement's defences – a succession of walls and ditches following the gentle slope of the hillside. The walls are made of earth and stones, and the moat is surprisingly deep.

"It says in here that there were two doors built into the rock faces on either side of us..." I continued to read from the information leaflet about the hillfort, but the men had wandered off to play at being Celts.

Inside the final mound, the village nestles in the hollow of the high ramparts. Low slate walls delineate the various buildings, crushed closely together. Some are the traditional Celtic round houses, others larger, rectangular structures. In the centre is a building the leaflet described as being owned by a 'strongly Romanised family, of economic power'. Here, Roman glass, pottery and other imported goods were unearthed. These finds suggest the settlement was not only still thriving during the Roman occupation of the peninsula, but was ruled by a Roman, or Romanised, leader – maybe a local tribal leader who gained citizenship of Rome.

In one corner of the settlement there were steps leading down to what was described as a well, though there was no water in there when we visited. The buildings huddled against the north wall were the best preserved and, I thought, had the most favoured position, facing the winter sun.

The first artefacts were discovered at the Viladonga site in 1911 by two men working the land. Amongst others, there was a gold torc, or Celtic armband, made of twisted gold wire which is now in Lugo's provincial museum. The first archaeological excavations of the site began in 1971 under Manuel Chamoso Lamas.

"The settlement covers an area of four hectares and is a key site for understanding the evolution of the Celtic hillfort during and after the Roman era in Galicia," I read – largely to myself.

The video, back at the information centre, where we sheltered as the storm blew itself out, was a well-told recreation of the settlement's history, narrated in English.

"The site's guide says; 'The greatest time in the history of this fortified settlement came in the 2nd and 3rd centuries. It prospered under the Romans and was probably self-sufficient.'"

No one replied to my information dump.

"Finds of cattle and other animal remains, ground corn, and grinding stones, as well as hand thrown pots, more torcs, and many Roman-era coins, point to a collaborative and prosperous city." I continued trying to educate my friends and family.

The on-site museum had a good collection of artefacts to chase away a cloudy day, and the staff were friendliness itself.

"*¿De dónde sois?*" asked the lady at the desk who gave us tickets.

"We're from Taboada," I said, pointing to ourselves. "And our friends live near here."

"Ah!" she said, turning to Dawn and Greg. "You are the English. You are very welcome. Here." She lifted two thick tomes off the desk at the side of her and handed one to each couple. I nearly dropped mine.

"Erm, thank you. How much are they?" I asked, handing the doorstop to hubby.

"No, nothing. They are a gift. I hope you are very happy here in Galicia."

"We are!" we chorused, staggering outside with our burdens.

"What on earth is it?" asked S, once we were outside.

"Museo do Castro de Viladonga," I read from the front. "I think it's about the site and the museum."

"Is it in Galego?" was my hubby's next, and obvious, question.

"Yes. But there's an English translation at the back. And French and German too."

"It's a generous giveaway!"

22 Celtic castros – Iron Age settlements

"Wow!" Our friends were impressed, I could tell.

Our afternoon was an indulgent one, lazing around at our friends' lovely home, drinking homemade sloe gin and sloe *augardente* (augardente is a local firewater, bottles of which are often given to us by kindly neighbours, and perfect for fruit-based liqueurs), nibbling on serrano ham and olives and playing an hilarious game of Trivial Pursuit whilst listening to our joint favourite artist on CD.

"But must you sing along?" groaned S.

"Yup!"

SECTION ELEVEN -
THE CLEAR CANTABRIAN SEA

23 Foz, and the Lucense coast

"What about heading north?"

"Okay, where?"

We were at it again. Mum had been living in Galicia for almost two years and it was time to head off to explore more of our adopted region with her.

"We've never done the bit in between Ribadeo and Ortigueira."

The Lugo (or Lucense) coast borders the Cantabrian Sea, and is known as the *rías altas* or high rivers. The first time we set foot in Galicia it was along this coast. Or to be exact, along a rather high and narrow road bridge over the river Eo into Ribadeo – the gateway to Galicia and the first resort on the *rías altas*.

The Lucense coast, and Lugo province, gives way to Coruña province at the Ría de Barqueiro, near to Ortigueira. From here, the Galician coastline turns southwards through Coruña and Pontevedra provinces for the rest of its 1,498 kilometres (930 miles) to the mouth of the Miño river, and the border with Portugal. Of the four provinces that make up Galicia, only Ourense has no coastline.

We were all up early on a warm and sunny morning at the beginning of March for our trip 'up north'. The road towards our provincial capital of Lugo passes through areas of semi-wild scrubland; in March, the heather and gorse were just beginning to bloom. Not for the first time, I marvelled that nature always blends her colour palette perfectly. The soft hazy purple of the heather and deep gold of the gorse harmonised with the dark green broom and the clear blue of the sky. I marvelled – and I muttered that there was nowhere to pull off the road to take a picture of this iconic spring scene.

Beyond Lugo, we followed an arrow-straight road northwards.

"We're calling in to see Dawn and Greg," I told Mum, as S drove along the quiet road. "They have a load of DVD cases for us. For our film club."

S had started the film club years earlier after friends returning to England donated a large number of DVDs to us. His club had grown over the years, and his daughter often sent us packages of DVDs she'd watched. It was easier and cheaper to send these without the plastic cases so the offer from our friends in the north was very welcome.

Dawn and Greg had a small house in a tiny hamlet equidistant between Lugo and the Lucense coast. It was a perfect stopping point.

Dawn greeted us at the door. "Hiya, come in. I'll put the kettle on."

See! I said it was a perfect stopping point.

From Dawn and Greg's, we tootled towards the coast, pausing in A Pontenova to admire the huge lime kilns which dominate the skyline of the little town.

These brick-built, squat circular towers were used to process iron ore for steel export to Britain and Germany. The ovens are the precursors of the blast furnaces of the 19th century, but iron-working has been in place in A Pontenova since at least the 15th century. The town, which forms part of the Eo River Biosphere Reserve, was well-placed for the industry, having the basic resources needed within easy reach. The river provided water; the forests, the wood to make charcoal to fuel the kilns; and of course, iron itself was found in great quantities. The whole area has large iron ore deposits but the mines around A Pontenova were the most productive.

In 1905, a train line was built to transport the huge amounts of steel produced here. The rail line sadly closed in 1964 and was dismantled. There are, though, a number of walking routes to discover more of the area's mining past. I made a note to return one day to

23 Foz, and the Lucense coast

walk the Ruta dos Fornos (oven route) and Ruta das Minas (mines route).

"Shall we take a look at The Cathedrals?" I said, as we turned left along the coast.

La playa de Augas Santas is a beach on the Cantabrian coast better known as As Catedrais, or The Cathedrals. Ten kilometres west of Ribadeo, these natural rock sculptures are part of the NATURA 2000 European network of protected natural spaces. Over fifteen kilometres of Lugo's coastline and 29 hectares of marine and land habitat are part of this protected area.

"Where the power of the sea unites with the patience of time," I read.

"That sounds a bit flowery."

"It's cos I'm translating the Spanish. It's always flowery! True though," I added, gazing at the huge architectural shapes on the sands below us.

At low tide it's possible to wander amongst, below, and around the sculptured rocks – the power of the waves indeed working with eternity to wear away the softer rocks, leaving huge caves, arches and buttresses of slate and schist some thirty metres high.

We'd parked up on a high and windy cliff above the beach. The tide was partially in, the water as turquoise as a tropical sea.

"Though much colder," said S, in response to my mumbled musings.

"Can we go down?" asked Mum, peeping nervously over the barrier set at the cliff edge. "It's a long way."

"I think the tide's coming in so we'd better not. Don't want you floating off to France," I joked.

Mum shivered.

We drove further along the coast, admiring the surprisingly calm Cantabrian Sea off to our right, and arrived at Foz just in time for lunch.

We parked near to the fishing port, along the Ría de Foz, and mooched along the front for a while towards the open sea. This end of town was compact and pretty, the *ría* calm and unruffled. In a small plaza there were a number of cafes. The Bar A Funcional had outside tables beneath a wooden-beamed gazebo. The menu of *tapas* and *raciones* seemed a perfect choice on this sunny day.

"This is lovely," said Mum, nibbling on a slice of *jamón*.

I lifted a *chipirón* from the platter in front of me and nodded. "It is, isn't it?"

After lunch, we followed a *paseo* along the river towards the marina. I posed with Mum alongside some of the gleaming white yachts, and next to a group of granite-faced men sitting with their legs crossed.

"D'you think he minds me sitting on his knee?" I asked Mum, patting a granite hand.

"He looks a bit cross," replied Mum. She nodded at a third stoney-faced figure, standing facing us.

"He's just jealous!"

A little further along the waterfront was a small fenced-in area. Scratting in the dirt was a collection of white and electric-blue peacocks. The male fanned his tail at us before jostling his ladies away.

We walked on.

"Oh, don't slip," said Mum.

The waterfront here had no barrier and a sheer drop into the azure water of the *ría*. S, of course, took this as a challenge and pretended to skate around the edge of the dock before mock-pushing Mum into the briny water; a moment captured on film for use in future law suits!

We walked along the *paseo,* looking down on a small, town beach hidden in the lee of the *ría*, until Mum's legs were aching.

23 Foz, and the Lucense coast

"You two wait here, I'll go see if I can find us a hotel. But behave!" I warned, as I turned uphill away from the seashore.

Foz seemed surprisingly lacking in hotels, or we were in the wrong area, but the Hotel Islas Novas was smart, and friendly. A small boutique type hotel, it had beautifully designed rooms and breakfast was included.

"The rooms are a cut above our usual style," I admitted when I returned to the deadly duo. "There are comfy chairs in an alcove and reading lights next to the bed. Sure you two can be trusted in such a fancy place?"

"You can always take us somewhere twice," said S.

"Yeah, the second time to apologise! What about you, Mum? I still haven't forgotten the convent at A Guarda."

"I blame the brandy," replied Mum, artlessly.

"Me too," I mumbled.

Our room looked out over the deep, sandy bay of Praia da Rapadoira, the town's largest white sand beach, and the red painted *paseo* alongside it.

"What do you want to do this afternoon?" I asked Mum after we'd checked in.

"I think I'll have a siesta, if you don't mind. My legs are wobbly."

"We did walk a fair way. Do you mind if we go for a walk then?"

"No, of course not. Will you wake me when you get back?"

"We might," I teased.

We'd noticed that the long *paseo* continued beyond our walk this morning, following the ocean shore westwards. We were eager to explore further.

The large beach I'd seen from our window faced north into the Cantabrian Sea; its edge along the *ría* was protected by a walkway, which bordered the marina and the small beach we'd passed earlier.

The footpath was intersected by tiny *rías* – narrow, deep, and sunless. High above the sea was a footbridge across one of the many channels.

"I love this bridge,"
"And the flowers too."

The clifftops were edged by *Mesembryanthemum* which spilled into the Cantabrian Sea. I'd already surreptitiously stolen a few cuttings of the pretty pink daisy-like flower which grew in huge mats all along the cliffs. I felt sure I could get them going back at home.

"They'll look good in pots."

We walked as far as La Playa de Llás, a pretty beach with low sand dunes backing it and rock pools glinting in the afternoon sun. The seashore along this coast is well-known for its frequent collections of seaweed and this beach is said to be the most iodine-rich beach in Spain.

"There are lots of properties for sale," I said. "I like this one."

A large villa stood on the cliff road with views out to the clear Cantabrian Sea. It had three floors and a large garden.

"Bet it's windy in winter," countered S.

As we walked back through the town, I spotted an estate agent's window.

"Oo, can we have a look?"

S rolled his eyes.

"It'd be a good investment. Mum could buy a little holiday flat too. Better than keeping her money from her house in a bank."

The lady in the agency was keen to show us some properties.

"I'm Lourdes. I can show you places this afternoon if you like. We have some very good properties today."

"Okay. But nothing ridiculously expensive, and no flats in complexes," said S, firmly.

We set off in Lourdes' car. The first flat she showed us was tiny with an internal bedroom and hardly any light.

"Oh," I said, disappointed. "It's so dark. I hate these internal tunnels."

23 Foz, and the Lucense coast

"Ah, yes. They are normal in Spain. I may have one with a kitchen internal?

"Mmm. Okay."

We headed back toward the docks area, and an older apartment block overlooking the fishing port.

"Here are the fiestas in summer," said Lourdes, pointing at the car park opposite.

We climbed to the second floor.

"At least this one has a window," I said.

The long thin living room had a full height window overlooking the car park, and the *ría* beyond. The tide was out, so there were pools of water broken by sandy ridges. The main bedroom looked out in the same direction.

"It's a nice view," I said.

"It's the sea," replied S, unimpressed.

The second bedroom also had a window, looking on to a small covered terrace at the back where a washing machine was plumbed in. The kitchen looked directly into the windows of the flat opposite; I felt I could almost reach out and touch hands with the neighbour. But the views at the front were good and the second room at least had a window!

"It's better," I admitted.

"It's tiny," said S.

"This *piso* is very good value. Only 90,000 euro for two full bedrooms."

"What are the charges," S asked, suddenly.

"It is fifty euros *por* month for the maintenance, *más* the ground rent of forty euros."

I stared.

"Thank you," S said politely as we got out of Lourdes' car back in town.

She handed us her card and waved a merry goodbye.

"I didn't realise," I said.

"I remember Mercedes saying how expensive the maintenance costs are on the flats."

"Come to think about it, so did María. And then there's the extras, if say the roof needs repairing."

"And the electricity for the common areas."

I was adding up in my head. "That's over a thousand a year just in costs. We could go on a lot of mini breaks for that."

"And you'd have to holiday in the same place every time if you had a flat."

"Good point." I sighed. "You're right, as ever."

"I thought you were the one who's always Wright."

I smiled. "Born that way! Come on, let's go get Mum."

We told Mum about our adventures over a delicious burger and a few vinos at the Bar O Ribeiro in town.

"Sounds exciting."

"Not really. I do love noseying at houses, but as usual himself was the sensible one."

The bar was a modern, glass-fronted building and the burgers were enormous.

"I can't finish this," said Mum. "Do you want some?"

"No way! Ours are huge too."

"But the man will be mad at me."

Our waiter had been a large, jolly chap, with a twinkle in his eye as he'd told Mum she had to eat it all up after her eyes had widened at the sight of her giant's meal.

"He's coming now. You'd better hide." I laughed as Mum blanched.

Breakfast the next morning was a decent enough buffet. There were the usual meats and cheeses, and a very acceptable *tarta de Santiago.*

It was another sunny day. The light glinted off the still water below, and some brave soul was sunbathing in the angle of the stone walls around the smaller Tupide beach.

We drove Mum around the headland where we two had walked the day before, and ambled with her across the little foot bridge over the mouth of the *ría.*

23 Foz, and the Lucense coast

"Oh! This is pretty," she said, leaning over the low sea wall to pick a sprig of the *Mesembryanthemum*.

"I've already pinched some of those," I laughed. "I'll plant them when I get home. You can have some if they go."

"Like mother like daughter," muttered S.

"True." I smiled at Mum. "Go and sit on that stone wall down there near the sea so I can take your photo."

Mum complied, sitting on a semi-circular terrace area halfway down a cliff. It was a pretty spot and Mum looked happy and relaxed.

Further along, giants' fingers stuck up out of the sand. I expected a huge stone Titan to lift his arm and grab us at any moment.

"That, or it's the buried Statue of Liberty from Planet of the Apes."

We drove along the coast towards Burela, where we stopped for a coffee and a wander along the *paseo*.

"There were some flats for sale here," I began.

S looked at me sideways.

"Just saying." I smiled. "Actually, you have to let me read from the estate agent's brochure. You know it was in English?"

"So she said, yes."

"It's hilarious. I don't know why they don't spend money on a proper translator. It's such a posh glossy brochure but anyone English would be put off by things like 'this little sailor town' and…"

"Probably only you, Miss Pedantic."

"I've got a novel called The Viveiro Letter," I said, as we entered the pretty coastal town of the same name a little while later.

"Was it set here?" asked Mum.

"No, in Mexico. It's probably a common name. Good book though."

We parked at the docks once more before heading into the old town. The fishing port here seemed industrialised compared to that at Foz. There are more tourists in Viveiro, tripling the usual 16,000 population over the summer months, though in March it was still quiet.

Viveiro was designated a city in the 19th century but was an important commercial port as long ago as the Middle Ages. For this reason, the town was fortified with thick stone walls and wooden gates which could be sealed from within. Most of the wall has been subsumed into modern buildings and only three of the gates now remain, but the Porta de Carlos V is impressive enough to stand alone, reminding me of the Arc de Tríomphe.

Built of dark grey granite with a castellated top, and a stone-carved shield above a perfectly formed archway, it is at once grand and awe-inspiring.

The old town winds up narrow roads, the tall buildings blocking out the sun, to the 14th century Gothic stone-built church of San Francisco. Mum went inside while we waited on the street, admiring the tall, octagonal, clean granite stonework and soaring, narrow, leaded windows. Against the bright blue of the spring sky, it looked stunning.

Squashed between renovated houses opposite where we stood, was an impossibly narrow roofless building, moss growing thickly on the derelict beams and pigeons perched in groups on the rafters. A tiny glassless attic window peeped back at us from on high, framed by the moss and greenery. Beyond, rendered old stone buildings with a few tiny windows framed in wood leant next to bright, white-painted renovated houses.

"I can see why people like Viveiro so much. It's very pretty."

From Viveiro, we drove across the 15th century Puente de Misericordia to Covas beach on the other side of the *ría*. It was a long walk to the water, through sand dunes of sharp tufted grass. Mum and S immediately set about collecting stones and shells.

Mum wrapped her finds in her jumper to carry them back to the car, looking like Dick Whittington with her stick and bundle over her shoulder; the cat awaited at home, with a rapturous welcome and a miaow which lasted until his bowl was filled with choice leftovers from our trip.

24 The Ortigueira Peninsula

March 2021 – we had been no further than our nearest shopping town for months, but, at last, Galicia was open in its entirety for us to visit. But where to go? With an as yet unvaccinated 89-year-old in tow we wanted to be careful and stay safe.

"What about a contactless coastal trip around the Ortigueira Peninsula?"

"Perfect! I'll pack a picnic. I bet we won't see a soul."

The wild, northwest tip of Galicia is incredibly scenic but so remote that it rarely gets busy even in the height of summer. This though was not summer; it was one of those Galician days that make you think summer is on its way, only to have your illusions shattered a few days later by icy winds and rain. For the moment though, it was ideal picnic weather. I'd made a quiche, and packed plenty of cake and fizzy drinks.

It was already 18ºC as we made our way towards the coast on that fine spring morning. The hedgerows and fields were alive with colour and birdsong.

Beyond Lugo, we turned onto the new two-lane expressway towards Ferrol, the once bustling port town of Galicia where modern shipbuilding and ancient military batteries share a harbour.

The AG64 was deserted. This was not a Covid-related emptiness though, just a normal Galician-road emptiness. New roads, which few people use, are being built with abandon all around us – until Galicia will become one large spider's web of empty tarmacadam. Bizarre.

Actually, we did meet a traffic jam on the old road to Ferrol once. It was mid-morning and the old road, a narrow, one-lane affair, wound down the hill towards As Pontes de Garcia Rodriguez. The line of lorries in front of us came to a halt and there we sat, admiring the tall chimneys of the electricity producing plant at As Pontes

24 The Ortigueira Peninsula

for fully thirty minutes. There are worse views to be had, and worse places to have to sit in line. We found out that the jam was due to poor timing on our part; the main freighter had docked at Ferrol and the lorries were queuing to board. We've not met another traffic hold up since.

Now, the new AG64 whizzed past the tall smokestacks on its way to Ferrol. We turned off as we saw As Pontes Lake (Lagoa de As Pontes) in front of us, glimmering azure in the sunshine, to take the minor road towards Ortigueira.

From As Pontes the AC101 becomes narrow and curving once more as it climbs into the Sierra de Faladoira where the most populous things are the 120-metre-high wind turbines marching into the distance, and the wild horses and cattle which graze at their bases.

The road passed through granite outcrops; the only trees were pine plantations, the rest rocky scrub. At one of the pull-ins we stopped for our midmorning cake, admiring the sleek fat cattle and the silent white behemoths which turned slowly above our heads.

Wind ruffled but sun warmed, we continued toward Ortigueira.

Our friends, Cris and Steve, lived in Ortigueira for a number of years and were kind enough to issue us frequent invitations to visit. Through our friends, we were introduced to many of the beaches of the area and the Celtic music festival, held each July. On this occasion, we were heading for one of the many, finger-like peninsulas which create this 'pearl of the rías'.

Our drive took us first to the coastal town of Cariño, situated on the northeast side of the peninsula. We parked by a school, and a locked building declaring itself the sports hall – which had apparently been repainted at a cost of just over 19,000 euros. I suggested to S that we could've tendered for 10,000 and made a darn good profit; it wasn't a large building. From the side of this magnificently repainted structure, we walked along a red tarmacked path towards the sea.

The beach at Basteiras had obviously been upgraded for the summer hordes of tourists. As well as the new red path, there was a boardwalk across the sand dunes towards the ocean. Mum found this nice and easy going until we reached the part where strong winds had blown a heap of soft sand into undulating waves, directly across our path. She doggedly continued, her stick sinking into the miniature dunes. In contrast, the beach itself was firm and dry – and totally deserted.

It was a long beach, stretching some 1,000 metres from the jetty on one side to the tree-clad hills on the other. Sadly, for Mum, it was a beach devoid of stones or shell. There were; no treasures for us to have to carry home. Only small heaps of seaweed marred its pure surface.

At the jetty end a lone figure walked past, their head at the height of our feet. What I'd thought was a walkway, level with the beach, was actually a wall. The path beyond was some six feet below it – an easy jump for us, but not for an 89-year-old. Mum, with S' help, bravely walked along the top of the narrow wall until the path rose to meet it some little way ahead. Rescue mission successful, we wandered to the end of the pier where two fishermen were loading their catch. Then we turned around – full into the wind.

It was only a hundred metres back to the red path but the wind buffeted us mercilessly. I stopped to take a cutting from a beautiful smoke bush but decided against having our picnic lunch on the beach here. Sand and quiche just don't mingle.

Instead, we followed the map up towards a viewpoint.

That is, we tried to follow the map.

Unfortunately, Galician maps leave much to be desired in terms of accuracy. I had two maps I was trying to follow, both courtesy of the local tourist board in Ortigueira. One showed a road called Ruta de las

24 The Ortigueira Peninsula

Miradores (viewpoint route) the other didn't, but it did show more detail around the town of Cariño. As we circled the town, twice, I wished our friends still lived here to guide us. Or that Galicia could produce just one decent cartographer.

Eventually we followed the signs for the Cabo Ortegal, the northernmost point of the peninsula. We didn't want to go there but hoped there may be a turn off on the way for the road we did want.

The roads through Cariño old town were narrow, cobbled, and one-way. By the time we'd gone round the tiny plaza a second time, people were beginning to wave to us. I felt like royalty – or an English idiot! The turning we needed, which we'd dismissed the first time round as being highly improbable, was a sharp right onto a one vehicle width, steep, straight, cobbled street between terrace houses whose front doors all opened directly onto the narrow lane. At the top we popped out on to a twisting road past the cemetery and up into the hills. I do love Galicia.

The road wound through pines and planted eucalypts (the scourge of the Galician coast) ever higher. At one point the direct route was closed and we were directed down into the pine plantations before snaking upwards again. Eventually we reached the top, having seen one other car the whole way. At a small viewpoint there was a single wooden bench facing the sea, way below us.

Up here the wind was strangely non-existent as we unpacked our picnic. We sat companionably on the bench, and the low stone wall in front, chomping cheese and onion quiche and drinking fizzy drinks.

Using my not very trusty map, I worked out what we were seeing. In front and below was Cariño and the beach we had walked along that morning, now a tiny speck. The way up the mountain was obvious from our vantage point. To our right was the *ría* separating this peninsula from Ortigueira, the town itself just out of view around the corner. To our left was Cape Ortegal and, again hidden from our angle, its lighthouse – signalling to ships the dangers of this rocky coastline.

Sated with quiche we sat for a while enjoying the peace and the view, until S pointed to a cloud bank rolling in from the south.

"Looks like it might be foggy over the other side," he said, as the cloud roiled and grew.

"Better make the most of this viewpoint then," I replied.

We packed away our empties, and left the pastry crumbs on the low wall for the birds.

"Not that there are any birds."

"But there must be some?" said Mum.

"Well, either way, something will eat the crumbs," replied S, popping the coolbox back into the car.

Heading across the peninsula, we soon descended into that cloud bank. The road was still in switchback mode, though leveller than previously, winding through rocky outcrops and low-grazed scrub. A lone cow loomed out of the mist, right in the middle of the road. She stood for a long moment before deciding to let us pass, wandering on to another part of the scrubland. Beyond were a group of horses, shaggy manes and thick coats testifying to their year-round existence up here in the wilderness. The dense fog made everywhere seem mystical and mysterious, something Galicia does so well.

We were heading for the tourist and pilgrim town of San Andrés de Teixido. There is a strange Galician saying which states that if one doesn't visit San Andrés during one's life then you will return after death, slithering in the manner of a snake or a lizard. Not a fate any of us fancied, so off we went.

San Andrés is said to be the second most important pilgrimage site in Galicia after Santiago de Compostela. The sign for parking began way out of town, though we had no problem parking in the dedicated bus area along with another three cars – the only visitors on that beautiful sunny day.

The mist which had coated the tops just beyond the *mirador* had vanished as quickly as it had arisen and San Andrés, on the opposite coast to Cariño and facing out to the Atlantic, was sunny and calm.

The steep road down into the village was pedestrianised, so Mum had to walk. She was pretty fit for an almost 90-year-old and managed admirably, even refraining from poking all the various touristic tat on sale in front of one of the white-mortared stone houses.

One of the unique features of San Andrés is its reputation as a 'white village'. This, though, is not white as in the rendered white houses of the south of Spain. The houses of San Andrés are built of dark granite, the stones plastered thickly between in white-painted mortar.

Galicia has a number of styles of pargeting. In Taboada the traditional render was in the form of birds and animals swirling around the stonework, though few buildings retain it now. When we were house hunting in the Ourense hills, the typical plasterwork seemed to be thick, white straight lines across the uneven granite stones, each with a thinner red line through the centre. I admit, I hated it as it seemed to detract from the beautiful stones themselves. I'm quite pleased we didn't buy in the area as I would've had to destroy the 'traditional' artwork for my own aesthetics.

In San Andrés, though, the thick white plaster seemed in keeping with its surrounds. The little 16th century church was plastered in the same way. It sat looking out to sea, a huge palm tree next to it and the usual Catholic Church gold leaf ornamentations within.

Below was another tiny chapel, lit with votive candles and entered by a set of curving stone steps. Below that was the wild Atlantic Ocean, many metres below. San Andrés is said to sit on the highest cliffs in Europe.

The village itself was obviously set up for tourists. There were stalls in front of the shops, and *percebes*, the goose barnacles which are a delicacy here, advertised in every window, along with local honey and razor clams. Of the tourists - there was one other couple with their dogs.

At the top of the steep path back to the car we allowed Mum a comfort break and a *vino tinto* at a deserted café. We sat outside and watched the owner's small child being introduced to a tiny scrap of a boxer puppy. We had seen what I assumed to be the pup's mother on the way in. She was lying on the warm stone path, not shifting for anyone. This pup couldn't have been more than six weeks old and was shivering in fear as the tot poked it and gently kicked it until it stood up. I was pleased they were introducing the child to animals early, as so many Spanish children seem terrified of dogs, but I wished they had done so in a less frightening way for the poor pup.

Mum having long since downed her huge glass of red wine, we made our way back to the car and headed for our next beach at Cedeira.

Not far outside of San Andrés we found another viewpoint. It was marked as the Cross of Teixido, a waypoint on the Camino de San Andrés de Teixido - a walking route from San Adrián to San Andrés, and beyond to Ferrol.

We walked over to the tall stone cross set on a rocky outcrop above the track, admiring the wild beauty of the landscape around us for a moment. Mum sat on the edge of the stone plinth, windswept as the clean, fresh air blew in our faces.

On the way back to the car, I noticed a memorial plaque against a large granite rock. I made my way over. I was amazed to find the plaque, written in English and

Spanish, was a memorial to the English actor Leslie Howard. He of the crisp accent and old-fashioned good looks in *Gone with the Wind* and the 1938 version of *Pygmalion*. According to the memorial, Leslie Howard had died when the KLM Dutch Airlines passenger plane he was in was shot down off the Galician coast by the Luftwaffe in June 1943. He was fifty years old.

I Googled Leslie Howard's death, once I was back at home. I discovered there is still controversy over whether Howard was an English spy, and so targeted by the Nazis (he was definitely a propagandist of high regard), or whether the Luftwaffe was simply patrolling a 'sensitive area' of coastline (previous KLM Lisbon to Bristol flights had also been attacked). It was all quite mysterious and intriguing.

Back in the car, my map was actually doing the business until we reached a wide T-junction with no signposting.
"Which way?" asked S, who was driving at that point.
I am supposed to be the better navigator as I can actually see the map, and don't get carsick staring down at my lap.
"No idea. This map doesn't show anything resembling a T-junction, and certainly not one this big." I held my finger up in the air and closed my eyes. "That way," I said, pointing right. "Cedeira has to be at the coast."
Wrong.
The route we took soon went from wide, smooth main road to tiny, twisting lane through a small village (not on the map) and then up in to the hills again.
"I don't think this is right," said S. "That's kilometre three. We started at kilometre one so I'm thinking the other way. Markers usually start at the biggest town."
Far too logical, but ultimately correct.
We turned around and headed onto the new, wide road towards Cedeira. By now it was after five. We parked up and went for a walk along the neat and tidy promenade, keeping the beach to our left. The sea was

so far away it was almost out of sight from the town. It left a damp and muddy stretch of sand which reminded me of childhood holidays in Skegness, trying to find the sea whilst avoiding falling in the muddy gloopy pools left behind.

We left Mum happily sitting on a bench whilst S and I walked further along the front towards the marina and fishing port where we admired a statue to La Virgen de Carmen del Mar, the patron saint of fishermen. Deciding against abandoning my parent, still sitting on her bench, we collected Mum before making our way toward the main road home.

By this point our fuel indicator was flashing 'too low'. The changes of gear necessitated by all the ups and downs and twisty roads had taken their toll. Although I knew we had over fifty kilometres of driving left, the flashing light always panics me so I set to looking for the nearest fuel stop. Unfortunately, the wilds of the Coruña coast doesn't seem to have a great profusion of service stations.

"There's one just before the AG64," I said. "I didn't see a services on the motorway."

At that moment we came to the roundabout for the new fast road and a small sign pointing to the right with a petrol pump on it.

As we coasted round to the pumps, I realised all the lanes had a 'no entry' sign on them. The helpful chap on duty said we had to go all the way back around to enter from the other side. This had not, I might add, been signposted from the road.

The pump was one of the new-fangled, self-serve ones which are slowly gaining ground here. Luckily, as most Galegos prefer someone putting fuel in the car for them, there is always a helpful assistant to show you how to use the machine – and to put the fuel in. Things aren't changing that much here, for which I am always grateful.

24 The Ortigueira Peninsula

With no more need to map read, I took over driving for the rest of the way home. The sky was blazing a pink splash in the east, reflecting the setting sun. That sun was also in my eyes each time I turned a corner, blinding me momentarily. Still, the view was glorious and the purple heather shone in its glow. It had been another beautiful, and safe, day of exploration in this magnificent land.

SECTION TWELVE – WALKING THE CAMINOS

25 Los Caminos de Santiago

We first arrived in Galicia along one of the Caminos de Santiago – the North Coast Way, or Camino del Norte. From Asturias, we had to cross the mouth of the river Eo into Galicia. Our only way across was a high road bridge. The day was blustery, the windsocks fluttering horizontally, and multiple lines of traffic whizzed past inches from our packs.

The Ways of St. James are a perfect means to see more of Galicia, whether walking, cycling, riding, or even driving. We certainly had an epiphany walking the *Camino*. I loved Galicia from the first moment we set foot on her granite rocks (once we'd crossed that bridge, that is) and we have been here ever since.

Legend has it that the tomb of the apostle, St. James the Greater, was discovered in the 9th century, in a field near to what was to become Santiago de Compostela. A hermit was praying in the forests when he saw '*a brilliant light from the stars falling from heaven*'. The stone tomb of Santiago (St. James in Spanish) was discovered in that 'field of stars'.

For the Asturian king, Alfonso II, the discovery of the tomb of Santiago came at just the right time. He needed help from nearby regions to defend his expanding kingdom against attacks from the southern Moors. What better reason to send assistance to a neighbouring Christian than to help protect the relics of one of the apostles of Jesus?

Pilgrimages to the site began shortly after the serendipitous discovery of the relics. During its heyday of the 11th, 12th and 13th centuries, many thousands visited the tomb of St. James each year. Spiritual indulgences for those who made the pilgrimage helped the Way to flourish, and a complex network of routes to the city grew. Together, these routes are known as the

Way of St. James, or the Jacobean Route. Los Caminos de Santiago were declared a European Cultural Itinerary in 1987 and the Spanish, and then French, Ways were declared UNESCO World Heritage Sites in 1993 and 1998 respectively.

The pilgrim route to Santiago de Compostela (St. James of the field of stars) is still one of the most important of Christian pilgrimages; thousands of *peregrinos* converge on the capital of Galicia from all corners of Europe, and the world.

There are currently six main Caminos de Santiago which pass through Galicia, plus a further two important Jacobean routes within the region. Over the years since we moved here, I've hiked, wandered along, stood on, or crossed, every one of these routes. I'd like to share some of my memories from those occasions and a little information about the different Ways, in the hope you too might make the journey to Galicia and share her wonders.

One of the first pilgrims to make the journey to venerate the site of the relics of St. James the Greater was said to be Alfonso II himself, using an ancient network of Roman roads from his court in Oviedo, the capital of Asturias. This 300-kilometre route is now called the Camino Primitivo (Primitive Way) or simply, the Original Way.

The Camino Primitivo is said to be one of the toughest of the Ways, with steep inclines and declines over the course of a single day. Parts of this route have changed little since those medieval pilgrimages; with stone churches, Roman remains, tiny isolated villages, and splendid views.

The Original Way enters northeast Galicia over the Alto do Acebo, 1,030 metres (3,380 feet) above sea level, before dropping down to the Roman-walled city of Lugo.

The Camino arrives in our provincial capital over the river Miño, across the Roman-medieval stone bridge. I love the views of the old city from the river. Lugo stands proudly on its hilltop; the effectiveness of the great, stone defensive walls is obvious as they rise above the mount.

From the river it's a steep climb to this UNESCO World Heritage city, 100 metres above. The centre of Lugo has an old-world feel, in keeping with its 2,000-year history. Its old stone buildings and cobbled streets, and its 12th century cathedral of Santa María, have an air of permanence.

The Camino Primitivo also passes over the mountains via A Fonsagrada and the Alto de Cerredo some 960 metres (3,150 feet) above sea level.

A Fonsagrada must be one of the most photographed villages on local TV. Being so high it often has snow into June, and each year the news stations show weary pilgrims trudging through snowdrifts. TV reporters stand shivering in short dresses, gloves and scarves, their cheeks red, their eyes watering, interviewing residents and commenting on 'how cold it is' in this high and bleak settlement. A Fonsagrada is definitely a place to pass through in the warmer months.

The best known, and most walked, cycled, or ridden, route to Santiago de Compostela is the French Way (Camino Frances). There are four principal routes through France towards Compostela, three of which cross the Pyrenees at the ridge of Roncevalles.

The French Ways enter Galicia via the Sierra de Ancares and the mythical heights of O Cebreiro, 1,300 metres (4,560 feet) above sea level, before continuing along 135 kilometres of Galician soil to reach the Cathedral in Santiago.

The Camino Frances is first mentioned in the Codex Calixtinus, an illuminated medieval manuscript which includes a guide for pilgrims. This guide, dated to 1135 CE, is said to have been written by the French monk and scholar Aymeric Picaud.

Picaud gave step by step details of his pilgrimage on horseback across France and Spain, listing drinking fountains, monasteries, and other points of religious interest. He also included expected weather conditions, perceived dangers, places to find a bed, and curiosities along the way – he was, in short, one of the first travel guide writers.

In 2018, we walked a short stretch of the Camino Frances. Our friends were walking the Camino and invited us to join them for the day. It was a misty April morning in Galicia when we roused ourselves at 8.15am to drive the short distance to Palas de Rei.

I was initially wary of walking a stretch of road that we know so well from our years of collecting visitors from the airport. For much of its length from Palas de Rei, the French Way criss-crosses the N547. We often saw *peregrinos* in varying states of repair: marching along, carefree and cheerful; stumbling forward, heads down, walking poles at the ready; or limping bravely, heads held high, focused on a distant spire.

I was, then, pleasantly surprised that most of our short hike that day zigzagged through tiny villages, meandered along green lanes beneath chestnut trees, and zipped beneath the new motorway on quieter tracks. We stopped for a welcome drink midway and arrived, not too footsore, in time to join Mum for lunch in Melide.

It was a magnificent *menú* at the hotel-restaurant Carlos. The *liebre* (hare) in a red wine sauce seemed to linger on my taste buds; the wine was fresher, and the desserts sweeter after our *camino.*

The Northern Route (Camino del Norte), which we walked in 2004, became popular in the Middle Ages. Despite military religious orders watching over pilgrims there had been numerous attacks by brigands across the high, bleak *meseta* of the French route. The Way along the Cantabrian coast was considered safer. It is certainly more picturesque to my mind – with its ups and downs to cross each tiny *ría*, its seaside towns, and its constant view of the sea off to the right.

Like the Primitive Way, the North Coast Way originally began in the Asturian capital of Oviedo. Our own journey along the Camino del Norte, began in the Asturian coastal city of Gijón. It was a delight for the senses and an agony of blisters from carrying too much stuff.

A quick tip for would-be *peregrinos* – don't pack the kitchen sink! Next time I'll just take my trusty bumbag and a spare T-shirt.

The English Way, or Camino Inglés, was, as its name suggests, followed by pilgrims from Britain and northern Europe who crossed the sea to one of the main Galician ports to begin their pilgrimage.

The English Way begins in the ports of either A Coruña or Ferrol in the northwest of the region. It is the shortest of the six official Caminos de Santiago eligible for the coveted *Compostela*, at just 119 kilometres (74 miles) long. I've stood on the Camino Inglés in both cities, explored the coastal town of Pontedeume and the beautiful Fragas do Eume, and visited the medieval capital of Betanzos, on its hill above two rivers. There are some beautiful spots along this Camino and it's one six-day hike I'd like to complete someday.

The Caminos de Santiago begin not only from France and Spain, but as far afield as Riga and Istanbul, Helsinki and Naples, Athens and Budapest.

The longest journey I've heard about someone making was during a serendipitous meeting...

We'd collected a friend from the airport at Santiago and were just joining the motorway home when we spotted a boy and a girl by the side of the road, overloaded with rucksacks, thumbing a lift. They gratefully piled into the car, telling us that they had just completed their *camino* and were hitching home.

"And where is home?" I asked.

"Kraków, Poland. We left eight months ago."

I almost crashed the car.

Over a coffee they told us the rest of their story.

"We have always wanted to walk the Camino of Santiago. We left the day after our wedding."

At this revelation, I stared. The girl looked incredibly young, with her blonde ponytail and shy smile; the boy bore a striking resemblance to a first-year Harry Potter, complete with thick framed glasses and lack of facial hair. The girl giggled and showed me her shiny gold wedding band.

"It's our honeymoon," she said.

"And you have been walking ever since?"

"Yes," said the boy. "It is amazing to see the different countries. Spain, we like very much. Switzerland was hard."

"With the hills?"

"Yes. But also, it is very expensive."

"And how many kilometres have you walked?"

"Over three thousand."

We dropped them, at their insistence, at a motorway junction in the middle of nowhere. They were confident they could catch a lift to Madrid that day. I wasn't so sure they'd have much luck from the wilds of Galicia, but then again, they'd made it that far. What a beginning to a marriage they'd had, and what memories they'd stored up for their continuing journey together.

The Winter Route (El Camino de Invierno) is the newest of the official Caminos de Santiago. Inaugurated on the 2nd of March 2010, the year we got married here in Galicia, it begins in Ponferrada, in the region of Castilla y León, and follows the Sil river valley into Galicia. This particular route was often used by medieval pilgrims in the winter months, as an alternative to the difficult

25 Los Caminos de Santiago

ascension of O Cebreiro or having to cross the flooded valleys of Valcárcel - where old rickety bridges were often washed away.

Historians document the existence of a secondary Roman road from Las Médulas, in Castilla y León, along the valley of the Sil. Unknowingly, we'd walked a little of this route when we visited the site of the Roman gold mines there. The track was steep, the views stunning, and the air clean. This secondary Roman road eventually joined the Via Nova, or Via XVIII, which passed through the district of Valdeorras (valley of gold) at the foot of the peak of Manzaneda.

There are other Roman mines along this particular Camino. Near the town of Quiroga is the tunnel of Montefurado - an intriguing work of engineering. In the 2nd century CE, the Romans dug through granite rock at the side of the Sil to create a tunnel and divert the river. This made the extraction of gold from the old river bed far easier. In the 2nd millennium CE, my hubby made a go of panning for gold in the river there - jumping down steep hillsides and getting thoroughly filthy. He found no gold, but had a fun afternoon.

The Winter Route passes through many of our best-known localities: Monforte de Lemos, where the route crosses the Roman bridge near the centre of town; and Chantada, a mere fifteen kilometres from our home. Chantada has an intriguing old town of cobbled streets and ancient stone buildings, and is where we swim or walk every week.

The Camino de Invierno zigzags down a steep Roman pathway to another Roman bridge across the river Miño at Belesar (where we caught the catamaran to the Cabo de Mundo one summer's day for Mum's 85th birthday), before winding its heart-stopping way back up the other side. It passes over the heights of O Faro, rich in wind turbines, and passes near to the chapel, A Ermida da Nosa Señora do Faro, which we hiked to in 2009 with a walking group. I guarantee the views from there are well worth the puffing and panting to arrive.

At Lalín, the winter route joins with the Via de la Plata (the Silver or Southeast Way). The latter is the longest of the pilgrim routes through Galicia, passing diagonally from the southeast through three of the four Galician provinces. The main route of the Silver Way is an extension of another Roman road, called Via de la Plata, connecting Emerita Augusta (Mérida in Estremadura) to Asturica Augusta (Astorga in Castilla y León).

This is the route used by the Moor known as Almanzor, a 10th century military leader and chancellor of the caliphate of Córdoba, to attack Santiago in 997 CE. During that attack, Santiago's cathedral was sacked and its bells stolen. In 1250, these old Roman roads began to be used as a way for pilgrims to reach Santiago from Andalucía and Estremadura. And, along this route, Santiago's cathedral bells were returned to their rightful place, over 200 years after their theft.

The second Camino de Santiago from the south is the Portuguese Way (Camino Portugués). This route enters Galicia, via the medieval capital of Tui, across the river Miño. The Camino Portugués began to be used in the late Middle Ages, when pilgrims would walk from the Portuguese cities of Braga, Coimbra, Oporto and Chaves to the holy city of Santiago de Compostela.

The Portuguese Way uses part of yet another Roman road, the Via XIX, the backbone of Roman Gallaecia. This road was built in the 1st century CE and is sadly much subsumed by the N550 main trunk road north. Our friends Debs and Al have walked this route a number of times and say it is one of the best walks they've done.

Although the official route of the Way crosses the Miño at Tui, slightly upriver, we once met a German man in Caminha, at the mouth of the Miño, who was walking the Camino Portugués. He had been hoping to catch the ferry across the river to A Guarda in Spain and view the Castro de Santa Trega on his way to Santiago. Unfortunately, that day was the local annual triathlon which involved a swimming race along the river. The ferry was suspended. We gave Hans a lift to the next nearest bridge inland and waved him on his way.

In Fisterra (Finisterre in Castilian), the westernmost point of Galicia, *peregrinos* traditionally bathe in the sea and burn their old clothes as a sign of purity. Many pilgrims also stay to watch the sun set over the Atlantic Ocean.

Pilgrims can extend their *Camino* to the 'end of the world' and beyond, along the Fisterra-Muxía Way – a triangular loop which is an extension of any of the Caminos de Santiago. From Fisterra, the Way continues along the coastal road to Muxía and the Santuarío de Nosa Señora da Barca, before completing the triangle to return to Santiago.

The Ruta do Mar de Arousa e Río Ulla is a short route which follows the direction that legend says was taken by the stone barge bearing the remains of the apostle Santiago in the 1st century CE. Beginning in either Cambados or Aguiño, the route follows the south or north shore respectively of the Ría de Arousa northeast to join with the Camino Portugués at Padrón.

Padrón, or Iria Flavia as it was known in Roman times, was the previous bishopric of the region, from where Bishop Teodomiro set out to discover St. James' remains in that 'field of stars'.

The legends of the apostle may be remarkable, even improbable, but the Ways to reach the capital of Galicia are all, without doubt, a joy to discover.

26 *A Casa do Campo* – a walk through the seasons

The Caminos de Santiago are certainly the best known of the walking routes in Galicia, but the region is crisscrossed with tracks and way-markers. These routes can extend for hundreds of kilometres or, quite literally, be a walk in the park – but they all showcase the varying landscapes and beauty of our adopted home perfectly. I've included in this book a few of the many routes we've had the privilege to walk and there are many more on my to-do list for the future.

Sometimes though, the familiar, seen with different eyes and the changing of the seasons, can be equally beautiful and soul cleansing. If the strict lockdown which Spain imposed at the beginning of the Covid-19 outbreak in 2020 taught me anything, it was to appreciate the beauty in our surroundings with new eyes.

It's late September as I write this – the start of my favourite season, autumn. Autumn in Galicia is such a magical time of year. All around is the smell of woodsmoke and roasting chestnuts, and the crunch of fallen leaves underfoot.

Across the valley, above the little water mill, the foliage of the fruit trees will soon change colour and the valley will be awash with hues of golds and scarlets, burnt umber, Lincoln greens and autumn browns. The lonesome pine trees will stand out, deeper green against the autumn palette.

A Casa do Campo is the last house in our tiny hamlet. If we turn left out of our gate, the tarmacked village road soon peters out to packed earth as we meander beneath the boughs of ancient sweet chestnut trees. The trunks of those trees are gnarled and knobbly – some are even completely hollow. I love to gaze at them, wondering what tales they could tell in their 200-year-old lives.

26 A Casa do Campo – a walk through the seasons

One of our regular walks begins below the branches of those trees, and where better to end our exploration of Galicia than in my own back yard? It's a truly magical spot at any time of the year, so sit back and enjoy a walk with me, through the seasons in Galicia.

Beneath those first chestnut trees, the track twists and turns. In summer, the packed earth is dusty dry; in winter it becomes a mudslide as the rains fail to penetrate its hard crust. In autumn, *Colchicums*, or autumn crocuses, flourish here, and by November the chestnuts are already starting to fall from the branches of the trees.

The ground underfoot is thick with crisp leaves. I'll collect some of those leaves later in the year, to use as a mulch on my vegetable beds and to turn into leaf mould compost, but for now I love to kick my way through them on our walks.

Past the tiny waterfall on our little *ría*, is my favourite tree – not a chestnut, but a huge oak which stands regally on the corner, alone and aloof. Beyond are two red, square pegs partly buried in the ground. These mark the spot where a motorway bridge was to be built. I was devastated when I first heard the news, not long after we moved in to *A Casa do Campo*. Thankfully, in the fifteen years since, no more has been done. Those markers are almost invisible now, and I remain optimistic that the necessary money will never reach its destination.

Beyond the red markers, the chestnut woods give way to low rocky cliffs on the right and a steep-sided valley of birch and gangly oak trees on the left. Down beyond the trees is the river which runs along the bottom of our valley, and the second water mill on that *río*. The *molino* has a brand-new roof, though it is sadly not a working mill.

The fresh, antiseptic scent of pine heralds a dense wood on our left. The ground below the conifers is thick with needles. The view through the trees is dim and mysterious. Not much grows in these woods but the native red squirrels dart about, their bushy tails twitching as they gather pine nuts.

Further still, the track crosses a small bridge over yet another stream before climbing to the little village above us. It's a pleasant walk around the village with its stone-built church and granite houses. The views from this height are spectacular on a clear day and the water in the village trough is fresh and cool. An old apple tree stands sentinel on the corner, its crisp, red fruit begging to be scrumped.

Shall we?

The village road crosses back over the *río* as the latter passes beneath. Just beyond, a quiet track turns off to the left, paralleling the river on the south side of our little valley. A large field on the right used to have the best display of field mushrooms I've ever seen in autumn. Sadly, it was ploughed up some years ago and they have not yet reappeared, though I remain hopeful.

Winters in Galicia can be cold. From up here, at the highest point of our walk, we can see the snow-capped mountains which form the Galician border with Castilla y León to the east. It's strange that in summer those mountains are invisible against the horizon, but come winter they rise again, gleaming white in the sunshine.

It's been a while since we had snow in our little valley. Six years in fact. It was the 4th of February 2015 – a date I vividly remember due to its almost disastrous consequences for our journey to the UK that year.

On those rare occasions that we do have snow, I enjoy plodding through snow drifts along these tracks. I always make a tiny snowperson effigy on the doorstep, and I love to be the first to jump into a pristine drift and create snow angels.

Back down in the woods, there is colour and sound throughout the winter. The tree trunks are speckled yellow and green with lichen and spongy mosses. The larger pale-green lichen hang down from branches like old men's beards whilst ivy winds around the trunks and bright ferns grow in the hollow insides, living off the rotting wood.

In the bare trees, birds still flit around, catching small insects or grabbing fat beetle grubs. The woodpeckers' hammering echoes off the hillsides whilst blackbirds chatter, kicking up the dead leaves hunting for worms and grubs. The brightly coloured robins, heroes of every sweet Christmas card, become more territorial – chasing away rivals for the slimmer winter pickings.

I always stop here to feed the two adorable donkeys, alone in a field. They come running now when I whistle, looking for a carrot, or an apple scrumped from that tree. My generosity assuages my guilt and ensures my pockets are lighter for the rest of my walk.

Spring comes early to our little valley; the fruit trees start to blossom from late February. First are the peaches and nectarines, which show tiny pink, fragrant blooms on bare branches. Later the plums join in, just in time for the bullfinches to return and steal the buds – pecking each one before spitting it out in a carpet of pink and white. Buzzards soar overhead, twisting and diving in their mating dance, and the blue tits nest once more. Occasionally we'll spot a shy roe deer in the field before it bounds away with a flash of white rump.

In the woods, the tiny wild daffodils peep through the leaves, and along the track wild violets bloom – a splash of purple against the brown mud. Tiny geraniums flourish in the centre of the track, safe from tractors, while pale-lemon primroses peek shyly from the banks.

Nature's spring palette is of soft mauves and bright golds against a backdrop of deep, rich green. Heather blooms on the hillsides and honey-scented gorse bushes provide an early splash of golden yellow along the woodland edge. Tall, stately, white-flowered asphodels spring up below the chestnut trees, and if I'm lucky there may be some early chanterelles for lunch.

The track forks here: to the left it winds downhill through a new eucalyptus plantation and back to the second mill on our *río*. Further on, our village is laid out below us, across the river. Our second rebuild, *A Casita,* is to the right of the group, the skylight windows glinting in the sunshine. Our own *A Casa do Campo* is off to the left, screened from view by a line of too tall eucalyptus trees. Those trees are growing so big now we soon won't be able to see the village at all!

From here we could make our way downhill back to the *río* and the first water mill – the one we can see from our house. But today we're taking the longer circuit.

The track is narrow here, with little sign of civilisation as we follow the north-facing ridge. Hazel trees join the chestnut trees overhanging the track, providing shade and delicious fruits, before we come to another tiny hamlet.

My favourite house in this village is in its own piece of woodland. It reminds me of Hansel and Gretel, though this house is of granite stone rather than gingerbread! Across from it is another renovated house. They've done a lovely job; the new bronze gutters gleam in the sunshine. Next door is the very antithesis of this house – an old, almost completely derelict property slowly sinking back into the landscape.

I often wonder how long it will take all signs of humans to disappear after we are extinct? Our own *A Casita* was disappearing into the brambles and vines when we bought it. It had been empty for 25 years. Near to our house is another which collapsed some eight years ago. Already the elder trees are growing in the old lounge, the brambles suffocating the kitchen. Another five years maybe and it will have disappeared. I quite like the idea of nature reclaiming itself.

On the right, in this village, is another house which looks like it may collapse soon. The chimney obviously leaks and the wall is black with mould. The house is empty but alongside it sits a beautiful chestnut wood,

26 A Casa do Campo – a walk through the seasons

its trees hundreds of years old. The wood is enclosed by a new and rather expensive looking green metal fence. It seems strange to spend so much on a fence for trees yet leave a house to fall down – especially as the fence ends at a large opening, ungated and easily accessible.

It is quite common here to see a gate at the edge of a field, surrounded by... nothing. No hedge, no fence, just a simple gate saying; 'This is my patch'.

When our friend Pepe wanted us to cut some of his trees for firewood, he walked us up and down looking for the boundary of his family's land.

"That tree wasn't here before," he said, impatiently, to a small oak sapling. "There should be a stone here somewhere."

"How big a stone," I'd asked.

"Oh, about this big," he'd replied, moving his hands a foot apart as if looking for a particular small stone in a bramble-infested chestnut wood was an easy task. There were rocks everywhere in that woodland – I'm not sure we ever did find the right one.

From the last village we head east, towards another small hamlet. This one is big enough to host its own fiesta for its saint's day in June, albeit a small one.

The food is good. Last time we walked there, the wine was a euro a cup. Our first plastic cup was a third full, our second half full, and the third almost overflowing. So much for optics and measurements.

The *orquesta*, or salsa band, had set up on the tiny square. It was a small truck-come-stage by Galician standards, but the enthusiasm from the performers made up for its lack of size. The entertainment, and the food of course, was free. There was a huge barbecue grill sending flames up in to the trees. Pounds of *chorizos* filled the air with their spicy aroma. There were pork ribs and bacon, mounds of fresh artisan bread, and hands digging in. Even Galician appetites couldn't eat all the offerings that night – we left with a catty bag or two and a spring in our step.

From this tiny hamlet the track meanders downhill again, back towards the *río*. The woods here are, unusually, oak rather than chestnut – rather straggly, tall and arched. In summer, myriad butterflies flit around our legs, fluttering up as we pass and landing back on the track behind us, our movement a temporary nuisance. There are gatekeepers and speckled walls, tiny blues and regal red admirals enjoying the dappled shade.

Beyond the oak wood are open fields. In spring and early summer, the track is lined with wild flowers. Tiny geraniums and heavenly blue snuggle up to periwinkle and powder-blue, wild lupins. In the meadows, cuckoo flowers sit erect, their pink flowers nectar for butterflies, their leaves food for the orange tip caterpillars, whilst mounds of stitchwort create a cloud of green and white on the margins. In the damper spots, celandine grows freely, cheering in late winter with its sunny yellow blooms. Beneath the trees, bluebells grow.

To the right, up on a hill, is our local market town of Taboada, its white painted apartment buildings gleaming in the sun. In front of us is a tall mound with a copse of pines growing out of the top like a spiky hairdo. That is our local *castro.*

As we walk, we criss-cross rivulets which in summer and autumn form tiny waterfalls. In early spring though, it's a different matter altogether. Melt water from the surrounding hills rushes down the river, swelling it until the torrent washes away the track itself.

At the bottom of the hill, a left takes us towards home. To get there, we need to cross back to the north side of the river over a small bridge.

When we first bought *A Casa do Campo*, the bridge here was a mound of tumbled boulders with earth piled on top to allow tractors and other brave souls to pass. One year, the council decided to rebuild the bridge – which always needed repairs in winter due to the flooding river. They built a smart concrete structure; it

26 A Casa do Campo – a walk through the seasons

lasted less than a year before the winter rains washed a hole in it. The broken part is now covered with a large sheet of rusting metal, disguising the gap beneath.

This is a 'proper' road and I once drove over that bridge… but only once. The concrete top is wider than a car, though not by much, but has no parapet, no upstand, nothing to indicate to the driver where the drop might be. It's a truly terrifying experience, wondering if the wheel is going to accidentally slip over the edge and take us with it.

Last spring, the river broke its banks and completely flooded the road. The bridge disappeared below the waves which gushed along the roadway, happy to escape their boundaries. The water was deeper than my wellies and swirled menacingly. We had to walk home the long way round that day.

In summer the *río* is a pleasant place to watch the dragonflies and demoiselles. Fool's cress grows thickly in the stream and pond skaters twirl in the pools left by the receding water. Some of our volunteer helpers have enjoyed bathing in the river, which stays cool beneath the chestnut trees.

From town, it's a pleasant amble back home. The downhill walk to the house was one of the things which sold *A Casa do Campo* to us all those years ago. It's still a joy to wander out for an evening in town then walk home in the complete darkness of a summer's night. Our friend Luisa asks how we manage without a torch, but the moon is bright enough to show our way as we wind beneath yet more ancient chestnut trees. The night-time snufflings are particularly loud. I'm never sure if we'll meet a badger, a fox, or a wild boar on the road home. We have seen all three over the years.

Bats flit around the streetlights in the village, hunting for moths, and on a damp night we have to stop frequently to rescue the pretty orange and black salamanders, which like to sit in the middle of the road waiting for an insect to land on their nose. Sadly, a car is as likely. In summer, house martins return to nest below our neighbour's eves and tiny female glow worms sit in the ditches shining a beacon for the males to find. They create a fairy light far bigger than one would expect from their dumpy grub-like bodies.

A Casita is on the left-hand side as we enter the village, just down a tiny track. It's painted sunshine yellow, and is always cheering in the worst weather. If it's a sunny day, you can bet Mum will be busy weeding. A bit of rain and the weeds go wild around here – and Mum does like a tidy garden. Unlike me. I like a few 'weeds' for the birds and the insects. That's my excuse anyway and I'm sticking to it.

Just fifty metres beyond Mum's little *casita* is *A Casa do Campo*, our 'country' home.

We are just in time for tea – and a well-deserved slice of cake.

Please consider leaving a review:

I hope you have enjoyed my tour of some of our favourite places in Galicia in these pages. If so, I'd be delighted if you could post a review on Amazon or Goodreads. A few words will do. Reviews really do mean so much to Indie authors and each (nice) one makes me smile. The links are below. Thank you.

Goodreads
https://smarturl.it/GRpulpopigpeppers
or
Amazon
https://smarturl.it/PulpoPigPeppers

If I've also encouraged you to maybe visit our little piece of rural Spain then I'm doubly delighted. There is so much to be discovered in Galicia, and if you ever find yourself nearby, rest assured, the kettle will be on and there's always cake in the tin at *A Casa do Campo*.

To download your free photo album which accompanies the stories in this book please copy the link below:

Travels around Galicia, the album
https://smarturl.it/travelsaroundGalicia

If you'd like to read my *Writing Home* series of travelogue memoirs, here's the universal link to book one: *Plum, Courgette & Green Bean Tart* which will take you to your local Amazon store

https://smarturl.it/PlumCourgetteBean

DISCLAIMER

This book is not intended as a travel guide. The trips in here have all been made by us, and my recollections are genuine as far as my memory allows. Some trips were many years ago. I cannot guarantee any prices mentioned, nor that some of the establishments even still exist, but I hope you will find inspiration in these pages. If you do discover a treasure I've missed in our beautiful green land, please do let me know; I'd love to hear from you.

You can email me at lisarosewright@msn.com

COMING NEXT

What happens when you take the country souls out of Galicia and throw them on an unsuspecting world?

Find out in this new memoir from Lisa Rose Wright.

Lisa and hubby S are leaving their home in the wilds of Galicia in NW Spain. But only temporarily, as they embark on a trip round the world. It's S' 70th birthday coming up and Lisa has the perfect holiday planned.

From the frozen wastes of Japan to the steamy city of Singapore, and from Australia's outback to the heart of Santiago de Chile, Lisa and husband S travel the world discovering new places, and realising they don't remember familiar ones, on this trip of a lifetime.

Workawaying as volunteers on three continents, driving across Australia's notorious Nullarbor Plain and sailing to the end of the world – what could possibly go wrong with such a perfectly planned trip? And will home be best after all, or will Lisa and S be bitten by the travel bug? It doesn't take long to find out.

Want a sneak peek? Join my subscribers' list for exclusive material and free offers
https://lisarosewright.wixsite.com/author/

For updates follow me at
http://www.facebook.com/lisarosewright.author
http://www.twitter.com/galauthor_lisa

ACKNOWLEDGEMENTS

An Indie author can never succeed alone so here's my chance to say a great big thank you to all those wonderful people who have helped this book come to fruition.

To my beta readers, Pat Ellis, Liza Grantham, Julie Haigh, Beth Haslam, Val Poore, Anna Rashbrook and Alyson Sheldrake. Thank you for daring to read the first draft and for your incredibly helpful comments. You are all five-star heroes.

To our shy friend Ramón for his lovely chapter on his home city of Ourense, even if you wouldn't allow me to name you!

To the friendliest group on Facebook, We Love Memoirs, for support, and for lots of fun-filled hours when I should have been working but was instead online. If you love reading memoirs (or writing them), enjoy competitions and chatting with like-minded people, then I highly recommend this wonderful group. We can be found at http://www.facebook.com/groups/welovememoirs

To S, my blue-eyed husband, for alpha, beta and omega reading, and for always walking by my side.

And to you, my readers – without you this book would be just a dream.

ABOUT THE AUTHOR

In 2007 Lisa left a promising career as an ecologist catching protected reptiles and amphibians, and kissing frogs, to move to beautiful green Galicia with her blue-eyed prince (now blue-eyed husband).

She divides her time equally between growing her own food, helping to renovate two semi-derelict houses and getting out and about to discover more of the stunningly beautiful area she calls home.

Lisa is happiest outside in her *huerta* weeding, watching the antics of her chickens, or in her kitchen cooking interesting recipes on her wood-burning range.

Pulpo, Pig & Peppers – Travels around Galicia, is Lisa's fourth full-length travelogue memoir. She also has stories featured in Alyson Sheldrake's fabulous travelogue anthologies which can be found at https://www.alysonsheldrake.com/travel-stories-series/

You can read about Lisa and Stewart's adventures buying and renovating *A Casa do Campo*, their ancient derelict stone farmhouse; defying Spanish bureaucracy to marry in Galicia; and of their continuing adventures when 'Mother makes three', in Lisa's *Writing Home* trilogy. The series is available in hardback, paperback, eBook, and free with Kindle Unlimited at Amazon stores worldwide.

Printed in Great Britain
by Amazon